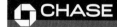

GREAT DECISIONS 2000

Printed by Dartmouth Printing Company
Hanover, New Hampshire

Cover design: Agnes Kostro

Cover photography: Tony Stone Images/
Peter Dazeley

CONTENTS

World map, full-color, up-to-date,
courtesy The New York Times Company Foundation.

‡ ‡ ‡

FPA gratefully acknowledges the contribution of text paper for this book by Westvaco Corporation.

**Preparation of this topic was underwritten by a generous grant from the Freeman Foundation*

FOREWORD

THE CURRENT RACE FOR THE WHITE HOUSE has ventilated the candidates' views on Social Security, education and health care—key domestic issues over which the President has a significant but by no means exclusive say. Discussion of foreign policy, however, has been notable for its absence. Yet foreign policy is preponderantly the business of the executive branch of the federal government and therefore an especially salient arena in which to evaluate presidential contenders.

The ultimate decision of who will become President rests with the voter, who is entitled to know whether candidates for this high office possess a strategic vision for America's role in the world and whether such a vision will capitalize on the current moment of American ascendancy to build a lasting democratic peace. As Charles Maynes observes in this issue of *Great Decisions:* "Foreign policy is always a mixture of the planned and the unexpected .... A nation will not be ready to exploit the unexpected unless it has a long-term strategy with respect to the international system it would like to see develop."

The increasing globalization of our society and our economy makes it imperative that we take the unimpeded view in shaping foreign policy. Such a foreign policy should be the embodiment of the best democratic impulses and values of American life. Articulating a coherent foreign policy, rather than allowing it to be driven by disparate special interests, is always a challenge in a democracy. A steady, forward-looking foreign policy requires the marshalling of a public consensus for responsible internationalism. Too infrequently do our politicians make the investment in public education necessary for such a consensus to emerge.

Nor can we shirk individually our responsibility to participate in the political process. As Alan Ehrenhalt observes in *Democracy in the Mirror*: "We like to pretend that politics and government are somehow alien institutions, operating by their own rules and unresponsive to popular concerns. In fact, the opposite is true. The political process plays by our rules and responds to our mundane hopes and fears—overresponds, most of the time. Politics is a mirror of our thoughts and attitudes. We may not always wish to face that difficult truth, but ultimately we can't avoid it ....The whole political system is you and I cavorting on the public stage." In other words, we get the foreign policy we deserve.

In *The Federalist,* Number 1, Page 1, Alexander Hamilton poses a central question of American democracy: "It seems to have been reserved to the people of this country, by their conduct and example, to decide the important question, whether societies...are really capable or not of establishing good government from reflection and choice, or whether they are forever destined to depend...on accident and force." From its inception in 1918, the Foreign Policy Association has sought to serve as a portal to provide the American public with the information needed to give the "right" answer to Hamilton's question. FPA has worked to strengthen American democracy by encouraging grassroots participation in the great decisions of foreign policy. Commending FPA in a letter to Major General Frank R. McCoy, then president of FPA, Franklin D. Roosevelt observed: "In a democracy, the government functions with the consent of the whole people. The latter must be guided by the facts. The Foreign Policy Association is performing a high duty in facilitating the lucid presentation of the facts of world problems and their impact upon the United States." By acting on its motto, "An informed public is an engaged public," FPA seeks to contribute to a future shaped by "reflection and choice." Never has this work counted for more than during this millennial election season.

Noel V. Lateef

U.S. Foreign Policy and the American Political System

THE CONSTITUTION has been described as an "invitation to struggle" between the President and Congress over the making of foreign policy.

- The President wages a yearlong campaign to win congressional approval for admitting three former Soviet-bloc countries to NATO.
- The President uses a seldom-invoked Constitutional provision—a "recess appointment"—to send philanthropist and businessman James Hormel as ambassador to Luxemburg.
- The President sees the Comprehensive Test Ban Treaty he had signed in 1996 defeated by the Senate 51-48.

How can a President provide effective leadership abroad if Congress blocks his policy initiatives? How can Congress give the President full rein over foreign policy without abdicating powers vested in it by the Constitution? In making foreign policy, should the President lead or be a coequal partner? Which branch of government determines the nation's foreign policy and which one is responsible for carrying it out? And what is the role of the public?

PETRICIC.CARTOONISTS & WRITERS SYNDICATE/ cartoonweb.com

America's foreign policy is the expression of its goals in the world and of how it proposes to achieve them. It is a reflection of the nation's interests, the most basic of which are sovereignty and independence. But there are many more: democracy, economic security, protection of human rights, environmental security.

Foreign policy is also an expression of how a nation relates to other countries. If the nation turns inward and chooses to have nothing to do with its neighbors, that choice is its foreign policy. Today such a choice is hardly practical because the world has become too interdependent for any country, least of all the U.S., to isolate itself. Every facet of life in America is affected by decisions made in other parts of the world.

And foreign policy is an expression of preferences for particular instruments, such as diplomacy or economic power or military force.

Compared to every other liberal democracy, the U.S. makes its foreign policy in a cumbersome way. The framers of the Constitution, wary of impulsive decisions that could embroil the country in war, built into that document a number of safeguards that have prevented tyranny, but sometimes at the cost of speed and efficiency. These safeguards frequently pit Congress against the executive branch, make it difficult to develop and implement a cohesive foreign policy, create uncertainty as to what that policy is, and give foreign governments and special interests an opportunity to apply pressure at many points, not just one.

The complexity of foreign policymaking has greatly increased with the blurring of the distinction between foreign and domestic issues. More and more the two overlap as a consequence of global interdependence and the breakdown of traditional barriers. Canada and the U.S. announce the Pacific Salmon Treaty, ending a protracted dispute over limits on catching salmon migrating between the two nations' waters. Following a trial in connection with U.S. money-laundering operations of drug cartels based in Colombia and Mexico, a U.S. District Court convicted three Mexican bankers and businessmen of conspiring to launder money for drug traffickers, proving a direct link between Mexican banks and the laundering of U.S. drug profits.

Economics—and especially trade—is one of the areas in which foreign and domestic concerns invariably intersect. U.S. tax policy is domestic, but it affects an American manufacturer's costs of doing business and the competitiveness of his products. American labor laws affect the number of workers hired, the number of jobs available in the U.S. and the number of Americans who are—or who are not—looking for work. In fact, almost every law relating to business or labor or farmers also has an impact, directly or indirectly, on American foreign trade.

Finally, developments that the framers of the Constitution could not have foreseen have added to the complexity of policymaking. These include the growth in the outreach and influence of information technology, political organizations and special-interest groups.

Congress, the President and Foreign Policy

THE U.S. Constitution divides power between the three branches of government: the legislative, the executive and the judiciary. It also gives each branch some check on the other. The President can veto legislation; Congress can override the President's veto; the courts can declare a law of Congress or an act of the President unconstitutional—although they have been reluctant to act on the issues of "high policy" that have traditionally been the realm of foreign affairs.

The Founding Fathers, conditioned by their colonial experience, were suspicious of executive power, which they equated with the oppressive British monarchy and colonial governors. They regarded Congress as the most "democratic" of the three branches.

Congress's power to tax and control government spending—the "power of the purse"—is possibly its most important. Although the President usually cannot spend money not appropriated by Congress, he has always been granted some latitude in emergencies. President Bill Clinton, during the Mexican peso crisis of 1994–95, circumvented Congress, which opposed a bailout for Mexico, by making a loan from funds at his disposal.

The Constitution assigns the Senate a distinctive role in the foreign policy process—to advise the President in negotiating agreements, to consent to them once they have been signed and to approve presidential appointments, including the secretary of state, other high officials of the State Department, ambassadors and career Foreign Service Officers. The Senate does not have to consent to or reject a treaty. The Senate can approve a treaty and in the process amend it or attach reservations. These must be approved by the other country or countries signing the treaty before it enters into force.

Since the Vietnam War, Congress has become more assertive in foreign affairs. This is partly a result of the breakdown of the postwar bipartisan consensus in foreign policy (the principle that politics stops at the water's edge); partly in reaction to what Congress saw as the executive's abuse of power; and partly due to the fact that money has become more important in carrying out foreign policy—and Congress controls the money.

The Senate used to confirm nominees routinely. That is no longer the case. "The nominating process is becoming a demolition derby," according to Marshall Adain, president of the American Foreign Service Association. "If you create a perpetual system that subjects people to abuse, you'll lower their incentive to stay." J. Brian Atwood, departing director of the Agency for International Development (AID), turned down his nomination to be ambassador to Brazil after clashing with Senator Jesse Helms (R-N.C.), chairman of the Foreign Relations Committee, over the Senator's plan to merge AID into the State Department.

The President's role

Under the Constitution, the President serves as head of state and head of government. In most other governments (Britain's and Germany's, for example), the two functions are separate. As head of state, the President is, in effect, the personification of the U.S.: its visible image, its official voice and its primary representative to the outside world. As head of government, he formulates foreign policy, supervises its implementation and attempts to obtain the resources to support it. He also organizes and directs the departments and agencies that play a part in the foreign policy process. Along with the Vice President, he is the only government official elected nationally. This places him in a unique position to identify, express and pursue the "national interests" of the U.S.

The President's specific foreign policy powers under the Constitution are few and restricted. He serves as Commander in Chief of the Army and Navy; nominates and appoints ambassadors and other public ministers, subject to the advice and consent of the Senate; and makes treaties, by and with the advice of the Senate, provided two thirds of the senators present concur.

The President's specific powers may be few, but his role in foreign policy, many believe, is crucial. "Only the President, by defining and articulating our interests," writes Lee Hamilton who served for 34 years as Democratic Representative from Indiana, "can restrain the experts and bring along voters and a reluctant Congress in support of American leadership." Harvey Sicherman, president of the Foreign Policy Research Institute in Philadelphia, noting that Clinton had declared himself a domestic President in his first term, writes: "The lesson of the past few years is that foreign policy cannot be conducted coherently unless the President imposes order upon it. . . . Above all, a presidency that educates public opinion, cultivates congressional consensus, manages international coalitions, and disposes of alert, decisive military power is not only compatible with a 'domestic presidency,' it is essential."

Treaty-making

The framers deliberately made treaty-making cumbersome so that the country could not enter into alliances lightly. Thomas Jefferson wrote concerning treaties, "...our system is to have none with any nation, as far as can be avoided." Behind that proscription was a fear of "entangling foreign alliances" that might lead to war.

The difficulty of convincing two thirds of the Senate to consent to controversial treaties has prompted Presidents to substitute executive agreements with other countries for treaties. (Executive agreements are either written or oral and they usually commit the parties to undertake certain steps or to accept obligations.) Most of the understandings and commitments between the U.S. and foreign governments today take the form of executive agreements, although these are nowhere mentioned in the Constitution.

Power to make war

Although the President is the Commander in Chief, the power to declare war rests with Congress. Did the Constitution intend that all uses of force be declared by Congress? Scholars disagree. In any event, Congress has only exercised the right in response to a presidential request. There have been only five *declared* wars in the nation's history (World War II, 1941–45, was the last declared war), a fact which illustrates both the changes in the nature of international conflict and the shift to the President of the power to employ the armed forces without a legal authorization by Congress.

The President also has the power to receive foreign ambassadors and, in effect, to recognize foreign governments. The President has two additional informal but influential powers in foreign affairs. One of these is the ability to determine the national agenda—or bring issues to the forefront of public attention and concern. The other—which ranks among the President's most potent weapons for controlling foreign policy—is the power to commit the nation to a particular course of action diplomatically. Once he does so, it can be extremely difficult for the President's opponents to alter that course.

The Policymaking Machinery

MAKING FOREIGN POLICY requires the participation of the President, the executive branch, Congress and the public. Conducting foreign policy, on the other hand, is the exclusive prerogative of the President and his subordinates in the executive branch. The distinction is fuzzy but important: you make policy when you decide to participate in a joint effort to restore peace to Kosovo; you conduct policy when you commit troops and matériel.

Until World War II, one agency, the Department of State, established in 1789 and the highest-ranking Cabinet department, and one individual, the secretary of state, who is directly responsible to the President, managed foreign affairs. The traditional functions of the State Department and its professional diplomatic corps, the Foreign Service, include negotiating on behalf of the U.S. government with foreign governments and in international organizations; defending the U.S. position in the world; reporting on and analyzing conditions in foreign countries and institutions such as the UN; representing the American people and current U.S. policies to the world; promoting relations with decisionmakers abroad; advancing U.S. trade and investment; and protecting U.S. nationals overseas from discriminatory and/or inhumane treatment. It currently employs nearly 25,000 people worldwide in just over 250 embassies, missions, consulates and branch offices.

The U.S. emerged from World War II a nuclear superpower with global interests. The National Security Act of 1947, among other things, created a Department of Defense, a permanent intelligence agency and a small Cabinet-level National Security Council (NSC), which includes the President, the Vice President, the secretaries of State and Defense and the chairman of the Joint Chiefs of Staff, to help the President manage and coordinate foreign policy. The NSC staff, headed by the President's national security adviser, consists of specialists in geographic areas and functional issues, such as arms control.

Policymaking machinery tends to expand or contract, depending on the exigencies of the situation. The outbreak of the cold war with the Soviet Union within months of the Allied victory in World War II put U.S. security and the containment of communism at the top of the nation's agenda. This meant that the Defense Department and the Central Intelligence Agency (CIA) frequently shared the foreign policy limelight with the State Department. A host of new agencies was also created to deal with security issues, from the National Security Agency, which collected, evaluated and disseminated intelligence gleaned from electronic communications, to the Arms Control and Disarmament Agency, which proposed, implemented and monitored measures to limit or reduce weapons of war.

COLD-WAR AGENCIES. Other agencies created during the cold war to deal with America's expanded global responsibilities were the U.S. Information Agency (USIA) and the U.S. Agency for International Development (AID). USIA planned and conducted informational and propaganda programs abroad. Its radio arm, the Voice of America, is a powerful shortwave radio network capable of beaming programs to most countries.

AID administers foreign economic assistance programs. In consultation with foreign governments, it formulates aid projects, establishes procedures for carrying them out and provides experts and other personnel.

THE PENTAGON. Military power serves as an instrument of diplomacy—as a means of achieving goals defined by civilian officials of the government. The head of the Defense Department is a civilian secretary who serves in the President's Cabinet. The principal military adviser to the President is the chairman of the Joint Chiefs of Staff, a strategy board consisting of the senior officers of the Army, Air Force, Navy and Marine Corps. The chairman is designated by the President.

When, where and to what extent the U.S. should use its armed forces to achieve its foreign policy objectives is a highly charged issue. Since World War II, U.S. troops have served in Korea, Southeast Asia, the Dominican Republic, Lebanon, Grenada, Panama, the Persian Gulf, Somalia, Haiti, Bosnia and Herzegovina, Kosovo and East Timor. In recent years, the will to send U.S. troops abroad has dissipated.

INTELLIGENCE. The "intelligence community" is a group of federal agencies that includes the CIA, the National Security Agency and the Defense Intelligence Agency. They collect information (for example, how many nuclear weapons China possesses), assess its accuracy and reliability, and disseminate the information to decisionmakers. In addition, the intelligence community, most notably the CIA, undertakes, with the approval of the President, clandestine operations. In October 1998, Congress and the White House approved the largest spending increase for intelligence in 15 years.

OTHER EXECUTIVE DEPARTMENTS. Since the earliest days of the Republic, the Treasury Department has played a major role in foreign relations. It is concerned today with the stability of the dollar abroad, foreign-exchange rates, commodity prices, debt service on foreign loans and bread-and-butter issues that affect the well-being and prosperity of the American people.

Other executive departments deeply involved in foreign policymaking are Commerce (which in 1995 the Republican majority in Congress hoped to abolish), the Office of the U.S. Trade Representative and, to a somewhat lesser extent, Labor, Agriculture and Energy. Particularly since the end of the cold war, the priorities on the U.S. global agenda have shifted pronouncedly from national-security concerns to the creation of new opportunities for trade, commerce and investment. Hence the consolidation of some of the cold-war agencies. In October 1998, both the Arms Control and Disarmament Agency and the USIA were abolished and their duties were assigned to the State Department. While AID still remains in business, its staff now reports to the Secretary of State instead of directly to the White House.

Formulation

George Washington once remarked that the U.S. ought to have the most successful foreign policy of any country in the world because it had so many self-styled secretaries of state. Since his day, the difficulty of developing a cohesive, relevant and feasible foreign policy has increased enormously.

Theoretically, the process of formulation should begin with a clear definition of the national interests, followed by a delineation of the policies that would promote those interests and the course of action by the various departments and agencies that would further those policies, as well as the allocation of the resources needed to carry them out.

In practice, no system is likely to produce a cohesive, viable and supportable foreign policy. The national interest is a cluster of particular interests, and the agencies and staffs involved may have very different views as to what it should be.

The American Political Process

THROUGHOUT MOST of U.S. history, a very small group of people conducted foreign affairs. In the minds of this "elite," public participation had no place in the management of foreign relations. It was Woodrow Wilson, a tireless champion of democracy, who was determined to "democratize" diplomacy—to do away with "secret deals" arrived at "behind the backs of the people" in favor of "open covenants openly arrived at." His ideas had a profound impact on the U.S. conduct of international relations long after his era. During World War II and throughout the cold war, when public support for America's foreign policy was critical, the role of public opinion rose to new eminence.

Not all members of the public exert the same degree of influence on policymaking. Social scientists tend to classify the public into three groups: the public-at-large or mass opinion, the attentive public and organized interest groups.

The public-at-large tends to have less interest in foreign policy issues than in local and family concerns. It tends to be poorly informed and sometimes distressingly ignorant. In a study conducted a few years ago, most high-school students could not identify the U.S. on an unlabeled map of the world. The public-at-large is also crisis-oriented. Its interest is aroused by vivid television coverage—for example, starving children or fleeing refugees—that demands some kind of response. Finally, the public's foreign policy outlook tends to change with some regularity—from isolationist to interventionist and back.

The attentive public—or elite opinion on foreign policy—represents perhaps 10%–20% of the American people. It consists of citizens who are genuinely interested and involved. They tend to be better educated and well-informed. Many communicate their views to policymakers in Washington. They write letters, sign petitions, visit their representatives. The attentive public helps focus the attention and arouse the interest of the apathetic. They participate in the activities of organizations like the Foreign Policy Association, World Affairs Councils, the United Nations Association of the U.S.A., the American Association of University Women and the League of Women Voters, which have contributed significantly to raising the level of public interest in and understanding of foreign affairs. The public-opinion elite also serves as a source of new and creative ideas for policymakers and as informed critics of prevailing policy. (As a service to readers, teachers and community activists, the editors have included at the end of each topic a list of resources—organizations that run the gamut from research to advocacy.)

The third category consists of organized interest groups. There are literally thousands of these. In addition to the "big three"—business, labor and agriculture—they represent every segment of society imaginable—religious denominations, war veterans, Foreign Service Officers, ethnic groups, environmental groups and human-rights advocacy organizations. Many individual business corporations with foreign interests maintain permanent offices in Washington, D.C.

Some of the most intensive and successful lobbying is conducted by executive agencies and officials of the U.S. government. The President has several White House assistants whose responsibility is "legislative relations." Their primary goal is to gain support for the President's foreign and domestic programs on Capitol Hill. The Department of State, along with nearly all other executive departments, has a Bureau of Congressional Relations, which monitors Capitol Hill.

Democratization of foreign policy

The foreign policy process has begun to change, and it is becoming more pluralistic, primarily as the result of the growing interdependence of the U.S. with the rest of the world. Decisions can no longer be made by the executive branch alone in consultation with a small group of foreign policy experts on the outside. Notes a report by the U.S. Advisory Commission on Public Diplomacy, a presidential commission created by Congress to provide bipartisan oversight: "America still needs diplomacy between governments, but policies and negotiated agreements will succeed only if they have the support of publics at home and abroad."

Once engaged, how can citizens make their voices not only heard but effective? What they need most of all is an understanding of the policymaking process. They can then develop an effective strategy for exerting their influence. This includes expressing their goals in a clear message and demonstrating that they have a strong political base and speak for key constituencies.

Governor George Ryan (R-Ill.) in October 1999 led a 45-member delegation of state, business, religious and university leaders to Cuba, declaring that he had "come here to build bridges between people." An opponent of the embargo, he planned to present more than $1 million worth of donated relief supplies. The Clinton Administration is encouraging direct contacts between the U.S. and the Cuban people.

Wider participation or pluralism in the formulation of policy brings new voices into the process, and as a result decisions are likely to be based on a broader consideration of the issues and a fuller assessment of the alternatives. But greater participation also makes the foreign policy process more cumbersome. Extensive public discussion does not necessarily lead to consensus; it can be divisive and inconclusive. It is especially unsuited to formulating long-range national strategy or addressing complex issues. But democracies are often unwieldy and untidy. As the British statesman Sir Winston Churchill once remarked, democracy is "the worst form of government except all those other forms that have been tried from time to time."

By the late Nancy Hoepli-Phalon, FPA's editor in chief 1981–98, with minor updating.

U.S. role in the world: what are the choices?

Throughout most of the 20th century, the goal of U.S. foreign policy was to contain communism. In the post-cold-war era, what will America's goals be? How will it pursue them?

by Charles William Maynes

THE WORLD VIEWS AMERICA AS THE MOST MILITARILY, ECONOMICALLY AND CULTURALLY DOMINANT NATION TO EXIST SINCE THE ROMAN EMPIRE.
HOW AMERICA VIEWS THE WORLD
HELLO? EUROPE? JAPAN? I COULD USE SOME HELP HERE!!
KAL CARTOONISTS & WRITERS SYNDICATE/cartoonweb.com

Asked if he felt indebted to Russia for helping crush the Hungarian uprising of 1848, the Austrian prime minister, Prince Felix Schwarzenberg, replied, "Austria will astound the world with the magnitude of her ingratitude."

Commenting on the course of British foreign policy, Lord Palmerston, prime minister of Britain in the mid-19th century, stated: "We have no eternal allies, and we have no perpetual enemies. Our interests are eternal and perpetual and those interests it is our duty to follow."

Any discussion of America's role in the world ought to begin with these two statements because they are among the most famous comments ever made in modern times about the nature of diplomacy. They reflect the way that the game of diplomacy has been played from the days of the ancient Greeks. Most governments throughout history have acted as amoral creatures, following no principles save self-interest in the name of advantage over others. The world of diplomacy has been a cold, heartless but logical domain where affection and even legal commitment have played a very limited role. It has been a world in which the strong did what they wished and the weak did what they were ordered to do. Will this be the world of the 21st century?

To act otherwise in the past was to court disaster. One's "friends" also followed Palmerston's logic. They also had no eternal allies. They also had no eternal enemies. They also might suddenly turn on their friends or embrace their enemies whenever such a move served the national interest.

In a world where no commitment seems eternal, necessarily principles will play a restricted role. The kind of honor that is appropriate to private behavior will not be seen as appropriate to the statesman. He will do what is necessary to protect his country, even if by most private legal and moral codes his actions would constitute illegal or immoral behavior.

All states, democratic and nondemocratic, have played this game, including America. During the period when the Nixon, Ford and Carter Administrations reached out to China, no one would deny that China, then in the Cultural Revolution (1966–76), was by far a much more totalitarian hell than the Soviet Union of Leonid I. Brezhnev in the 1960s and 1970s. Nevertheless, for strategic reasons, the U.S. sided with the morally less attractive state. The U.S. progressively entered into an informal strategic alliance with China against the relatively more benign but much more powerful and therefore much more threatening Soviet Union. Meanwhile, the Communist Soviet Union became the informal strategic ally of democratic India! It may truly be said that traditional diplomacy makes for ideologically odd bedfellows.

During the cold war, Hungary was in the Communist world and Guatemala in the free world, but the human-rights conditions in Guatemala were undoubtedly worse than in Hungary. Historians are now contending that "genocide" took place in Guatemala during the cold war, while in Hungary one had "goulash communism." Welcome to the world of what geopoliticians call

CHARLES WILLIAM MAYNES *became president of the Eurasia Foundation in April 1997. From April 1980 until April 1997, he served as editor of* Foreign Policy *magazine, one of the leading journals in the world on international affairs. Over the course of his career, Mr. Maynes has held positions in the Department of State, U.S. Congress and the foundation world.*

realism or balance-of-power politics.

In this hemisphere, the U.S. traditionally played the game of realism as aggressively as many others. Nevertheless, what distinguishes America is the existence of an opposing tradition that is probably more closely associated with the U.S. than with any other country. This opposing tradition asserts that the classic balance-of-power approach to international relations has led to disaster again and again and will do so in the future. Cold egoism in the international realm, it is pointed out, has brought an endless series of wars and over the course of the centuries has probably led to the death of hundreds of millions of people. A better approach, it might be argued, would be to introduce the principles of law, morality and reciprocal obligation into international affairs so that states would behave more honorably in the future than they have in the past.

Those who hold such views are often called Wilsonians because Woodrow Wilson, then President of the U.S., justified America's entry into World War I as an effort to bring law and honor to international relations. Realists, who hold the more traditional view of international relations, have long regarded Wilsonians as misguided or dangerously naive.

Many believe that one of the principal weaknesses of American foreign policy is a fatal addiction to legalism and moralism, which form the taproot of Wilsonianism. In his book *Diplomacy,* Henry A. Kissinger (secretary of state, 1973–77) suggests that at the turn of the century the U.S. had a chance to develop a mature, more European foreign policy. The country was emerging from the era of isolationism and faced a choice between a Palmerston-like foreign policy based on national interest, which President Theodore Roosevelt (1901–09) personified, and a foreign policy of legalistic internationalism, which Wilson espoused. According to Kissinger, Wilson won this argument and, in his view, American foreign policy continued to be handicapped by its historic inability to adopt the European approach to international affairs, one based on a quest for power and a determination to act according to the standard of national interest.

The Kissinger view is widely held among practitioners of international relations, that is to say, the people who are charged with the formal responsibility of managing the nation's affairs. There are, however, two major difficulties with the realist critique of American foreign policy. First, as Kissinger himself admits, the American people have never been comfortable with a pure balance-of-power approach to international affairs. And second, if it is true that balance-of-power politics is the appropriate way to manage international relations and the U.S. has difficulty following this approach, how can one explain that by almost any standard no state in the 20th century has had a more successful foreign policy than the U.S.?

Nazi Germany and the Communist Soviet Union, which followed realism's amoral code in the most ruthless fashion imaginable, have disappeared. Britain and France, which historically have championed this approach, have been reduced to middle powers. Japan, which struck the U.S. when the moment seemed opportune—a realist tactic—has virtually become an American protectorate.

Post–World War II debate

The realist point of view has always had strong academic champions. A key book published after World War II outlined the balance-of-power, realist view. In 1948, Hans J. Morgenthau of the University of Chicago published his enormously influential textbook, *Politics Among Nations: The Struggle for Power and Peace.* A refugee from Europe and a brilliant student of international relations, Morgenthau worried then that the U.S. might not live up to its new global responsibilities after World War II, just as many express this concern in the post-cold-war era. Morgenthau believed that for the U.S. to act responsibly, it would need to abandon its preoccupation with international law and institutions and embark on a foreign policy rooted in the concept of national interest. His book went through several editions and influenced several generations of students of international affairs to adopt the so-called realist approach.

Morgenthau explained the nature of a realist foreign policy in this way:

> "The lawyer asks: 'Is this policy in accord with the rules of law?' The moralist asks: 'Is this policy in accord with moral principles?' And the political realist asks: 'How does this policy affect the power of the nation?'"

The implication seems clear: If an action is illegal or immoral but advances the power of the state, it is permissible. Indeed, a statesman would be derelict in his duties if he failed to take the necessary action to advance the nation's self-interest simply because he feared that his decisions might be judged by others as illegal or immoral. It is this kind of logic that permits states to engage in actions abroad—aggression, assassinations or bribery—that would be considered crimes at home.

Morgenthau's book became the most influential textbook in international affairs in America, but the school he pioneered never totally won the debate. Most Americans continue to believe that law and morality should play a *central* role in American foreign policy. They feel that law and morality are in the country's national interest. Most realists make some accommodation to that national predisposition. They concede that a foreign policy without a moral and legal component will not receive public support.

Nevertheless, during the cold war it is fair to say that the realist school predominated. When a nation concludes it is in a war, its people expect its government to take decisions that might trouble public opinion more in peacetime. Particularly if a nation's very survival is at stake, there may be a general lowering of the moral code. In war, after all, the objective is to defeat the enemy, by killing him (or her) if necessary.

Indeed, it is now known from archival revelations made possible with the end of the cold war that standards were lowered in the struggle between the Communist and the democratic worlds, even among the democracies. As a secret report prepared as part of the 1954 Hoover Commission study on government noted with respect to America's struggle with the Soviet Union:

> It is now clear that we are facing an implacable enemy whose avowed objective is world domination by whatever means and at whatever cost. There are no rules in such a game. Hitherto acceptable norms of human conduct do not apply. If the U.S. is to survive, long-standing American concepts of 'fair play' must be reconsidered. We must develop effective espionage and counterespionage services. We must learn to subvert, sabotage, and destroy our enemies by more clever, more sophisticated and more effective methods than those used against us. It may become necessary that the American people will be made acquainted with, understand and support this fundamentally repugnant philosophy.

Many Americans were not comfortable with such views even at the height of the cold war; but if they were acceptable then, are they acceptable today?

With the end of the cold war, a debate that Morgenthau hoped his book could settle has, in fact, reopened. What is the balance between America's principles and its interests in a post-cold-war world? How can America's interests be defined now that the Soviet Union has disappeared and the U.S. towers over all other countries in the international system? Can America employ the same tactics against the weak that it felt forced to employ against the strong?

Should the U.S. seize its "unipolar" moment and make a bid for world hegemony, as some on the political right now urge? Should it embark on a policy of "hegemonic liberalism" as some on the political left now suggest? Or can the U.S. place its hopes for a better world in what some advocates contend are the allegedly certain and benign effects of "globalization." ■

The national interest

During the cold war, America's strategists thought they understood the national interest. It was to halt the spread of Moscow-controlled communism, full stop. They were particularly concerned with the spread of communism in Western Europe and Japan. Those two areas represented such massive centers of power and wealth that, were they ever to come under the control of Moscow, the balance of power in the world might tip decisively in Moscow's favor.

U.S. policymakers also worried about the spread of communism elsewhere. This fear drew the U.S. into two major ground wars in Asia, first in Korea (1950–53) and then in Vietnam (1965–75). The debate over those two wars was often framed in terms of law and morality. Nevertheless, the core dispute was whether the U.S. had the same national interest in opposing the rise of communism in mainland Asia that it did in opposing the rise of communism in Western Europe and Japan. In the end, even the strategists—led by Morgenthau—decided in the case of Vietnam that it did not.

Now that the Soviet Union has disappeared, American strategists suddenly find themselves at sea. What is the national interest in circumstances where the U.S. has no great enemy?

Balance of power for the U.S.

For most countries the concept of the national interest endures decade after decade, century after century. Most countries have no strategic choice. Geography and history frame the debate and predetermine the policy. In the case of the Britain of Palmerston's day, pursuing the national interest meant acquiring mastery of the seas so that no other European power could launch a successful military assault on the island. It also meant opposition to any power on the Continent, regardless of its ideological predisposition, that seemed within reach of uniting Europe under its leadership. A united Europe would in time be able to subdue Britain, only a few miles off the coast of the Continent.

Following this doctrine, Britain joined with illiberal Prussia and Russia to defeat Napoleonic France and then joined with liberal France and autocratic Russia to defeat the semi-democratic Germany of Kaiser Wilhelm II (1886–1918). Then it united with the totalitarian Soviet Union to defeat totalitarian Nazi Germany, only to quickly join with the U.S. in embracing defeated Germany as part of an alliance to contest the now-feared Soviet Union.

It is no accident that as soon as Germany reunited, with the fall of the Berlin Wall in 1989, some prominent British commentators immediately voiced concern that Germany might now achieve peacefully what it had failed to accomplish through arms—the domination of Europe. Nor was it an accident that French statesmen immediately began pressing the Germans to bind themselves irrevocably to the European Union, the 15-nation group formed in 1991 to promote political, economic and social cooperation. Both responses reflected centuries of British and French statecraft.

What does the concept of the national interest mean, however, for a country like the U.S.? For most of its history, it has seemed to enjoy a larger margin of strategic choice than other states. And today, with no visible enemy and towering over all other major states, it clearly has a wide margin of strategic choice.

The U.S. is strong enough that it could retreat from the world, venturing out occasionally to strike down those that would dare to challenge it in some fundamental way. The U.S. also has it within its power to enter the world scene with the goal of establishing a form of global hegemony. Provided it did not overreach by attempting to intervene in the internal affairs of too many states, it could hold the ring internationally, in effect becoming the world's policeman. No other power can challenge it militarily, and its economic resources are sufficient to buy the support of a number of governments.

Or the U.S. could reach out to key partners to establish the more orderly

JEFF STAHLER REPRINTED BY PERMISSION OF NEWSPAPER ENTERPRISE ASSOCIATION, INC.

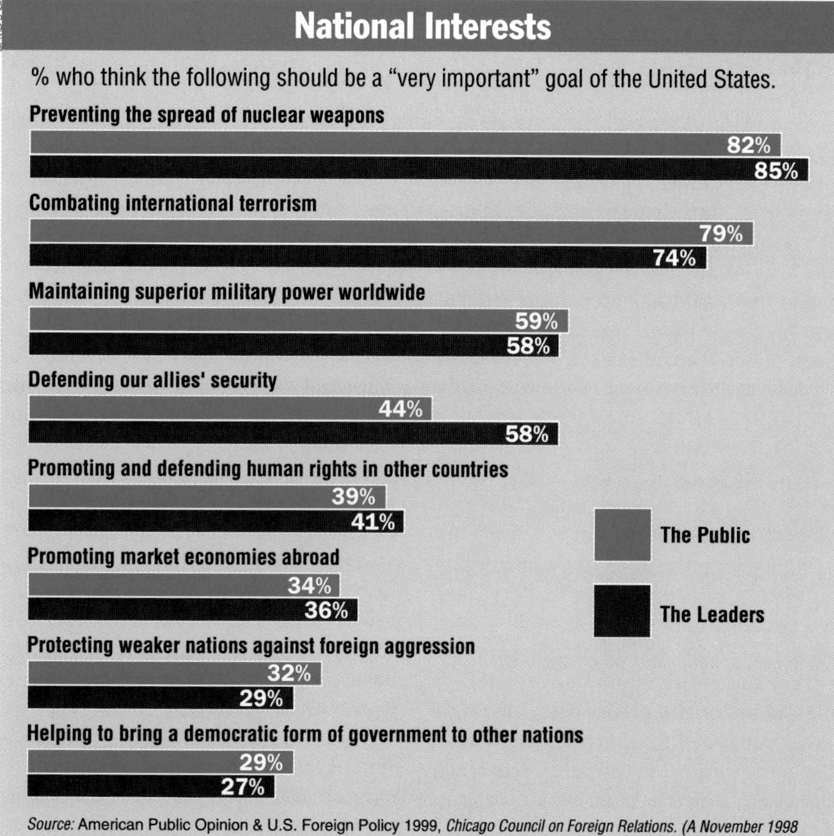

Source: American Public Opinion & U.S. Foreign Policy 1999, *Chicago Council on Foreign Relations. (A November 1998 survey of 1,507 citizens and 379 foreign policy opinion leaders.)*

and lawful world toward which its historical traditions have inclined it. The end of the cold war and the collapse of the Soviet Union seem, at least temporarily, to have freed the U.S. almost completely from history and geography.

The historical legacy

It is customary to argue that the U.S. has followed a diplomatic tradition different from other states from the beginning—pursuing for most of its history an "isolationist" policy that avoided involvement with balance-of-power politics. And some scholars cite this tradition as proving that the U.S. is different from other states in the way it conducts its international affairs.

But is that true? It is, in fact, possible to argue that the U.S. simply played the same game of power politics as every other state only a little more successfully. Thus, in the early days of the Republic, the more prudent and eminently realist policy was to find a way to avoid unnecessary risks in order to ensure the survival of the new state. Had the U.S. become swept up in European diplomacy, there was always a chance it would chose the wrong side; in that event, the American experiment might end. Hence George Washington in his famous Farewell Address wisely urged his compatriots not to become involved in European diplomatic quarrels.

The wisdom of Washington's words was apparent in 1814 when the U.S. found itself at war with powerful Britain and suffered the humiliation of having British troops occupy Washington, D.C., and burn the Capitol. America narrowly exited the war without serious damage to the future prospects of the country.

But it was not easy for America to stay out of European politics. After all, Europe was in the Americas in the form of British, French, Russian and Spanish colonies. A realist might thus argue that the primary U.S. goal should have been to drive these states from the hemisphere. And that is precisely what the U.S. over several decades set about to accomplish.

Its first break came from an unexpected source. Ironically, America can credit much of the subsequent success of its 19th-century foreign policy to the poor people of Haiti. A slave revolt erupted on the island, then the richest colony in the world, owing to its sugar production. Napoleon attempted to suppress the revolt and failed.

France's financial loss was America's diplomatic gain. Napoleon, short of cash and having lost the pearl of the French empire in America, decided to sell America most of the rest in the form of the Louisiana Purchase.

America then turned its sights on Russia. Troubling moves by Moscow in the Pacific persuaded President James Monroe to issue the Monroe Doctrine in 1823, which warned European states not to consider this hemisphere any longer open to colonization.

During the American Civil War, France made another bid to reenter the hemisphere. But when France exploited unsettled conditions in Mexico in the 1860s to install a pro-French emperor in Mexico City, the hapless Maximilian of Austria, Washington ordered troops moved to the Mexican border as soon as the course of the Civil War permitted. It was clear that if the Mexicans did not succeed in getting rid of Maximilian, which they did, the U.S. would have.

When Russia offered to sell Alaska and leave the hemisphere permanently, Washington paid $7.2 million in 1867 to remove another powerful rival.

To eliminate Spain, the U.S. through military pressure forced Madrid to sell the state of Florida to Washington in 1819 and at the end of the century, Washington provoked a war with Spain over Cuba that finally drove the Spanish from the hemisphere.

The final step was to put Britain in its place. A long-standing border dispute between Venezuela and British Guinea had festered for decades. The quarrel intensified when gold was discovered in the area. With the British refusing to arbitrate, by 1895 the U.S. felt strong enough to deliver to London a virtual ultimatum to agree to arbitration. London ceded to the American demand and Washington had achieved its century-long quest—total domination in its own hemisphere.

A more realist approach to national interest is hard to imagine.

The change

Viewed from this perspective, in other words, U.S. foreign policy may not deviate as much from the Palmerston norm as many popular accounts of American foreign policy suggest. Americans, like others, have followed their national interest quite deliberately and resourcefully.

Once America became master of its own hemisphere, however, its strategic situation changed. Bordered by two countries that could not challenge its superior position and guarded by two wide oceans, the U.S. by the early part of this century became one of the few nations on earth with true strategic freedom. It could decide whether to tend to its own knitting or to seek a world role.

It had the power to play such a role. It was by then the greatest industrial power in the world. It had a huge population, so it could raise large armies. It had major commercial interests to defend worldwide. With the completion of the Panama Canal, it had a two-ocean navy.

Nevertheless, isolation was also a credible option. The oceans were so wide and the U.S. so strong that no one could seriously challenge Washington in its own hemisphere.

For most of this century Americans have debated how to use the unusual degree of strategic freedom with which they have been blessed. First, they stood apart from the world. Then in World War I they launched a crusade for democracy. Following victory, they entered a decade or more of withdrawal.

The Japanese attack on Pearl Harbor in 1941 seemed to end the debate between isolationism and internationalism forever. It seemed clear that if the U.S. did not go to the world, the world would come to it. It could not remain safe by standing apart. ■

Six schools of thought

SINCE 1941 WASHINGTON has been resolutely internationalist. The issue now is whether it should continue to be so with the end of the cold war. America has again returned to a period of strategic choice and a debate has understandably broken out over the course America should take. At this point there seem to be six identifiable schools of thought.

Hegemonic realism

At the end of the Bush Administration, a draft Pentagon strategy paper, leaked to the press, called for the U.S. to exploit the demise of the Soviet Union to prevent the rise of any other power that could challenge America's position. It argued that U.S. policymakers should take steps not only to prevent the reemergence of another threat based in Moscow but also to make sure that America's allies, in particular Germany and Japan, remained in a dependent condition.

The American press judged the paper a bid for world hegemony. To end the ensuing public furor, the Bush Administration repudiated the paper as a policy document.

Repudiation, however, did not end the debate. The position expressed in the paper remains a legitimate option for the U.S. in the eyes of what might be called the hegemonic realists.

This school of thought begins with an observation. America has power unparalleled in the modern era. Perhaps not since the days of Imperial Rome or Ancient China has a single nation so dominated the international system as it has known it. Like Rome or China, the U.S. towers above others in military technology, economic development, political cohesion and cultural magnetism. America has arrived at an extraordinary position of power and influence.

Why not exploit that moment to entrench American superiority, argue writers clustered around the conservative weekly, *The Weekly Standard,* namely chief editor William Kristol and contributing editor Robert Kagan. Both held key positions in the Bush Administration. The case they make can really be traced back to arguments developed by Morgenthau in his seminal book. According to the realist case as presented by Morgenthau, "human nature, in which the laws of politics have their roots, has not changed since the classical philosophies of China, India, and Greece endeavored to discover those laws." If this statement is true, then it means that much better behavior cannot be expected from modern states than has been recorded in the behavior of ancient states. They were consumed with the struggle for power internationally and so will the U.S. be consumed.

International politics will forever remain a ruthless game of domination. There can be few rules except to do what is necessary to prevail. With such a pessimistic view of human nature, a few guidelines for policy develop:

- The U.S. should seek hegemony because if it does not, someone else will. Better America dominating others than others dominating America.
- The international system, inherently anarchic, needs someone in control. Today, the U.S. is the only power able to impose control on the international system. If America does not exercise control, there will be chaos.
- Others will strive to displace the U.S. from its position of superiority and some of them may be dangerous. The U.S. must use its superiority to retard others in their effort to develop weapons that can challenge it.
- Though no one likes a hegemon, America will be a better hegemon than others. On balance, it will exercise its power with some restraint. American hegemony will be relatively benign. At least it will be benign compared to the hegemony others might impose.
- Whoever dominates the international system militarily will be able, to a significant extent, to dictate to it politically and economically. This is an opportunity to spread the borders of democracy and free-market capitalism, the expansion of which should be in the American national interest.

Though the proponents of traditional realism acknowledge that ultimately other powers will rebel against American hegemony and at some point will coalesce to pull America from its perch, they argue that it is in U.S. interests to delay that moment as long as possible. They acknowledge that attempting this

KOPELNITSKY, CARTOONISTS & WRITERS SYNDICATE/cartoonweb.com

delay will be expensive. The editors of *The Weekly Standard* call for sharp increases of $80 billion in the already enormous American defense budget.

Prudent realism

A number of thinkers who also consider themselves realists are disturbed by calls for hegemony. They fear a backlash in Russia similar to the reaction in Weimar Germany, which led to the rise of Adolf Hitler. They also question whether the political culture of the U.S. is suited for the role of hegemon.

Adherents of this school argue for what might be called prudent realism. Former Department of Defense officials in the Clinton Administration like William Perry, Joseph S. Nye Jr. and Ashton Carter are concerned that the U.S. is losing sight of its true national interest, which is protection of the heartland. Instead, in their view, press sensationalism is diverting the nation's attention and energies into intervening in areas that are not critical to the nation's future.

These prudent realists divide threats to the U.S. into three categories.

- Category A: **Threats that will determine America's future.** Examples would be a Russia that begins to resemble Germany just before Hitler; a hostile China that begins to challenge America's position in Asia; the proliferation of weapons of mass destruction (WMD) to "rogue states" or terrorists who might strike the heartland; or catastrophic terrorism generally.
- Category B: **Major regional wars that might break out in Southwest Asia or Northeast Asia.** Here the prudent realists are thinking primarily of Iraq or North Korea, where either treaty commitments or policy declarations require the U.S. to take action to prevent aggression.
- Category C: **Important problems that do not threaten U.S. interests.** Examples, according to the prudent realists, would include Kosovo, Bosnia, Rwanda, Somalia and Haiti.

It is striking that virtually all of the world's attention in recent years has been given to Category C while very little has been devoted to Category A. The prudent realists would reverse that order. Nevertheless, their own understanding of the country in which they live causes them to acknowledge that powerful nations like the U.S. must do more to deal with humanitarian disasters than great powers in the past might have done.

Nye, for example, urges a differentiated approach to problems like Kosovo and Haiti. He realizes that American policymakers cannot just unplug their television sets and refuse to acknowledge that there is a humanitarian crisis, say, in Haiti. He calls for a variety of nonmilitary pressures, reserving force for only the most egregious situations and these he defines as those cases where America's "humanitarian interests are reinforced by the existence of strong national interests." He would therefore endorse the use of force in the Persian Gulf but would have preferred to have avoided the recent war with Serbia over Kosovo (although once the U.S. had entered, he argues, then it had to prevail for the sake of its larger interests in Europe).

Yet another prudent realist is Richard N. Haass, director of Foreign Policy Studies at the Brookings Institution, an important think tank in the nation's capital. He argues that according to the laws of the realist school, U.S. primacy cannot last forever. America's goal should therefore be to persuade other centers of power to support "constructive solutions" to the issue of how world society should be ordered in the future. He urges that the U.S. attempt to build an international order based on four premises: less resort to force to resolve international disputes; reducing the number of WMD; accepting only a limited doctrine of humanitarian intervention; and economic openness.

Again, a prudent realist.

Hegemonic liberalism

Hegemonic liberalism is the progressive's answer to the question of what to do with America's enormous and unchallenged military power. Most progressives are not enamoured of balance-of-power politics. They distrust a foreign policy based on the cold, traditional definition of national interest, an approach to international affairs that has led to repeated wars.

At the same time, many progressives recognize that the international system is hardly benign in character. There are states governed by evil people. Since America enjoys such superiority militarily, why not, the hegemonic liberals ask, act to eradicate that evil?

The case for hegemonic liberalism rests on what might in turn be called optimistic realism. Its proponents accept the harsh realities of international life but believe that at least America has risen above them. The world consists of the civilized and the uncivilized. It is the duty of the former to impose order on the latter.

Authors like David Rieff, deputy editor of *World Policy Journal,* urge the U.S. to exploit its military superiority to impose a world hegemony not over potentially dangerous powers like China, Germany, Japan and Russia, but over the so-called uncivilized powers. In Rieff's words, "our choice at the millennium seems to boil down to imperialism or barbarism."

In the last century, people talked of the "white man's burden." As this century draws to a close, the hegemonic liberals seem to urge America to assume a "decency burden." This school of thought holds that America is a decent country that happens to have enormous and unchallenged power. It should use that power to force others to adhere to a higher moral code.

Giving the hegemonic liberal position tremendous emotional force is the very disparity between America's military power and that of the rest of the world. The size of the disparity in itself creates an obligation to act. America is like the adult in a school playground who spots a large teenager mercilessly beating a five-year old. Does the adult not have an obligation to step in and stop the abuse?

Internationally, America resembles that adult.

Previously, it would have been impractical for America to act in all the cases championed by the hegemonic liberals. That is no longer the case. The U.S. defense budget is now 20% higher than the combined defense budgets of all of America's European and Asian allies together. The U.S. is the only country in the world that can project military power to any point on the globe within hours. Moreover, America is the only country in the world that now aspires to a world role. Consequently, when America does not act, it seems craven and heartless. Perhaps emotions like these persuaded the Bush Administration, which had earlier blocked even United Nations involvement, to order the U.S. military to intervene in Somalia in 1992 to feed the starving people there.

And, the hegemonic liberals ask, if the U.S. does not act, then why is it spending so much money on the military? Both the director of the Central Intelligence Agency and the director of the Defense Intelligence Agency have acknowledged in congressional testimony that the U.S. no longer faces any major threat to its security. China is decades away from any serious military competition with the U.S., even within Asia itself. It has only 149 strategic nuclear warheads compared with more than 7,000 for the U.S., and its conventional weaponry dates from the 1950s. Russia is a declining power. Its official gross national product (GNP) is now less than that of New Jersey and Pennsylvania combined, its conventional forces are melting away because the central government can no longer afford even to meet the payroll, and its defense production is now less than 15% of what it was in 1991.

The so-called rogue states of North Korea, Iran, Iraq, Syria, Libya and Cuba are certainly foreign policy problems but their combined GNP is about 2% of that of the U.S. Their weapons are antiquated, their economies are in ruins, and their diplomacy operates with no major friends or allies.

Reflecting these new realities, Michael Elliott, editor of *Newsweek International,* has written: "For many of those who live in the advanced democracies, the old definition (of national interest) no longer indicates what is worth fighting for, because in today's world no conceivable external military threat to those countries exists." He concludes: "For whatever wars the U.S. may wage in the next century, this can be said with certainty: None of these will look remotely like World War II. But a lot of them may look like Kosovo."

Of course, Americans could ignore stories of misery in some remote part of the world. But globalization and modern communications ensure that all will know that America did not act when it had the power to intervene. Like the adult in the schoolyard, America will enjoy no respect if it allows the bully to proceed.

Meanwhile, the legal bar to action has been lowered. According to traditional international law, states did not intervene in the internal affairs of others. This convention was the result of Europe's terrible experience during the religious wars of the 16th century. Wars then depopulated whole regions of Europe; millions lost their lives because states intervened in one another's affairs over the issue of religion. After decades of slaughter, the rulers of Europe decided that all were better off if a doctrine of nonintervention prevailed. Henceforth, no matter how brutally a sovereign might treat his citizens over the issue of religion, it was agreed that fewer people would suffer if others stood aside and watched the abuse take place than if they attempted to intervene.

This doctrine of nonintervention reigned unchallenged until World War II. Then came the shocking experience of the Holocaust. Its searing memory gave birth to a postwar human-rights movement that over time has shaken the convention against intervention. As Canadian scholar Michael Ignatieff has noted about the North Atlantic Treaty Organization's (NATO) military campaign in Kosovo in the spring of 1999, its legitimacy depended on "what 50 years of human rights has done to our moral instincts, weakening the presumption in favor of state sovereignty, strengthening the presumption in favor of intervention when massacre and deportation become state policy."

The dilemma for the U.S. is that the Ignatieff statement seems to impose equal moral obligations on all powerful states that aspire to be decent, but the reality is that in most crises America alone can act. Hence the moral pressure to respond seems to be directed primarily at one capital alone, namely, Washington.

This reality explains why in the 1990s the U.S. has taken the lead in organizing international interventions in Somalia, Haiti, Bosnia and Kosovo. When others have tried, they have usually failed unless the intervention was very close to the home country, as was the case with the Italian intervention in Albania. If the crisis is far afield or involves a significant logistical effort, only the U.S. has the aircraft and ships to support such operations on quick notice and at long distances.

There are political dangers in a policy of hegemonic liberalism just as there are in a policy of hegemonic realism. The rest of the world may not like either. Nelson Mandela, former president of South Africa and one of the world's most revered statesmen, probably spoke for many when he recently said that his country "cannot accept that a state assumes the role of the world's policeman." Other developments suggest that at some point more powerful states than South Africa will begin to coalesce in opposition to American presumption of hegemonic leadership. Meetings between senior Chinese and Russian officials regularly and pointedly condemn the concept of a world hegemon. French officials have begun talking about the U.S. as a "hyperpower."

AP/WIDE WORLD PHOTOS

U.S. SECRETARY OF STATE *Madeleine K. Albright met with Russian Foreign Minister Yevgeny Primakov (left) in July 1997 to ease tension aroused by the expansion of NATO.*

There are also questions as to whether the American people would support either "hegemonic realism" or "hegemonic liberalism" over a sustained period. George F. Kennan, the famous U.S. historian and diplomat, expresses the views of a significant number of Americans when he urges that the U.S. not engage in humanitarian interventions that would require our taking over the powers of government in a number of non-European countries. He contends that "neither dollars nor bayonets" could assure success. He also suggests that America would not have the staying power. He takes a somewhat different view of humanitarian interventions in Europe, of which the U.S. is "still largely a part," but even there he argues that issues like Kosovo are largely a problem for the Europeans themselves.

A new liberal internationalism

The Clinton Administration has been more cautious than the "hegemonic liberals." It has been reluctant to engage in humanitarian interventions although under political or diplomatic pressure it has launched several. Its fundamental approach, however, has been to trust history's "invisible hand" in the form of the alleged benign effects of the spread of democracy and free markets.

Research by scholars such as political scientist Michael W. Doyle has suggested that democratic states are much less likely than nondemocratic states to go to war against one another. Indeed, depending on the nature of one's definitions, it is possible to argue that democratic states have never attacked one another. (Britain and the U.S. were not "true" democracies when they went to war in 1812 because the electorates were sharply limited in both countries to property holders.) A corollary of the policy is that democracy depends on the development of a middle class, which to further its own interests will insist on an opening of the political process. Since the economic development of capitalism and free markets builds that middle class, the invisible hand thus ensures that politics and economics are linked.

Here, then, begins a virtuous circle that operates in America's national interest: Free trade and open markets lead to the development of a middle class; that middle class in turn brings pressure on nondemocratic governments to open up the political process; once that opening occurs, democracy develops; and finally, once a state becomes democratic, it will cease to war with its neighbors provided they, too, are democratic.

Following this logic, the Clinton Administration has favored the establishment of free-trade agreements with a growing number of countries around the world. It has also presented the issue of enlarging the membership of NATO as a step toward entrenching democratic gains in Europe.

Free trade supposedly contributes to the development of the middle class everywhere. This expanding middle class will gradually enlarge prospects for democracy worldwide, not just in Europe.

In the best of all possible worlds, every country will become democratic and peace will prevail.

In the case of NATO, the reasoning is more complicated. Some critics assert that America's most important long-run national interest in Europe today is to enhance the chances that Russia will make the transition to a democratic, free-market society. NATO expansion to the East greatly complicates the task of those fighting inside Russia for democratic change there. Democracy's enemies inside Russia are able to portray the West as taking advantage of Russia's current weakness to advance militarily toward its borders.

The Clinton Administration has tried to soften the impact of NATO enlargement by taking the position that additional states to the East will be eligible to join NATO and that at some point, assuming adequate reform, even Russia can become a member. Many question whether this is a realistic position. America's West European allies, as well as a number of U.S. senators voting for NATO expansion, tend to see the alliance in more traditional security terms. They would not favor Russian membership under any conditions. The question of whether NATO expansion will turn out truly to be in the national interest probably cannot be resolved until the political fate of Russia itself is more settled. If Russia becomes a true democracy, those in favor of NATO expansion will argue it had no effect. If Russia falters, the debate over NATO expansion is likely to endure for decades.

World-order liberalism

A venerable tradition in foreign policy holds that men go to war not so much because they are evil but because they are desperate. A realist believes with Morgenthau that war is an entrenched feature of the international system because it is part of the never-ending struggle for power. An idealist believes that men (and women) would cease fighting if they were not struggling to gain the necessities of life or if they had an alternative way of resolving their differences.

Certainly, many wars in history have involved a struggle over resources—access to water, land or treasure. Throughout most of history, the more land and people a sovereign possessed, the more powerful he became. Throughout most of history, the citizens of a conquered territory accepted the role of the conqueror. It was almost immaterial to whom they paid taxes since their lot in life was fixed anyway. More land, more people, more treasure—each and all meant more power. Kings sought all of them and accepted war as the necessary price of success.

In the post-cold-war era, however, conquest usually does not bring greater wealth but greater expense. Conquered populations do not acquiesce. They fight. They continue fighting until they are freed. Land and treasure are less important than well-educated and hard-working populations that can participate in the modern economy based on information. The path to power, in other words, lies more in internal development than in external expansion.

Of course, there are exceptions. Had Iraq seized Kuwait with its oil wealth, Iraq would have been richer. Egypt would fight to protect its main water source, the Nile River. Many Middle East countries would go to war to gain access to water. (It is ironic, however, that the cost of desalinization of seawater, though high, is still much cheaper than almost any major war one can imagine in the Middle East.)

Germany, by contrast, would not be richer or more powerful if it again tried to seize some of the territory of one of its neighbors. It would immediately be poorer and more vulnerable.

These are fundamental changes in the character of modern politics and economics. They give hope to some that for the first time in history the realists may be wrong. It may be possible to abolish war. Thomas L. Friedman, Foreign Affairs columnist for *The New York Times,* expresses this view graphically and somewhat tongue in cheek when he argues that no countries have ever gone to war with one another when their citizens could buy "Big Macs" on their own terrain. He further asserts that the poor of the world are more anxious to go to Disneyland than to mount the barricades against the rich.

These images are Friedman's shorthand for saying that the process of globalization has made war obsolete for a growing number of nations. Fail to participate in the global economy and a country will be poor. Join it and a country will not only be rich, it will be peaceful.

The world-order liberals suggest that the new security threats in the world are common to all and therefore all states have an interest in cooperating with one another in solving them. It makes little difference if one nation is slightly richer than another if both are breathing polluted air. Global warming will affect everyone. Free trade can bring greater wealth to all only if there are common rules that all accept.

A globalized economy cannot work without cooperation and accepted rules. All will be richer and more secure if they cooperate. And the rich have a special interest in the development of the poor. The rich countries are graying. Their older populations need investments with high returns. They are much more likely to find them if the developing world can resume the growth patterns of the early 1990s.

The hegemonic realists call for a significant increase in the U.S. defense budget. The world-order liberals would prefer that the U.S. significantly increase the amount of money it devotes to America's soft power—development assistance and international cooperative regimes to control the environment or to regulate the market.

All Americans of whatever school have a bit of world-order liberalism in them. America is fundamentally a commercial power favored by the status quo, which it wishes to protect. America therefore has a fundamental national interest in developing international rules and institutions that can guard that status quo.

President George Bush (1989–93) was expressing this attitude when he called for a new world order at the end of the cold war. So was the Clinton Administration when it talked of "assertive multilateralism." In each case, the fundamental assumption was that there should be international cooperation to maintain international peace and promote international commerce.

America first and alone

Patrick J. Buchanan, as part of his effort to seek the U.S. presidency in 2000, has proposed a populist, isolationist foreign policy that in his opinion would better serve the national interest than any of the schools mentioned above. Buchanan's analysis builds on the reality of American preeminence but instead of using that preeminence to establish some form of American-led global position, Buchanan would have the U.S. retreat to its own shores, ready to lash out at any power that dared to challenge the country in any fundamental way.

Like internationalism, isolationism comes in many shades. Not every isolationist would adopt the same policy, but as a general principle all isolationists would interpret very narrowly the dictum of Walter Lippmann (renowned editor and foreign affairs analyst) that national interests are those "for which the people of the nation are agreed they must defend at the risk of their lives." Most isolationists would offer U.S. security guarantees to very few countries. They would oppose U.S. involvement in any repetition of the Persian Gulf war and they would vehemently oppose U.S. participation in such peace-enforcement efforts as those the U.S. has undertaken in Haiti or the Balkans.

In the post-cold-war world, Buchanan believes the U.S. should:

- withdraw from the 1947 Rio Pact for collective security action between the U.S. and governments in Latin America,
- abrogate any security treaties that require us to go to war automatically in the event of an attack by a third party,
- and withdraw U.S. ground troops from Western Europe and South Korea.

All isolationists are extremely suspicious of American involvement in international organizations such as the UN and NATO and reject the concept that international law can bind the U.S. in its international behavior. In this regard, Buchanan argues that the "globalists" have replaced the Communists as America's "antagonists."

In a choice between being alone and well-armed, and allied and well-armed, isolationists would choose the former because allies imply obligations to others and this is precisely what isolationists do not wish the U.S. to assume.

U.S. foreign policy options

Foreign policy is always a mixture of the planned and the unexpected. The U.S. was planning to wage the cold war for decades to come. It was totally unprepared for its end. It is therefore no accident that there is considerable confusion within government and outside about the path that the U.S. should follow.

At the same time a nation will not be ready to exploit the unexpected unless it has a long-term strategy with respect to the international system it would like to see develop. The realist who expects the worst even from friends must have in mind some sense of the direction in which he would hope to encourage other states to move. So a debate about what constitutes America's national interest in this remarkable period following the end of the cold war is not a matter for academic experts only.

America has an enormous margin of strategic choice today. That fact explains why recent debates over foreign interventions have been so controversial. During the cold war, some Americans on the far left or far right might contest the direction of American foreign policy. But the Soviet threat, involving as it did the possibility of the very annihilation of the American experiment, concentrated the minds of policymakers and rallied support for the policies they urged.

With the end of the cold war, it was a matter of strategic choice whether the U.S. entered the Persian Gulf war. It was, in a sense, America's first volitional engagement since the attack on Pearl Harbor. From the Japanese attack on Pearl Harbor until the Berlin Wall fell, the U.S. believed its core security was threatened by states abroad that might well strike the American heartland. For the foreseeable future, it sees no such threats. Hence, a debate over intervention in the Persian Gulf war or in Haiti or Bosnia is to be expected.

W. GADOMSKI

At some point, however, if it wishes to shape the international system and not simply react to it, America must chose. It must decide through a consensus at the elite level and supported by a majority of the people what course it wishes to follow.

Using the yardstick of the national interest can help focus that debate so that Americans as a people one day reach that consensus. ■

Opinion Ballots are on pages 19–20

DISCUSSION QUESTIONS

1. Should the U.S. exploit its great military superiority vis-à-vis others to seek world hegemony? What is it about the character of the international system that makes you conclude that such a step would be in the nation's national interest? Would you be willing to support a major increase in U.S. defense spending to achieve that goal?

2. Should the international community attempt to take over certain territories that are not governed according to modern standards of human rights? What role should the U.S. play? Should it help finance such operations, provide logistical support, or participate with others in providing ground troops as we are in the Balkans?

3. Do you agree with George Kennan that the U.S. should not participate in a policy of "hegemonic liberalism" with the possible exception of Europe? In other words, is it in American national interests to intervene in Europe but not in Africa or Asia? Why?

4. Do you believe it is in the national interest to use America's current moment of dominance to try to change the character of the international system? Which is the best way to change that system's character—the promotion of policies of free trade and democracy as favored by the Clinton Administration or world-order measures that would strengthen organizations like the UN, the World Trade Organization, and regional partnerships?

5. Should the U.S., in the words of one "realist" skeptic, Michael Mandelbaum, professor of international relations at Johns Hopkins School of Advanced International Studies, engage in the "missionary work" of assisting failed states? If it does intervene, what is the responsibility of other powers to assist the U.S.?

READINGS AND RESOURCES

Albright, Madeleine K., "Challenges Facing U.S. Interests at Home and Abroad." **U.S. Department of State Dispatch,** Jan./Feb. 1999, pp. 15–18.*

Buchanan, Patrick J., **A Republic Not an Empire: Reclaiming America's Destiny.** Regnery Publishing, 1999. 437 pp. $29.95. The political commentator assesses U.S. foreign policy and international obligations, criticizing America's overexpanded role and intervention in world affairs.

Eland, Ivan, "Tilting at Windmills: Post-Cold-War Military Threats to U.S. Security." **Cato Policy Analysis** No. 332. Washington, DC, Cato Institute, 1999, 43 pp. Though serious military threats to the U.S. have diminished since the end of the cold war, the author states that the threat of the proliferation of chemical, biological, nuclear and missile technology by rogue states and terrorists remains large.*

Morgenthau, Hans J., **Politics Among Nations: The Struggle for Power and Peace.** New York, McGraw-Hill, 1993. 419 pp. $35.75. This updated abbreviated version of Morgenthau's classic work on international relations presents the major themes, issues and analyses of international politics.

Nye, Jr., Joseph S., "Redefining the National Interest." **Foreign Affairs,** July/Aug. 1999, pp. 22–35. Nye states that the information age has changed the nature of national interests and power. The U.S. needs to define American interests and redefine its policy in the world beyond moral values to ensure the success of the international system.

Rieff, David, "A New Age of Liberal Imperialism?" **World Policy Journal,** Summer 1999, pp. 1–10. Rieff examines the future of state intervention in the international system. He asserts that liberal imperialism may presently be the best choice for stability in the global arena.

Ullman, Richard H., "The U.S. and the World: An Interview with George Kennan." **The New York Review of Books,** Aug. 12, 1999, pp. 4–6. The interview provides many insightful opinions on various international issues affecting the U.S., such as its role in Kosovo and its relations with China and Russia.

ATLANTIC COUNCIL OF THE U.S., 910 17th St., NW, Suite 1000, Washington, D.C. 20006; (202) 463-7226; Fax (202) 463-7240. ■ A nonprofit, nonpartisan organization that conducts research to foster public debate about U.S. security and international economic policies. Publications include bulletins, reports, policy papers and the annual **Program Summary** (free). **www.acus.org**

CENTER FOR STRATEGIC AND INTERNATIONAL STUDIES (CSIS), 1800 K St., NW, Washington, DC 20006; (202) 887-0200; Fax (202) 775-3199. ■ CSIS is a public policy research institution dedicated to analysis and policy impact. Its goal is to inform and shape selected policy decisions in government and the private sector to meet the increasingly complex and difficult challenges that leaders will confront in the next century. **www.csis.org**

INSTITUTE FOR FOREIGN POLICY ANALYSIS (IFPA), Central Plaza Bldg., 10th fl., 675 Massachusetts Ave., Cambridge, MA 02139; (617) 492-2116; Fax (617) 492-8242. ■ Founded in 1976, IFPA is an independent research organization that examines political-economic, national security and defense industry issues confronting the U.S., including global trade and technology transfers. **www.ifpa.org**

U.S. DEPARTMENT OF STATE, Bureau of Public Affairs, Rm. 6808, Washington, DC 20520; (202) 647-6575; Fax (202) 647-6738. ■ The Department of State can supply information on almost any issue of political or geographical concern. Publications include the monthly **U.S. Department of State Dispatch. www.state.gov**

You can find links to this document and additional readings on our website at* **www.fpa.org/program.html

OPINION BALLOTS

Please feel free to xerox opinion ballots, *but be sure to submit only one ballot per person. To have your vote counted, mail ballots by June 30, 2000. Send ballots to:*

FOREIGN POLICY ASSOCIATION, 470 PARK AVENUE SOUTH, NEW YORK, NY 10016-6819

TOPIC 1 U.S. Role in the World

ISSUE A. Which of the following two American Presidents set the better model for U.S. foreign policy in the 20th century?

___ **1.** Woodrow Wilson

___ **2.** Theodore Roosevelt

ISSUE B. Do you agree or disagree with the following statements?

	AGREE	DISAGREE
1. The U.S. should exploit its great military superiority to seek world hegemony.	❑	❑
2. The international community should take over certain territories not governed by modern standards of human rights.	❑	❑
3. The U.S. should focus its foreign policy on Europe rather than Asia or Africa.	❑	❑

Your zip code: _____ _____ _____ _____ _____

Date: / /2000 *Ballot continues on reverse side...*

TOPIC 1 U.S. Role in the World

ISSUE A. Which of the following two American Presidents set the better model for U.S. foreign policy in the 20th century?

___ **1.** Woodrow Wilson

___ **2.** Theodore Roosevelt

ISSUE B. Do you agree or disagree with the following statements?

	AGREE	DISAGREE
1. The U.S. should exploit its great military superiority to seek world hegemony.	❑	❑
2. The international community should take over certain territories not governed by modern standards of human rights.	❑	❑
3. The U.S. should focus its foreign policy on Europe rather than Asia or Africa.	❑	❑

Your zip code: _____ _____ _____ _____ _____

Date: / /2000 *Ballot continues on reverse side...*

TOPIC 2 Russia

ISSUE A. How likely is it that Russia will become a civil society in the near future?

___ Very likely

___ Somewhat likely

___ Somewhat unlikely

___ Very unlikely

ISSUE B. Should the U.S. get tougher with Russia or be more accommodating over such issues as the war in Chechnya and the Balkan conflict?

___ **1.** Get tougher

___ **2.** Be more accommodating

Your zip code: _____ _____ _____ _____ _____

Date: / /2000 *Ballot continues on reverse side...*

TOPIC 2 Russia

ISSUE A. How likely is it that Russia will become a civil society in the near future?

___ Very likely

___ Somewhat likely

___ Somewhat unlikely

___ Very unlikely

ISSUE B. Should the U.S. get tougher with Russia or be more accommodating over such issues as the war in Chechnya and the Balkan conflict?

___ **1.** Get tougher

___ **2.** Be more accommodating

Your zip code: _____ _____ _____ _____ _____

Date: / /2000 *Ballot continues on reverse side...*

OPINION BALLOTS

ISSUE C Grade the postwar American Presidents according to how well they handled foreign policy.

	A	B	C	D	F
Truman					
Eisenhower					
Kennedy					
Johnson					
Nixon					
Ford					
Carter					
Reagan					
Bush					
Clinton					

ISSUE D. Which is the better way for the U.S. to change the international system—promote free trade and democracy or strengthen international organizations like the UN and WTO?

___ **1.** Promote free trade and democracy.

___ **2.** Strengthen international organizations.

ISSUE C Grade the postwar American Presidents according to how well they handled foreign policy.

	A	B	C	D	F
Truman					
Eisenhower					
Kennedy					
Johnson					
Nixon					
Ford					
Carter					
Reagan					
Bush					
Clinton					

ISSUE D. Which is the better way for the U.S. to change the international system—promote free trade and democracy or strengthen international organizations like the UN and WTO?

___ **1.** Promote free trade and democracy.

___ **2.** Strengthen international organizations.

ISSUE C. How important is it for the U.S. to pursue the following goals in dealing with Russia?

	VERY IMPORTANT	IMPORTANT	NOT SO IMPORTANT
Promoting democracy	❑	❑	❑
Improving the market economy	❑	❑	❑
Settling the nuclear legacy	❑	❑	❑
Strengthening the Russian state	❑	❑	❑
Integrating Russia into international organizations	❑	❑	❑

ISSUE D. The effect of U.S. policy to move Russia toward democracy and capitalism has mostly been:

___ **1.** Positive for Russia

___ **2.** Negative for Russia

___ **3.** Of little effect

ISSUE C. How important is it for the U.S. to pursue the following goals in dealing with Russia?

	VERY IMPORTANT	IMPORTANT	NOT SO IMPORTANT
Promoting democracy	❑	❑	❑
Improving the market economy	❑	❑	❑
Settling the nuclear legacy	❑	❑	❑
Strengthening the Russian state	❑	❑	❑
Integrating Russia into international organizations	❑	❑	❑

ISSUE D. The effect of U.S. policy to move Russia toward democracy and capitalism has mostly been:

___ **1.** Positive for Russia

___ **2.** Negative for Russia

___ **3.** Of little effect

Russia: report card on survival

In the 10 years since the collapse of communism, opportunists have plundered the country, leaving the economy in worse shape than ever. Can this scandal be halted? How can the U.S. help?

by Allen Lynch

REUTERS/ARCHIVE PHOTOS

A WOMAN HOLDS A FLAG *bearing the face of Vladimir I. Lenin. Thousands of striking workers gathered in Red Square on November 7, 1998, to demand unpaid wages and to call for the resignation of Boris Yeltsin.*

WHAT SORT OF A COUNTRY is Russia, now entering the 21st century and completing its first decade of post-Communist rule? What are the dynamics driving the Russian political and economic systems and Russia's engagement with the outside world, including American-Russian relations?

It is commonly accepted that modern democracy has a political-institutional foundation in the agencies and procedures of representative government; a sociopsychological foundation in the tolerance and civic spirit of the citizenry; and a socioeconomic foundation in economic well-being and a large and secure middle class. By these standards, it is most unlikely that Russia can in any foreseeable future become a liberal market democracy. Too many preconditions are absent: the rule of law, a stable and secure middle class, a broad commitment to individualism. Russia's primary political challenge instead is the establishment of a minimally competent state, one that is able to perform such elemental functions of government as raising revenue, enforcing the law among its own agencies as well as in society at large, controlling the military, policing the borders, suppressing internal rebellion, regulating monopolies and banks, etc. This is a cruel irony in light of Russia's historical struggle with overweening state authority. Yet the debility of post-Communist public institutions means that for Russians to have a chance at the development of the rule of law, the establishment of a reasonably strong state is as important as the emergence of a vital and democratically committed civil society.

In fact, Russian public life in the past decade has had less to do with the striving of state and society for democratic accountability and the consolidation of a capitalist economy than with a remarkably successful effort by strategically situated members of the old Soviet elites—economic, political and administrative—to seize Russia's wealth and consolidate their position as the new rich, at the expense not only of the Russian nation but also of the state itself. The nearly unimaginable plundering of economic assets by this post-Soviet upper class has undermined Russia's already precarious chances for a viable post-Communist transition and called into question its ability to execute its international responsibilities.

The outside world needs to view Russia with a clear eye if it is to deal with a reality that is far indeed from the optimistic premise of democratic and capitalist "transition" that has governed U.S. policy toward Russia throughout the 1990s.

ALLEN LYNCH *is an associate professor of government and foreign affairs at the University of Virginia and is the director of the university's Center for Russian and East European Studies.*

Historical legacies

Karl Marx famously observed that, while men make history, they do not do so in circumstances of their own choosing. Political, economic, social, cultural and other legacies decisively restrict the choices available to leaders and societies. How has Russia's distinctive experience, and especially that of the Communist era—which lasted for three quarters of the 20th century—shaped the country's post-Communist circumstances?

Consider that in 1913, the last full year of peacetime before the Revolution of 1917, Russia was at approximately the same level as Italy in such terms as life expectancy, infant mortality, lit-

eracy, per capita income and rail service; both were among the most backward major states in Europe. By the 1990s Italy was ranked among the top five industrial-technological powers in the world, while early post-Communist Russia was ranked last among major economies (49th out of 49 in 1996 and 59th out of 59 in 1999) in international competitiveness. In other words, the Communist years accomplished much less than is commonly supposed. This is not simply a question of Russia failing to improve its position vis à vis the Western powers, while nevertheless achieving gains over its previous condition. In some critical areas, such as male life expectancy, the Russian Federation is worse off than was the Russian Empire at the end of the 1890s. Thus, a Russian male teenager today has less chance of surviving to age 60 than did his great-grandfather in 1900. Ian Blanchard, a distinguished British economic historian, has calculated that, if the economy continues to decline at current rates, by 2005 per capita income will sink to the levels of the mid-19th century.

Russia's marginalization is not unique: Many European Communist countries found themselves in relatively worse economic shape after decades under communism. Per capita income in the Baltic states, about the same as Finland's in 1940, fell to one seventh of Finland's by 1989; Czechoslovakia, which had competed successfully with Germany in selling high-precision tools and finished industrial goods on the world market in the 1930s, had become by the 1980s, in the words of its own economists, a "museum of an industrial country."

What is unique to Russia is the extent to which its militarized economic structure, a legacy of the cold war, has distorted the allocation of resources, making it difficult to see how Russia can compete in the global economy—apart from a few natural-resource areas like oil and natural gas—in the foreseeable future.

A sense of the strain imposed by the military economy may be inferred from the fact that, with a gross domestic product (GDP) of at most one third that of the U.S. in the 1980s, Russia had a military machine that was comparable to, and in some areas superior to, that of the U.S. Nikita S. Khrushchev, First Secretary of the Soviet Communist party from 1953 to 1964, was once heard to say that the Americans built weapons with one hand and conducted business with the other, while the U.S.S.R. built weapons with both. Khrushchev and his successors failed to fully free up one of those hands for productive economic activity, with results that weigh heavily upon Russia's chances for quick economic recovery.

Finally, one should consider the enormous toll of violence on the Russian people throughout the 20th century, which has exhausted them, physically and psychologically. "Since the Thirty Years' War, no people have been more profoundly injured and diminished than the Russian people by the successive waves of violence brought to them by this past brutal century," the diplomat and Russian scholar George F. Kennan said recently, including two world wars, revolution and civil war. Add to this, he continued, "the immense damages, social, spiritual, even genetic, inflicted upon the Russian people by the Communist regime itself. In this vast process of destruction, all the normal pillars on which any reasonably successful modern society has to rest—faith, hope, national self-confidence, balance of age groups, family structure...have been destroyed. The process took place over most of an entire century. It embraced three generations of Russians. Such enormous losses and abuses are not to be put to rights in a single decade, perhaps not even in a single generation."

Natural assets

To be sure, it is not as if Russia has no tools to use in shaping its economic and political future; these include a nationwide system of secondary and higher education—one positive product of the Soviet era—as well as an impressive scientific establishment and potential in research and development. Moreover, Russia has an enormous natural-resource base, a highly educated, low-wage workforce, immense reservoirs of suppressed managerial skill and consumer demand, and impressive accomplishments in such fields as nuclear energy, outer space exploration and steel processing. Russia produces 17% of the world's crude oil, 25% to 30% of its natural gas (with more reserves than the rest of the world's combined) and 10% to 20% of all nonferrous, rare and noble metals; it is the second-largest producer of brown coal, third in timber logging, fourth in electric energy, cast iron, steel, iron ore, cereals and meat, fifth in black coal and mineral fertilizers. In such areas as production and reserves of gold, silver, diamonds, platinum, chromium, nickel, tin, lead, zinc, copper, rubber, sugar, paper and board, and bauxite, Russia is regularly among the top five in the world.

Despite its political problems, Russia possesses many of the trappings of a functioning constitutional democracy. These include a written constitution mandating separation of powers among executive, legislative and judicial branches of government; a federal structure that takes into account the country's ethnic as well as regional diversity; media that mirror the range of active political parties (this is less true of television, where the government plays an important role, directly and indirectly); and federal, regional and local elections since 1989 that have been on schedule and more or less free and fair.

Unfortunately, Russia's economic and political performance has not lived up to the promise of its resources and declared democratic commitment. The country remains mired in a decade-long depression with little prospect of participating in the global market as an industrial or postindustrial economic power. With a dollarized GDP comparable to that of the Netherlands (about $400 billion) and combined exports and imports similar to Denmark's, Russia's exports are dominated by the sale of oil and gas and are virtually nonexistent in other, value-added sectors. (Following the 1998 financial crash, which saw a 70% devaluation of the ruble, the dollar value of Russia's GDP was estimated to have declined from $446 billion to $329 billion. Russia's foreign debts increased from 28% of its GDP in January 1998 to an estimated 111% by December 1999 and a projected 116% in the year 2000.) Politically, nearly a decade into Russia's post-Communist "transition," the country is no closer to a genuinely responsive, not to mention constitutional or democratic political system, than it was at the end of the Gorbachev period in 1991. In fact, the extreme concentration of power in the hands of President Boris N. Yeltsin, exemplified by his sacking of four prime ministers in 17 months in 1998 and 1999, makes plausible the argument of the Krasnoyarsk governor and former national security chief General (ret.) Aleksandr Lebed: "Today, we have an authoritarian system of power. Until the president at the top does something, then nothing happens in the pyramid."

ILLUSTRATION BY ISMAEL ROLDAN

Political liabilities

What are the stumbling blocks? To a large extent, the political "transition," which generally corresponds to post-1945 North Atlantic forms, obscures the mechanisms and processes by which acquisition and distribution of public (and private) resources are controlled. Again, the chief force driving Russian politics since the late 1980s has not been a striving for democratic and market accountability but rather—spurred by the administrative chaos of the late Gorbachev period—efforts by strategically situated elements of the Soviet elite to convert their previous administrative control over economic assets into private ownership. In so doing, they have been able to insulate themselves from the consequences of Soviet collapse, which explains in part why the system collapsed as peacefully as it did. Not only did the disintegration of the U.S.S.R. not threaten their socioeconomic positions, it enhanced them; this helps explain the present anticommunism of former high-level members of the defunct ex-Soviet Communist party. (One gauge of the magnitude of the transfer of wealth following Soviet disintegration is the revenue from arbitrage transactions on the heavily regulated export market—where raw materials can cost as little as 1% of the world market price—which the Swedish economist Anders Åslund calculated at 30% of GDP in the first post-Soviet year, 1992.) Anatoly Chubais, Yeltsin's periodic first deputy prime minister in charge of the economy, has confirmed that special customs privileges awarded in secret by Yeltsin to his cronies, who paid Yeltsin back in 1996 with massive infusions of cash for his presidential campaign, cost the government more than $800 million. More broadly, although 57% of Russian firms were privatized between 1992 and 1996 in an effort both praised and financially supported by the Clinton Administration, the state received just $3 billion to $5 billion from the proceeds of these "sales." Essentially, the bulk of the Russian economy changed hands for the equivalent of title fees. In one of the most dramatic, but by no means atypical transactions, Oneximbank, controlled by Vladimir Potanin, one-time first deputy prime minister under Yeltsin and a friend of his personal bodyguard, in 1996 purchased the oil company Sidanko from the government for about $470 million at an auction or-

Russian Prime Ministers: a chronology

VIKTOR CHERNOMYRDIN

AP/WIDE WORLD PHOTOS

Dec.1992—March 1998

SERGEI KIRIYENKO

AP/WIDE WORLD PHOTOS

March 1998—August 1998

YEVGENI PRIMAKOV

AP/WIDE WORLD PHOTOS

Sept. 1998—May 1999

SERGEI STEPASHIN

AP/WIDE WORLD PHOTOS

May 1999—Aug. 1999

VLADIMIR PUTIN

AP/WIDE WORLD PHOTOS

Aug. 1999 and counting . . .

ganized by Oneximbank itself. In 1997 British Petroleum (BP) paid $571 million for a 10% stake, 20% of the voting rights and positions in upper management. The ratio of net worth to price of purchase was approximately 12 to 1, a fair gauge of the extent to which Russia's new capitalist class has plundered the nation. (By summer 1999, BP had written off $200 million of its investment in a company that was rapidly being stripped of its assets by its own management and suing for bankruptcy.)

Firms like BP haven't been the only victims of the predatory practices of the economic elite. The Russian Central Bank has channeled as much as $50 billion in state—that is, taxpayer—funds over the past seven years to Fimaco (Financial Management Company), a branch office that it established under Gorbachev in Jersey in the British Channel Islands, a noted banking and tax haven, to manage Communist party finances. These funds, which were sent abroad ostensibly to protect the Russian government from claims against unpaid Russian debt, were recirculated to buy Russian government bonds that provided returns of up to 200% to bondholders (compared with a normal 5%), before the Russian bond market crashed in August 1998. This scheme was managed most recently by the Central Bank director, Viktor Gerashchenko (also the last central banker of the U.S.S.R.). An audit released by Pricewaterhouse-Coopers in August 1999 indicated that the bank also transferred credits committed by the International Monetary Fund (IMF). While precise figures are difficult to come by, the IMF indirectly confirmed that at least $1.2 billion dollars of its funds were channeled to Fimaco. In the polite language of an IMF report on the matter, "the transfer of assets in the books of the central bank to Fimaco meant that the balance sheet of the central bank had given a misleading impression of the true state of reserves and monetary and exchange rate policies." These transactions reflect "a fundamental lack of cooperation on the part of the Russian authorities, and [are] a serious violation of Russia's obligations to the IMF," according to an IMF communiqué.

The scale of the diversion is suggested by the fact that the Russian government has not yet provided an adequate accounting of $4.5 billion the IMF gave it in July 1998. In the words of a *Le Monde* editorial, "one of the great countries on the planet, one of the influential members of the UN Security Council, misappropriated, like a common swindler, money from the international community through companies set up in faraway tax havens, so that a few oligarchs might enrich themselves." The IMF, which is believed to have known of the diversion, decided in mid-1999 not to give money directly to the Russian government, instead creating a $4.5 billion credit against previous loans. This allowed the money to move "from one IMF account to another," according to IMF head Michel Camdessus. The pretense of providing funding for the development of the Russian economy had been abandoned. As Camdessus put it, describing a conversation in August 1999, "I alerted President Yeltsin that Russia will be treated exactly like Burkina Faso" (one of the poorest countries in Africa).

This triumph of private over public interests, while helpful in constraining civil violence, has also constrained political and economic prospects, democratic or otherwise. In the final analysis, private interests have proven incapable of shepherding the nation through the necessarily painful aftermath of Soviet collapse.

This remains a historical development of extraordinary magnitude. By managing to dissociate economic power from sovereign power, the elite has undermined the distinctive pattern of autocratic rule that prevailed to one degree or another from the suppression of the princely "boyars" (aristocrats) by Ivan IV ("the Terrible") in the second half of the 16th century until the disintegration of the U.S.S.R. In other European countries during this time, political power, in the form of sovereignty over a polity, and economic power, in the form of control of land, resources and even people, were progressively separating, and it is precisely this distinctively Russian "patrimonial" system that was destroyed with the disintegration of the Soviet state. In principle, this means that Russia's path toward more typical European and North American patterns of political and economic development is now open. Yet the manner in which that path was opened by the Soviet boyars means that the journey will be long and arduous, with possibilities for side trips all along the way. What is surprising is not the difficulties that Russia has experienced in making a transition to democracy but that serious observers—recognizing the country's institutional and psychological legacies and the wanton privatization of the nation's wealth—should have supposed that democratic capitalism was a meaningful proposition for the Russian Federation at least in the short term.

Crisis of the state

The persistent inability of the Russian state to raise adequate tax revenue has compounded its inability to govern effectively in many other spheres. For example, severe underfunding of the military is reflected in lengthy arrears in pay to servicemen. The intermittent interruption of electric power to Russian military bases—including those with nuclear responsibilities—for failure to pay electric bills, also has seriously degraded the state's capacity to suppress internal rebellion, as the disastrous Chechen war of 1994–96 shows. In recent years the military has not purchased a single new combat aircraft from Russian manufacturers, even while they eagerly ply their wares in China and other countries able—unlike Russia—to pay cash. Following the financial crash of August 1998, the central government lost even more of its capacity to fund its far-flung military, and as a result in many areas military forces have become regional rather than national entities, as it is often the regional rather than the federal government that now supplies clothing, food and housing to locally based army units. Similarly, underfunding of the police agencies has greatly facilitated criminal penetration of the law enforcement establishment, where officers and patrolmen earn a small fraction of salaries in the legal (and illegal) private security business.

In general, cash-starved government agencies increasingly must draw on their own resources if they are to survive in the austere post-Communist budgetary environment. Often, individual ministries and private enterprises have been able to flout governmental restrictions with impunity, even when serious international consequences are involved. Several Russian factories engaged in the production of ballistic-missile components have been selling to Iran and India despite Russian treaty commitments not to do so; the U.S. has in turn imposed sanctions against these firms, to the chagrin of the Russian government. The Ministry of Atomic Energy has aggressively marketed its nuclear reactors to Iran in an $800 million deal that provides critical off-budget cash but has provoked an American protest against threats to the nuclear nonproliferation regime. The Russian government has in this case stoutly backed its own ministry on an issue where the U.S.S.R. and the U.S. managed to cooperate quite well.

Economic devastation

Space limitations prohibit a comprehensive description of the economic consequences of the crisis of the Russian state, which were underscored by the financial crash and default of August 1998. But in brief:

- "There should be no pretense. The Russian economy and living standards of the Russian population have suffered the worst peacetime setbacks of any industrialized nation in history," the UN's International Labor Organization recently declared. Between 1991 and 1996, Russia experienced an industrial-sector decline worse than America's Great Depression of 1929–33. Its GDP declined 4.8% in 1998 alone. (The devaluation of the ruble by two thirds in August 1998 temporarily stimulated domestic production in a number of areas, and the recovery of world oil prices—adding an estimated $3.8 billion to Russia's federal budget revenues in 1999—has since benefited the critical energy sector; yet absent the consolidation of a reliable legal structure, which is the precondition for large-scale investment, such gains cannot be sustained across the economy for any length of time.)
- According to the World Bank, Russia's top 30 banks have negative equity amounting to $10 billion to $15 billion. The failure of banking reform has enabled many Russian banks to "transfer their remaining assets to other financial structures while leaving their liabilities to creditors." *In extremis,* the "unpaid staff of failed Russian banks have ripped out furniture and computers and sold them on the streets."
- Most transactions, including the payment of salaries (when they are paid), are negotiated not with money but by bartering. Where money is involved, suitcases of cash are far more common than instruments of credit, even when distances are great.
- The International Institute for Management Development, of Switzerland, and the Geneva-based World Economic Forum have both consistently ranked Russia dead last in economic competitiveness. The two organizations reviewed over 100 criteria for the leading economies of the world, including openness to foreign trade, government budgets and regulations, development of financial markets, flexibility of labor markets, quality of infrastructure, technology, business management and judicial institutions. The World Economic Forum concluded: "Russia is isolated from world markets, taxation is high and unstable and there is a general disdain for the infrastructure, technology and management."
- The Economist Intelligence Unit has regularly listed Russia as the riskiest foreign investment destination among countries that it tracks.

The decomposition of the Russian state has undermined not only foreign but also domestic confidence. Despite its privileged position in terms of natural resources and workforce, capital investment in Russia in the mid-1990s was just 24% of the 1990 level. The consequence: The capital stock of the

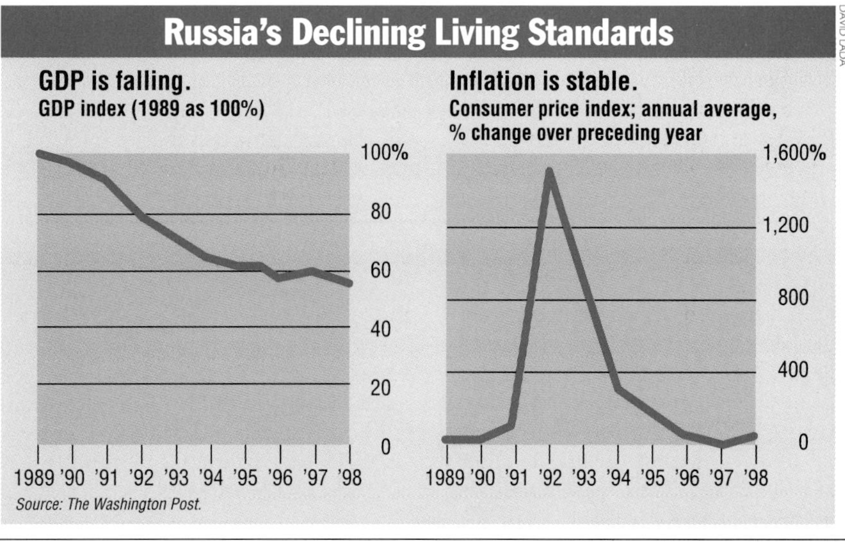

Source: The Washington Post.

country is rapidly wearing out. The average age of industrial equipment in 1995 was 14.1 years, compared with 10.8 in 1990, and 8.5 in 1970. Wealth is being accumulated in a parasitic rather than productive fashion and bears little comparison with early capitalist development in the West, which was distinguished—as Karl Marx approvingly noted—by massive and productive capital investment throughout society. The implications of this draining are dramatic: While a team of Russian economists recently prepared a best-case scenario, in which Russia might attain its 1990 GDP around the year 2008, the reality is that their worst-case scenario—in which Russia attains its 1990 GDP in 2015—may in fact be optimistic. ■

U.S. interests and choices

THE PLUNDERING of Russia's economic resources was made possible initially by the disintegration of Communist authority under Gorbachev and then quite consciously as state policy under the "reformist" government of Yeltsin, aided by the U.S. government and its democratic allies in Europe, Japan and Canada. The three pillars of post-Soviet economic reform—price liberalization (and the four-digit inflation that ensued), privatization (and the ravaging of the economy) and austerity (reinforcing widespread impoverishment)—were as much imposed upon the population as was Stalin's brutal "Revolution from Above" in the late 1920s and 1930s. The Nixon Center's president, Dimitri Simes, observed that initially, in 1991 and 1992, Yeltsin and his economic advisers Yegor Gaidar (prime minister in 1992) and Anatoly Chubais (who directed the privatization program) could not count on the backing of groups that had no hope of acquiring private wealth (i.e., the legislative and popular majority), so they attempted to create a new class of property owners who could be relied on to support radical change because it benefited them personally. But without adequate legislative foundation (because the legislature would not support the new policy), this meant market reforms by presidential decree; also absent were significant new investments, domestic or foreign, and a credible mechanism for restructuring former government enterprises. Yeltsin did not prepare the people for a period of hardship, and the majority of the population had no real stake in the reform process and thus little enthusiasm. "Had Yeltsin, Gaidar and Chubais accepted what every politician in the West takes for granted," Simes wrote, "namely, that voters cannot be forced to make major sacrifices against their will and that imperfect but democratically sustainable reforms are better than more radical changes imposed autocratically—they would likely have found many opportunities for dialogue with those elements of the Russian political spectrum who are supportive of reform but uncomfortable with shock therapy." Instead, the distinguishing mark of Yeltsin's presidency was his use of tanks in October 1993 to destroy the Parliament, thus resolving Russia's most important policy dispute by bullet rather than ballot. Russia's subsequent authoritarian constitution, which concentrates power in the hands of the (elected) executive, is a direct consequence of that failure of policy.

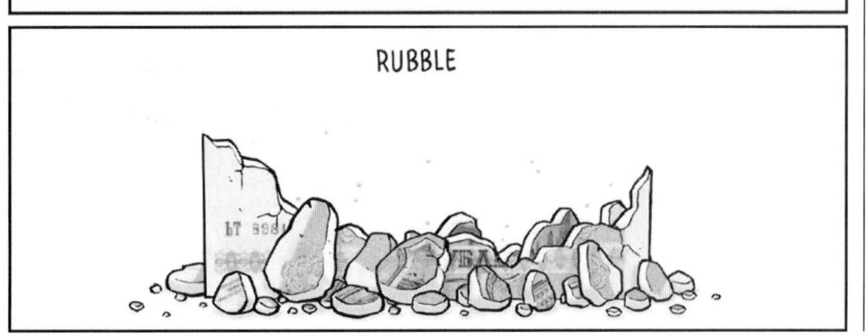

U.S. support…

The U.S. throughout the Clinton years has given Russia political and material support, in effect making the U.S. party to a faction that has lost what electoral support it once enjoyed. In the process, the U.S. has become more controversial in Russia today than it was under the Soviets (among the people).

U.S. support has come to mean support for a particular vision of how a free-market democracy might unfold, one associated with the immediate abolishment of price controls, rapid and comprehensive privatization of the economy, and tight state budgets and restricted monetary policy during a prolonged depression. Because such policies were supported by a small cohort of Yeltsin associates and opposed consistently by democratically elected Parliaments, their implementation has polarized the political system, isolated the president's party vis à vis the legislature and public opinion and, by concentrating power in an executive branch determined to push unpopular policies, set back the very cause "democracy" was supposed to advance. To the extent that ordinary Russians identify U.S. support with the violent suppression of the Parliament, the impoverishment of large sectors of society and the rise of a wealthy, politically connected elite, the foundation for liberal market reform, not to mention those directly associated with Yeltsin's government, becomes weaker—along with the pro-Americanism that took hold in the early 1990s.

It is important to stress that U.S. support for "reform" has not been limited to rhetoric: The U.S., along with international financial institutions that it strongly influences, have repeatedly provided Yeltsin's government with invaluable political cover and material resources. In October 1993, Clinton used diplomatic channels to indicate to Yeltsin that the U.S. understood his position in his physical confrontation with the Parliament, thereby emboldening him to resort to force of arms to resolve a political disagreement. In December 1994, on the eve of the Russian Army's invasion of Chechnya, Clinton specifically noted in public that the Russian-Chechen conflict was entirely Russia's internal affair, again reassuring the Yeltsin government that Russia would not have to pay a significant price in its relations with the U.S. for the large-scale (and in the end disastrous) use of force. In May 1995, Clinton traveled to Moscow, but not to London, in celebration of the 50th anniversary of the end of World War II, again underscoring the depth of the Administration's commitment to Yeltsin's government. Indeed, a year later, during a meeting of the Group of Seven advanced industrial democracies in Moscow, which was designed to emphasize Western financial support during a presidential campaign, Clinton went out of his way to compare Boris Yeltsin to Abraham Lincoln, and the war in Chechnya to America's Civil War. In spring 1996, the Clinton Administration sent four political campaign strategists—including Richard Dresner, who had worked with Clinton's personal "guru" Dick Morris when Clinton was running for governor of Arkansas—to assist in Yeltsin's reelection campaign, a fact that the Russian government strove successfully to keep secret until after the elections.

Most controversially, perhaps, the U.S. government, through the U.S. Agency for International Development (AID), effectively turned its Russian program over to a single group of reformers within the Russian government, the one associated with Chubais, Yeltsin's privatization chief. Through a subcontractor, Harvard's Institute for International Development (HIID), AID channeled $40 million in direct funding and $300 million in indirect funding to agencies controlled by Chubais. The majority of HIID contracts were awarded without competitive bidding.

IN OCTOBER 1999 *Russian soldiers look out from a trench near Gudermes, the second-largest city in Chechnya. In an effort to stem further disintegration of the Russian Federation, Boris Yeltsin had originally ordered the invasion of the breakaway province in 1994.*

Chubais's political power was critically dependent on his ability to tap foreign capital for the creation of a pro-Yeltsin upper class through rapid, comprehensive privatization of the Russian economy. U.S. and other aid agencies became the foreign constituents that were lacking at home. AID ultimately invested $58 million dollars in the privatization effort. In its 1996 annual report, AID praised the campaign, noting that 150,000 firms were privatized in 1994 alone. But, in the absence of parliamentary or popular support, this effort required rule by presidential decree. HIID drafted many of these decrees, making the U.S. government a direct party in the most controversial aspect of economic transformation. In 1997 the Russian Parliament denounced the program on a vote of 288-6. The social anthropologist Janine Wedel, who has closely studied Western aid to post-Communist Europe, observed, "Building lasting, nonaligned institutions is a tough assignment in any context. To foster reform, donors need to work to develop a market infrastructure that all relevant parties can support—not just one political faction." Through its efforts to shape the Russian economy, Wedel continued, the U.S. has helped to make it "virtually impossible to conceive of a pro-reform Russian nationalist." The discussion of Russia's national identity and interests is increasingly framed in opposition to the West, and in particular the U.S.

...and Russian backlash

Domestic backlash, which has made untenable an explicitly pro-American platform, has been compounded by Russia's increasing international isolation. The decision to expand the North Atlantic Treaty Organization (NATO) to include the former Soviet satellites Poland, Hungary and the Czech part of former Czechoslovakia, followed by NATO's air war against Serbia in spring 1999, has created something of a siege atmosphere in the Kremlin. Indeed, Russian leaders interpreted the war in Serbia as "Case Study No. 1" of the world after NATO expansion, that is, a world in which NATO rather than the UN Security Council—where Russia wields a veto—determines war and peace, including intervention against the wishes of a sovereign state. The Russian General Staff's decision to hurriedly send 200 troops to the Pristina airport in Kosovo in June 1999—made without the involvement of the Defense or Foreign ministers—reflects a widespread sentiment that Russia still counts for something in world affairs.

Likewise, Russia's renewed war against Chechnya in the fall of 1999 has been framed in anti-American terms. Defense Minister Igor Sergeyev told a group of Russian generals on November 12, 1999, that the U.S. wanted to

Key contenders in Russian elections

RUSSIA IS SCHEDULED to hold parliamentary elections on December 19, 1999. (Previous elections were held in December 1995 and December 1993.) A two-round presidential election will be held in June and July 2000 to choose a successor to Boris N. Yeltsin, who is constitutionally barred from seeking election to a third term. (Yeltsin was elected president of the Soviet-era Russian Federation in June 1991 and reelected as president of the independent Russian Federation in July 1996.) Key issues include: (1) whether the presidential election will in fact be held, given evident concerns in the president's office about political and legal retribution against Yeltsin, his family and aides, once out of power; (2) establishment of a national consensus on economic and social policy in a more statist and protectionist direction; (3) modification of the constitution to allow for a more balanced relationship between president and Parliament in favor of the latter; and (4) the nature of relations with the West in light of Russia's failure at economic reform and NATO's expansion eastward.

Although 28 parties are registered for the December parliamentary elections, key contenders include: the Communist party of the Russian Federation—the largest party in the Russian Duma (or Parliament)—which together with allied parties frequently commands a majority; the Union of Right-Wing Forces, a liberal coalition of economic reformers (including the former privatization chief, Anatoly Chubais, Sergei Kiriyenko, prime minister for five months in mid-1998, Yegor Gaidar, prime minister in 1992, and former Deputy Prime Minister Boris Nemtsov); Fatherland-All Russia, a moderate nationalist alliance that includes the powerful mayor of Moscow, Yury Luzhkov, important regional leaders and Yevgeny Primakov, the popular prime minister before being fired by Yeltsin; the Nationalist Unity party; Yabloko, a small, independent liberal party headed by the economist Grigor Yavlinsky; Our Home Is Russia, a pro-government party headed by former Prime Minister Viktor Chernomyrdin that has done poorly at the polls in the past; and the former "Liberal-Democratic" party, since renamed the Zhirinovsky Bloc after the demagogue Vladimir Zhirinovsky, whose fortunes have dropped steadily (4% support in mid-November 1999 polls) since securing nearly one fourth of the votes cast for political parties in the December 1993 parliamentary elections. Former General Aleksandr Lebed, who negotiated an end to the Chechen war in summer 1996, has seen his presidential prospects plummet since being elected governor of Krasnoyarsk province in spring 1998.

Finally, one should mention the prime minister as of the time of the writing (November 17, 1999), Vladimir Putin, who has seen his popularity skyrocket to 29% (high by Russian standards) after unleashing a massive military offensive

"weaken" Russian control of the Caucasus: "The U.S. national interests require that the military conflict in the north Caucasus, fanned from the outside, keeps constantly smoldering." General Sergeyev has not been publicly contradicted, underscoring the extent to which the U.S. has lost the benefit of the doubt in Russian politics.

Russia is very different from the rest of Eastern Europe in this respect. As the Romanian political scientist Silviu Brucan has observed, "...while the mechanisms of the world economic system compels the [smaller] East European nations to play by the rules of the world market, the referee being the IMF, the dynamics of power politics generates in a great power like Russia the will to resist, and gradually oppose, the tendency of the Western powers to assert their supremacy." (Similarly, the Russian Revolution itself can be seen in part as the reaction of a backward peasant nation against the industrial system of the West, and Stalin's "socialism-in-one-country" campaign as a desperate attempt to disconnect Russia from that overpowering world system in order to industrialize and become powerful.) If, according to this feeling, Russia is not included by the West, it can still compel Western attention. The general shift from pro-Western positions, a key part of Russia's experience with Western-aided economic "reform," has rendered such interventions noncontroversial among Russian elites. The burden of proof in Russian politics is now squarely on those arguing that the West, including the U.S., should be given the benefit of the doubt.

The U.S. and Russia

Gone is much of the sentimental glue that bound the two countries together in the early 1990s, creating an anti-Communist, pro-reform consensus. While both governments remain committed to a harmonious relationship, important constituencies in Russia see less and less to gain from it. It is not hard to imagine how actions like the dispatch of Russian troops to Kosovo or a prolonged war in the north Caucasus could trigger an anti-Russian backlash in the U.S. Congress, thereby raising the domestic cost of a pro-Russian policy for the U.S. Administration, and triggering recriminations and tensions in both Moscow and Washington. (Republican presidential hopeful George W. Bush Jr. has stated that Russia should receive no U.S. aid as long as the indiscriminate Russian bombardment of Chechnya continues.) The Russian-American relationship is thus at its most fragile point since the mid-Gorbachev period.

This is not to say that its collapse is inevitable. For the first prolonged period since the late 19th century, there is no ideological animus driving Russian-American differences. Moreover, key groups of Russian economic elites, especially in the energy and metals sectors—which together account for 56% of exports—depend on Western markets and thus reasonably harmonious relations with the leading industrial democracies. The Russian state is deeply indebted to the Western financial community, private and public: Russia's total debt, forecast at $157 billion by the end of 1999, is equivalent to about 93% of Russia's post-devaluation GDP. Any hope for continued debt rescheduling, not to mention forgiveness of Soviet-era debt (about 70% of the total), also requires good relations with the U.S. and other creditor states, which are close U.S. allies. Finally, Russia under Yeltsin, anxious to avoid the active hostility of the U.S. and its allies, has sought to preserve lines of communication even while tacking to the increasingly nationalist domestic winds. For all of the public airing of differences between Russia and the U.S. over NATO expansion and the Balkans, Russia remains committed to the joint Russia-NATO Council, established in the wake of NATO expansion, and has been an active member of a six-nation Contact Group devoted to coordination on Balkan issues. A bilateral commission in Chechnya following a series of four terrorist attacks against Russian officers and civilians, which included the destruction of two apartment buildings in Moscow and nearly 300 deaths. Putin, a career KGB official who was previously head of the fiscal oversight Control Commission of the presidential administration, is Yeltsin's preference for the next Russian president and would presumably insulate Yeltsin, his family and entourage from prosecution and legal harassment once in office. Whether he can in fact be elected may depend on upon whether, in the run-up to the presidential election in summer 2000, he can make peace as dramatically as he is currently waging war. (Dramatic peace initiatives in the previous Chechen war were also launched in the months before the summer 1996 Russian presidential elections.)

The Communist party will back its chairman, Gennady Zyuganov, as presidential candidate; Zyuganov received 40% of the vote in 1996 in a run-off with Yeltsin, although recent polls indicate that the Communists cannot advance their constituency beyond a second-place finish for the presidency, especially since their ally, the Agrarian party, has joined the Fatherland-All Russia alliance. The Fatherland-All Russia party is likely to nominate Primakov as its candidate; polls taken before the onset of the second Chechen war in fall 1999 indicated that he was far and away the most popular politician and likely to win the presidential election.

It is unclear whom the reformist Union of Right-Wing Forces alliance will nominate; the coalition does not appear to believe that it can achieve more than a nominal representation in Parliament; furthermore anyone identified with privatization, price liberalization and liberal reform in general is unlikely to be elected president. (Party Chairman Chubais is unlikely to run for office, parliamentary or presidential.) Yavlinsky is highly regarded for his integrity but will have to make some political allies to be sure of advancing beyond the 5% threshold needed to guarantee his party representation in the Parliament.

In terms of foreign policy, the Communist party suspects a Western conspiracy to undermine Russia but sees its primary challenge as reestablishing Russian power within the territory of the former U.S.S.R. The Union of Right-Wing Forces remains the most Western-oriented of parties and factions, although its leaders have adhered to the Russian consensus against NATO expansion and NATO's war in Serbia. Fatherland-All Russia's leaders, as exemplified by Primakov, would pragmatically seek to balance Russia's interests within central Eurasia with harmonious economic and strategic relations with the advanced industrial democracies.

Whoever comes to power will have to contend with the considerable constraints that Russia's economic weakness and the contraction of its military place on Russia's international ambitions, even within the area of the former Soviet Union. ■

headed by the U.S. vice president and the Russian prime minister has had success resolving differences over issues like arms sales to Iran, exploration of outer space, nuclear disarmament and trade. In the absence of territorial disputes, ideological conflict, intense economic friction or irreconcilable geopolitical interests (Russia is the only major power against which Americans have not gone to war, from the colonial period on), there is every reason to expect that intelligent diplomacy—that is, negotiation—can safeguard Russian-American relations.

Even in the event of a serious lapse, there is little prospect of a return to anything like the cold war. Russia has already lost a great deal of power and can no longer threaten regions of vital interest to the U.S.; where Russia still matters, in the former U.S.S.R., U.S. interests are relatively small. The danger of frayed relations lies in the difficult and costly matter of obtaining Russian cooperation in areas where it is key. For example, since 1992 the Russian Parliament has refused to ratify the START II nuclear disarmament treaty signed by Yeltsin and President George Bush in 1993, thereby barring the way to further collaborative disarmament. It has refused not because of substantive objections (Russia is disarming anyway due to the dilapidation of its nuclear industry) but rather as a political protest against what the nationalist-minded Parliament deems undue deference to the U.S. and as a way of protesting developments over which Russia has little control, such as NATO expansion; uncertainty over U.S. intentions regarding the 1972 Anti-Ballistic Missile Treaty, which restricts each country's ability to shoot down the other's missiles; and the NATO war against Serbia. (Similarly, the basis for U.S. Senate opposition to the SALT II nuclear arms-limitation treaty in 1979 was not the substance of the agreement but the broader context of Soviet-American relations. President Jimmy Carter shelved the treaty after the Soviet invasion of Afghanistan, knowing that under the circumstances the treaty could never be ratified.)

Democratic reforms are not a necessary prerequisite to solving problems critical to the U.S. There are, however, several crucial areas where Russian-American cooperation is indispensable to satisfying vital U.S. national interests. These include:

- ■ managing military and civilian nuclear stockpiles in a world where one nuclear power may no longer be assumed to be stable;
- ■ containing the proliferation of nuclear weapons and other weapons of mass destruction given conflicts between Russia's commercial interests and its obligations under the Nuclear Non-Proliferation Treaty and other international agreements;
- ■ ensuring that the vast stretches of south central Eurasia that were once part of the U.S.S.R. not become a haven or conduit for global terrorism;
- ■ making the vast untapped energy resources of the Caspian Sea basin available to the rest of the world through transportation and distribution networks that correspond to producer and consumer interests; and finally,
- ■ establishing sufficient stability along Russia's transcontinental southern borderlands to minimize the international fallout from the inevitable regionalization of the Russian Federation, as the global implications of letting Russia disintegrate would be catastrophic.

Each of these challenges, complex as they are, can be tackled whether or not Russia becomes a liberal state on the American model. U.S. insistence that Russia follow the U.S. example domestically as a precondition for healthy Russian-American relations could jeopardize, through backlash in Russia, every item on this security agenda, and this in spite of the fact that they are as much in Russia's as in America's interests. ■

Opinion Ballots are on pages 19–20

DISCUSSION QUESTIONS

1. Should the U.S. government use its resources to influence specific Russian domestic policies and the fortunes of specific Russian politicians? under all circumstances? under no circumstances?

2. What do you see as the relationship between Russia's domestic institutions and its international behavior? Can a nondemocratic Russia have normal diplomatic relations with the U.S.?

3. Is Russia, in fact, a democracy, or heading toward it? What difference does the answer to this question make to you? to the Russian people?

4. How important do you consider U.S. relations with Russia now that the Soviet Union no longer exists?

5. What is your best-case scenario for Russia's political future? your worst-case scenario? What would have to happen to bring either of those scenarios closer to realization?

6. How much international, including Russian and UN, oversight of U.S. nuclear weapons would you tolerate in order to establish outside control over Russia's nuclear weapons?

READINGS AND RESOURCES

Albright, Madeleine K., "U.S. Strategy for Responding to Russia's Transformation." **U.S. Department of State Dispatch,** Oct. 1998, pp. 1–5.*

Åslund, Anders, "Russia's Collapse." **Foreign Affairs,** Sept./Oct. 1999, pp. 64–77. The author reexamines the key factors behind Russia's economic problems and discusses prospects for reform.

Boilard, Steve D., **Russia at the 21st Century: Politics and Social Change in the Post-Soviet Era.** Fort Worth, TX, Harcourt Brace College Publishers, 1998. 224 pp. $29.75 (paper). Boilard displays a modern approach to examining the Russian Federation and offers a thorough analysis of contemporary Russian government and politics.

Brucan, Silviu, **Social Change in Russia and Eastern Europe: From Party Hacks to Nouveaux Riches.** Westport, CT, Greenwood Publishing, 1998. 136 pp. $49.95. The former Romanian ambassador to the U.S. and the UN describes the social history of transition from communism to capitalism in Russia and Eastern Europe.

Gaddy, Clifford G., and Ickes, Barry W., "Russia's Virtual Economy." **Foreign Affairs,** Sept./Oct. 1998, pp. 53–67. The authors examine the realities of the Russian economic crisis and the need for reforming current lending practices, which if continued will provoke further economic and political instability.

Lloyd, John, "The Russian Devolution." **The New York Times Magazine,** Aug. 15, 1999, pp. 31–41+. A look at the failure of reforms in Russia since the fall of communism and a discussion of the key factors and players behind this failure.

Mandelbaum, Michael, ed., **The New Russian Foreign Policy.** New York, Council on Foreign Relations, 1998. 215 pp. $17.95. An outstanding collection of chapters on various aspects of contemporary Russian foreign policy, all of which trace the trend away from the pro-U.S. premise of the early 1990s.

Simes, Dimitri K., **After the Collapse: Russia Seeks Its Place as a Great Power.** New York, Simon & Schuster, 1999. 272 pp. $25.00. This former adviser to President Richard Nixon examines Russia since the collapse of the U.S.S.R. and the dynamic relationship between Russia and the U.S.

Wedel, Janine R., **Collision and Collusion: The Strange Case of Western Aid to Eastern Europe, 1989-1998.** New York, St. Martin's Press, 1998. 288 pp. $27.95. Wedel examines Western aid efforts in Eastern Europe and the often debilitating effects of this aid on recipient countries.

HARRIMAN INSTITUTE, Columbia University, 420 West 118th St., New York, NY 10027; (212) 854-4623; Fax (212) 666-3481. ■ The institute specializes in teaching and research on Russia, the Soviet bloc and post-Communist states. It publishes **The Harriman Review,** a quarterly. **www.columbia.edu/cu/sipa/REGIONAL/HI/home.html**

INSIDE RUSSIA (THE HERITAGE FOUNDATION), 214 Massachusetts Ave., NE, Washington, DC 20002-4999; (202) 546-4400; Fax (202) 546-8328. ■ The Heritage Foundation in collaboration with its Moscow office created the Inside Russia program to support research and debate on the politics and people of Russia in transition. The program offers conferences and lectures, publications, commentary and interviews and various links including Moscow Talk Radio and Dateline Moscow News Update. **www.insiderussia.org**

ISAR: A CLEARINGHOUSE ON GRASSROOTS COOPERATION IN EURASIA, 1601 Connecticut Ave., NW, Suite 301, Washington, DC 20009; (202) 387-3034; Fax (202) 667-3291. ■ ISAR supports initiatives that empower citizens throughout the former Soviet Union to create a more just and sustainable society. It seeks to build coalitions among U.S. groups interested in grass-roots activities in the former Soviet Union. Offers technical assistance and training and publishes **Surviving Together,** a quarterly journal which covers environmental and other activities in Eurasia. **www.isar.org**

KENNAN INSTITUTE FOR ADVANCED RUSSIAN STUDIES (WOODROW WILSON INTERNATIONAL CENTER FOR SCHOLARS), One Woodrow Wilson Plaza, 1300 Pennsylvania Ave., NW, Washington, DC 20004-3027; (202) 691-4000; Fax (202) 691-4001. ■ Academic center that fosters advanced research on Russia and the former U.S.S.R. by scholars, government officials and the press. Publications include a monthly newsletter and **Occasional Paper Series.** **wwics.si.edu**

You can find links to this document and additional readings on our website at* **www.fpa.org/program.html

Indonesia in aftershock: prospects for recovery

The fourth-largest country in the world is torn by political, economic and civil strife. Is it likely to recover anytime soon? Should the U.S. care?

by John Bresnan

AGENCE FRANCE-PRESSE

NEWLY ELECTED *President Abdurrahman Wahid, the surprise choice of Indonesia's national assembly in an October 20, 1999 vote, clasps hands with Vice President Megawati Sukarnoputri, daughter of Indonesia's first president.*

INDONESIA IS A NATION in aftershock. The financial crisis that swept the newly emerging markets in 1997 produced its most devastating effects in Indonesia. The currency lost two thirds of its value. The banking system collapsed. Unemployment spread rapidly through the cities of Java. Inflation went through the ceiling. Old grievances, long submerged by prosperity, rose to the surface, and social relations across ethnic and religious lines broke down in violent events in widely separated locations. Rioting and looting occurred in the capital and other major cities in May 1998, and Suharto, the country's president for 32 years, was forced to resign. That was the shock, the undoing of a highly centralized, highly personalized system of power that had turned the governance of this huge nation, the fourth-largest in the world, spread across a vast archipelago, into an increasingly corrupt and repressive regime.

The aftershocks are still occurring. International pressure led to a referendum in the eastern half of the remote island of Timor, a former Portuguese colony, that rejected autonomy within Indonesia in favor of independence. This was followed by an effort by local militias, backed by the Indonesian army, to leave a legacy of devastation for the embryonic state. Most foreign aid was suspended owing to either the East Timor events or a major banking scandal or both. Elections in June 1999 created a Parliament divided between five major parties with no clear winner. Only in October 1999, 17 months after President Suharto's fall, did a national assembly select as president a surprise candidate, a respected Muslim leader, Abdurrahman Wahid, a champion of tolerance, inclusion and self-respect. By this time, a student-led movement in the far north of Sumatra had gathered mass support demanding a referendum on independence for the province of Aceh, leading to widespread fears that the whole of Indonesia might break apart. President Wahid and his broadly based coalition government stirred cautious hopes, but faced daunting challenges.

These developments have left the Indonesian elite battered by foreign criticism, uncertain who is to blame, and, as this is written in mid-November 1999, pressed to act quickly to do several things all at the same time: preserve their national unity, repair their economy, and reform their public and private institutions. As if these domestic tasks were not enough, President Wahid has expressed an interest in building a new coalition of Asian states, including India and China, to help balance the unparalleled role of the U.S. in Indonesia's recent affairs. But he also, within weeks of

JOHN BRESNAN *is senior research scholar in the East Asian Institute of Columbia University. He has made many trips to Indonesia and has written extensively about that country.*

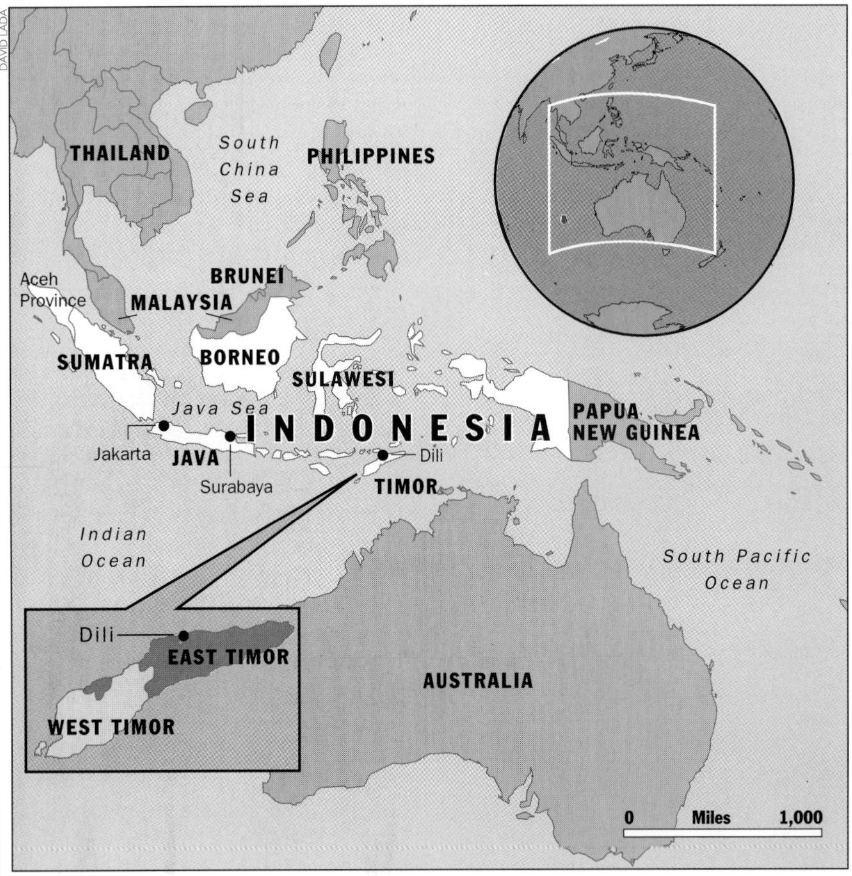

his election, was in Washington to meet with President Bill Clinton, asking for American help—economic aid, as was to be expected, but also support for helping Indonesia to become a nation under the rule of law.

All this has come very hard for one of the societies that created "the East Asian miracle." That was no miracle, of course, but it was no mirage either. It was real and it was the result of the interplay of public policy, private investment and profitability. The Indonesians doubled average per capita income, in real terms, three times over three decades. They did it by putting the country's resources into economic and social development, not into political monuments or expensive military hardware. Food production spiraled upward. Educational advances were unrivaled in the developing world. Population growth slowed markedly. And the country consistently stood by tolerance in the midst of exceptional ethnic and religious diversity.

Suharto's role

So what went wrong? Suharto bears a large part of the responsibility for the corruption of the state, which gathered force particularly through the 1990s, and which was at the heart of the loss of confidence in the economy in 1998. He approved every contract, investment or loan of any significance. He granted private monopolies to his cronies and children. They in turn used their ties with him to obtain generous loans from state banks. In this way the whole national bureaucracy was in time engulfed in the corruption. When confidence was lost in part of the state structure, it was quickly lost in the entirety.

Suharto's notorious corruption posed a dilemma for the U.S. It felt compelled to participate in the International Monetary Fund (IMF) bailout of the Indonesian economy in October 1997 because the contagion was spreading to Wall Street, and the global financial system was at risk. But the IMF was up for refunding by the U.S. Congress, where Suharto and the IMF were equally unpopular. The Administration assured Congress that it would exact a price from Suharto and his family for the bailout. Suharto agreed in writing to the terms set by the IMF, but he had no intention of following them. He complained to former Vice President Walter F. Mondale that he was being victimized. For months he did nothing as the economy slid further downward. The IMF finally cut off the flow of funds to force Suharto's hand. When he did act, it was to raise the price of fuel for cooking and transport, hitting ordinary citizens, while he continued to shield his family and friends. That action led directly to protest demonstrations, police and army firing on unarmed students, still wider rioting, looting, arson and Suharto's own downfall.

In addition to Suharto, the IMF bears some responsibility for the severity of the crisis in the Indonesian case. The IMF experience had been chiefly in Latin America, where the problem was typically that a government had spent more than its income and needed to go through a period of austerity. That was not what had happened in East Asia; in fact, the governments that eventually fell under IMF control—Thailand, Indonesia and South Korea—had been running budget surpluses. Yet the IMF imposed the same measures it had applied in Latin America: it demanded bigger government budget surpluses, which reduced the supply of money and credit, and deepened the forces of depression. In addition, in Indonesia, for reasons that have not yet been adequately explained, the IMF and the Indonesian government closed 16 commercial banks. Indonesia had no deposit insurance system, however, and the closing of the banks led depositors in the remaining banks to withdraw their funds in a panic, pushing the banks into collapse.

Indonesia's private banks and corporations, along with foreign private investors and lenders from the U.S., Japan and Europe, contributed to the severity of the crisis as well. All through the 1970s and most of the 1980s, the price of oil was high in international markets, and Indonesia's oil exports played a key role in financing its economic and social development. By the 1990s this was no longer the case, and Indonesia needed a new engine of growth. It found one in foreign borrowing. Foreign banks and investment houses were searching globally for high rates of return. And Indonesia's private corporations were aggressively in search of capital for expansion. Private greed led to imprudent deals. Indonesians borrowed foreign currency to invest in domestic expansion, and they borrowed for one to three years to finance long-term projects. They were taking a risk on the ability and willingness of the foreign parties to roll over the debt when it came due, and they were taking a risk on the strength of the Indonesian currency to buy the foreign currency at the old rate of exchange. Both sides knew that these risks were unhedged.

The cost of the collapse is still being reckoned. At this writing, the Indonesian currency is still trading at less than half its value in June 1997, before the floating of the Thai baht set the crisis in motion. As a result, most Indonesian corporations have not been able to pay their debts to foreign banks, or have been unwilling to do so. (They also have not filed for bankruptcy because there is no functioning bankruptcy system in place.) The banking system has not yet been recapitalized and so is not yet functioning either. Exports of manufactured goods are still not returning to past levels, in spite of exchange rates that are highly favorable. The gross domestic product (GDP), which fell by 13.8% in 1998, is expected to drop again in 1999. The prospect is for a slow climb back over a period of another five years.

U.S. involvement

The U.S. has found itself deeply involved in Indonesia's affairs in spite of a history of official policy that has given Indonesia a low priority in American strategic thinking. The U.S. became involved in the financial crisis of 1997-98, in the Indonesian parliamentary elections of June 1999, in the referendum in East Timor of August 1999, and in the formation of a coalition government in October 1999 because the process of globalization is making the world a smaller place. And it became involved because the U.S. could not afford not to do so.

Indonesia has since its emergence as an independent state been what Yale historian Paul M. Kennedy calls a "pivotal state." It matters greatly to other states in its region. It is strategically located astride the sea-lanes between the Pacific and Indian oceans, through which the U.S. Navy reaches the Persian Gulf, through which Middle Eastern oil reaches Japan and the rest of East Asia, and through which Australia ships the bulk of its exports. With a population of more than 211 million, Indonesia comprises 40% of the population of Southeast Asia, and is key to regional stability and prosperity.

But ever since its ignominious retreat from Vietnam in 1975, the U.S. has not been able to maintain a consistent view of Southeast Asia. The Indonesian case is a prime example. Indonesia has come across the horizon of Washington policymakers only from time to time, most often as a problem, only very occasionally as an opportunity. The U.S. Treasury opted for the financial bailout of Indonesia because it feared for the world markets. The U.S. Department of State played an active role in Indonesia's first unrigged elections in 44 years because it saw an opportunity to promote democracy, a key Clinton addition to the U.S. foreign policy agenda. The U.S. Congress focused on East Timor because a number of members of both houses were concerned about Indonesian military abuses there; over the years the Congress had virtually eliminated military contacts between the U.S. and Indonesia. There has been no overall strategy for dealing with Indonesia, and little coordination. The scandals that have plagued the Clinton White House have inhibited U.S. engagement. And the division of control of the executive branch and the Congress between Democrats and Republicans has been a source of further instability in U.S. policy.

Three-part U.S. interest

The U.S. interest in Indonesia is strategic, humanitarian and political. The U.S. agonized over whether and how to intervene in the East Timor case because it did not want to earn the enmity of the fourth-largest population in the world and the globe's largest Muslim population, and because it could not ignore the human tragedy that was occurring among a tiny and defenseless population that the U.S. had the means to help defend. The U.S. also did not want to take any action that might worsen the disarray that already existed in Indonesia's political life, fearing that the situation could easily collapse into further violence in cities like Jakarta, the nation's capital, with a population of 8.8 million. Nor did the U.S. want to impede the political transition that was taking place in Indonesia, which could lead to its becoming the third-largest democracy in the world, and one of the few with a predominantly Muslim population (87%).

The U.S. strategic interest has changed as the world has moved into the new era of globalization. Analysts now consider Indonesia's control of the sea-lanes as being chiefly of economic concern. The thinking is that closing sea-lanes is a blunt instrument, causing pain to friend and foe alike, and therefore seldom attempted. Moreover, should the sea-lanes be closed, shipping would almost certainly go around the area of obstruction, increasing transportation costs but not requiring a military response. That is what happened when the Suez Canal was closed; shipping

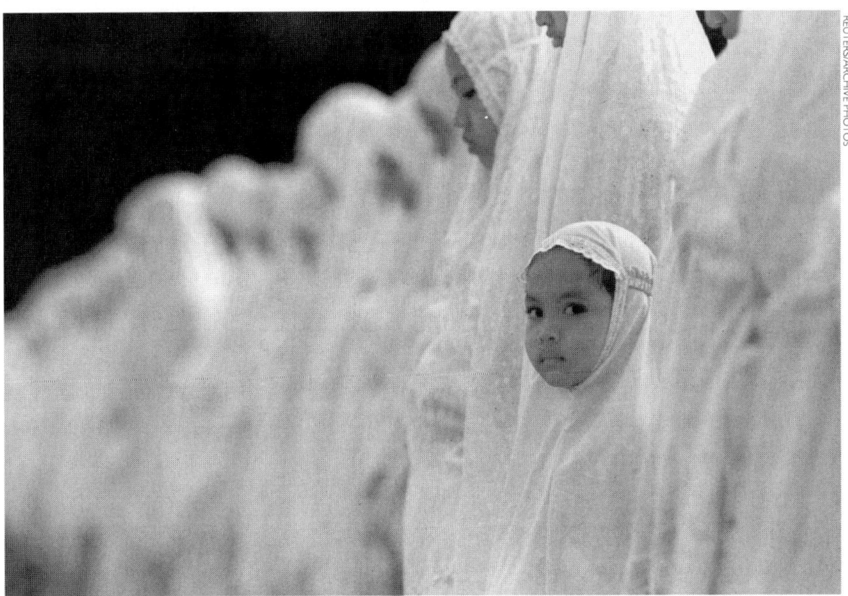

REUTERS/ARCHIVE PHOTOS

A YOUNG MUSLIM GIRL *takes part in an early morning service celebrating Eid at the Al Azhar Mosque in Jakarta, Indonesia. That country contains the world's largest Muslim population.*

simply went around Africa. The U.S. does have economic interests in Indonesia, chiefly in oil, natural gas, minerals and banking. But these, while of great importance to the Indonesian economy, are of only limited importance to the U.S. economy. Perhaps the strongest argument for a U.S. interest in Indonesia is that country's vital importance to Australia and Japan, and to Thailand and the Philippines, all U.S. treaty allies.

A principal characteristic of U.S. policy toward Indonesia, then, is that U.S. attention tends to be episodic, responding to developments in Indonesia as they occur. The U.S. seems to be unable to maintain any degree of continuing engagement, or to have a clear set of priorities in mind, and thus is unable to stay focused on a set of goals it can pursue in a pro-active manner. This is the worst possible position for the U.S., because it is thus regularly obliged to deal with situations about which it is not well informed and to act before it is well prepared. The U.S. has only a relatively small embassy in Jakarta, at the western end of the island of Java, and consulates in Surabaya, at the eastern end of Java, and on the island of Bali, with no representation anywhere else in the vast Indonesian archipelago. (The recent increase in attention to Indonesia has led to some hope of improving the U.S. presence in the coming year.) The U.S. also has had no one with resident experience in Indonesia at a political level in the government in Washington. (With the recent return to Washington of the U.S. ambassador, J. Stapleton Roy, who will serve as assistant secretary of state for intelligence and research, there will be the first opportunity in years to have the advantage of firsthand familiarity with Indonesia represented in the process of policy formulation.) Unlike governments such as those of Japan and Australia, the U.S. seems to be unable to mobilize the expertise of the private sector except, again, episodically. This situation is not unique to Indonesia. It is common to the entire class of "pivotal states."

In this environment, the U.S. has recently faced three major decisions in regard to Indonesia that posed questions that go beyond that country. The U.S. faced the question of how to respond when the Indonesian police and army failed to bring the marauding militias of East Timor under control, an event that galvanized the UN Security Council to a rare consensus on peacekeeping. The U.S. faced the issue of how it should act as a member of the executive board of the IMF when a financial scandal raised questions about the ability of the government of Indonesia to manage international aid in a manner free of corruption. And the U.S. was confronted with the problem of how it should deal with the army of Indonesia: whether as a political force to be reckoned with in the future of Indonesia or as a pariah to be isolated from normal relations. All three of these issues arise in settings beyond Indonesia. They are major concerns somewhere in the world at all times in the current era of international relations. Nevertheless, as the Indonesian case demonstrates, the U.S. response is not likely to be uniformly the same across the geopolitical horizon. Circumstances matter, and cases differ. ■

Implications of the East Timor tragedy

THE HORROR OF RAMPAGING Timorese militias, the killings of hundreds, perhaps thousands of people, the flight and enforced removal of hundreds of thousands more, the physical destruction of homes and public buildings, the targeting of religious leaders and structures, all these images remain clear in the mind's eye of anyone who was following the international news in September 1999. Less clear were the answers to several questions: Was the mayhem planned, and if so, why and by whom? Why did the Indonesians not stop it? Why was the international community not better prepared? Why did it take the U.S. so long to act? And was the outcome that resulted the best that might have been expected?

East Timor was a colony of Portugal until 1975. Following the overthrow of a dictatorship in Lisbon, a reformist Portuguese government declared that East Timor's colonial status would end, and set October 1976 for popular elections to an assembly to determine East Timor's future. Two groups of Timorese quickly formed, one favoring independence, and the other favoring integration with Indonesia. Faced with some prospect that the pro-independence party would proceed without waiting for a vote, Indonesian forces invaded East Timor on December 7, 1975. The UN Security Council on December 22 called on Indonesia to withdraw. Thus a population of 600,000, long ignored by its colonial masters, and occupying the eastern half of an infertile island in a remote part of the Indonesian archipelago, became an object of international dispute.

The U.S. was unfortunately implicated in the Indonesian invasion. In December 1975, President Gerald R. Ford, accompanied by Secretary of State Henry A. Kissinger, was visiting Jakarta on a tour of Southeast Asia designed to reaffirm the American commitment to the freedom of the region in the wake of the collapse of South Vietnam. Suharto told them of the planned Indonesian invasion. Kissinger later acknowledged that he had told the Indonesian president that the U.S. assumed the Indonesians would do what they had to do. The Indonesians began their invasion the following day, using equipment provided by the U.S., in contravention of the U.S. terms under which it was sold. It is not true, however, as some have argued, that the U.S. gave a "green light" for the Indonesian invasion. There is no evidence that Suharto sought U.S. approval, and indeed it would have been out of character for him to have done so. But it is true that, in the cold-war spirit of the time, the U.S. did not object to or criticize the Indonesian invasion. Washington contented itself for years with noting that Indonesia had de facto control of East Timor and that an act of self-determination had not taken place.

From the very beginning, the Indonesian army earned a reputation for extreme brutality in its behavior in East Timor. Especially following a cemetery massacre in 1991, members of Congress protested the Indonesian abuses in East Timor. In the pre-Timor years, the U.S. had developed a close working relationship with the Indonesian army, and it became customary for senior officers to have some period of training in the U.S. In the post-Timor years, the Congress whittled this relationship down to next to nothing. By the time the East Timor case erupted in 1999, there was not much left but a few joint humanitarian exercises a year, each requiring the personal approval of the secretary of defense.

Indonesia and Portugal were gradually coming to an agreement on East Timor under quiet goading by the secretary-general of the UN. Then in early 1999, B.J. Habibie, successor to President Suharto, was stung by a letter from John Howard, prime minister of Australia, letting him know that Australia was no longer prepared to recognize Indonesia's sovereignty in East Timor. An impulsive man, Habibie announced that Indonesia would unilaterally proceed to determine the wishes of the East Timorese people. The government of Indonesia would offer them a considerable measure of autonomy, and if they did not accept that, would consider East Timor as no longer a part of Indonesia. It was subsequently agreed that the UN would conduct this act of self-determination, and voting was eventually set for August 30, 1999.

Opposition of army leadership

The Indonesian army leadership opposed this decision, and, having been overruled, attempted to subvert it. Military intelligence personnel organized militias in each of East Timor's districts, armed them, and set them loose on a campaign of intimidation. The aim apparently was to keep enough people from voting to produce a questionable outcome. But on August 30, more than 98% of the registered voters cast their ballots, and more than 78% of these voted against the Indonesian proposal—in effect, voted for independence. At this point, the army stood aside as the militias began a rampage of terror, murder, arson, looting and destruction. People fled the towns for the hills. Some 200,000 fled or were forced to flee to neighboring West Timor. UN personnel were fired upon and two were killed; Catholic priests were shot dead. Indonesian army forces were reported to observe these actions without opposition and even, in some cases, to join in.

Speculation took several directions. One was that the Indonesian army leadership in Jakarta gave general approval for a certain amount of postelection violence in order to provide an object lesson—either to the civilian government, or to the people of other separation-prone provinces. Another was that the militias were intended to create a semblance of civil war as a basis for a division of East Timor into two sectors, one of which, adjoining West Timor, would remain with Indonesia. Whatever the intention, the violence quickly got out of hand, and army personnel were unwilling to stop it. General Wiranto first assured foreign governments that he would quickly bring the situation under control, but after a personal visit to East Timor concluded he could not do so. Finally, on September 12, after almost two weeks of chaos, a humiliated Indonesian armed forces commander agreed to cede responsibility to foreign troops.

All through these two weeks, the U.S. government faced growing pressure to act. The case of Kosovo was very much on American minds—the first time the nation has gone to war to stop ethnic cleansing of a minority people. Was East Timor another Kosovo? The U.S. had no vital interest in East Timor. There was no Asian counterpart to a North Atlantic Treaty Organization needing to prove it was relevant in a post-Soviet Europe. On the other hand, the international community had never recognized East Timor's incorporation into Indonesia. And allowing the militias to nullify the results of a UN referendum was not a precedent that anyone wished to permit. But Security Council members also were not prepared to send troops to face a possibly hostile Indonesian army. So the issue became that of obtaining Indonesia's consent to intervention by an international force.

Pressure on the Indonesians to accept an international force in East Timor came from several sources. Australia was prepared to lead the international force. Five ambassadors sitting in the Security Council traveled to Jakarta to speak directly to Habibie and Wiranto, and went to Dili, the capital of East Timor, to see the situation firsthand. The governments of four of Indonesia's neighbors in Southeast Asia—Singapore, Malaysia, Thailand and the Philippines—volunteered to contribute to the peacekeeping force. Russia and China, often opposed to humanitarian intervention, made clear they were prepared to join a unanimous vote in the Security Council. The Indonesians must have begun to see that they faced the condemnation of the international community.

President Clinton said publicly that

AP/WIDE WORLD PHOTOS

IN EAST TIMOR, *a man wearing traditional headdress is lost in a sea of voters waving their voter registration papers while they line up at a polling station for the historic UN-sponsored vote to determine the region's status.*

the Indonesians must end the violence or permit an international force to do so. Officially, the U.S. did not wish to go further, concerned not to add to the growing xenophobia in Jakarta. Congress was meanwhile threatening to legislate economic sanctions on the already devastated Indonesian economy. Every day of inaction, it was pointed out, also meant the loss of lives in East Timor. As the Indonesians continued to stall for time, Clinton finally did threaten to halt support for Indonesia from the IMF, which would bring most international economic transactions to a halt. But he did so speaking privately to General Wiranto by way of the chairman of the U.S. Joint Chiefs of Staff, General Henry H. Shelton. And this seemed to provide the final push. The Indonesian army and then the Indonesian government capitulated.

Australia pressed the U.S. to play a strong supporting role in the international force. Australia had historic ties to East Timor; the East Timorese had saved Australian lives during the Japanese occupation of the island during World War II. But the Australians did not want to risk a possible confrontation with the armed forces of Indonesia without the support of the U.S. Some in Washington believed that the U.S. should provide

Financial corruption

As the U.S. was threatening to withdraw the support of the IMF unless the Indonesians accepted international peacekeepers in East Timor, the IMF and the World Bank were already warning that their support of the Indonesian economy was in jeopardy. The reason was persistent corruption in the Indonesian financial system. The most notorious case involved a payment of $70 million by a nationalized bank, Bank Bali, to a company connected with Indonesia's ruling party to recover loans already guaranteed by the government. Critics charged that the money had been siphoned off to help pay for Habibie's run for the presidency in October 1999.

The collapse of the financial sector was the central feature of the Asian crisis of 1997–98. In Indonesia, the collapse of its currency, the rupiah, led to widespread closures of banks crippled by panicked withdrawals of deposits and mountains of nonperforming loans. On the advice of the IMF, the Indonesian government set up the Indonesian Bank Restructuring Agency (IBRA) in January 1998, with extensive powers. IBRA closed 66 banks and took over an additional 12. In bailing out several other banks, it forced the owners to put whatever assets they had into special holding companies, giving it indirect control of an estimated 25% of Indonesia's annual economic output. IBRA was to sell off these assets to help finance bank recapitalization. To do so it would have to remove the management of the assets from the families of their powerful owners. Not surprisingly, little of this has happened as yet.

It also was possible that the Bank Bali scandal was only the tip of an iceberg. In August it was reported that several senior managers of the country's largest private bank, Bank Internasional Indonesia, which is part of the Sinar Mas group, the country's second-largest family-owned conglomerate, were forced to resign after failing an ethics evaluation. It also was reported that $250 million was missing from the books of Semen Cibinong, the country's third-largest cement producer. The absence came to light in discussions with the company's creditors, which included the Export-Import Bank of the U.S. A survey of businessmen ranked the Indonesian economy among the most corrupt in the world, along with Russia's, Colombia's and Nigeria's.

The Bank Bali scandal posed a serious quandary for the IMF. Together with the World Bank, it had paid over $10 billion to Indonesia as part of the $40 billion rescue package assembled in 1997. The World Bank was already holding back $600 million in loans for Indonesian poverty relief following charges that relief funds were used to sway voters in the June 1999 parliamentary elections. Obviously these international lenders had to be concerned if money designated to salvage Indonesia's banks and its poorest people was ending up in the pockets of corrupt officials who helped create the problems the international institutions are now trying to resolve. But they had little alternative but to make the payments of some $2 billion that were already scheduled. Indonesia's economy and government depended from day to day on this flow of funds. Continuing the flow was essential if the IMF and World Bank were to recover the funds they already had paid out.

The election of Wahid to the presidency resolved this dilemma, opening the way to cleaning up the Bank Bali case and the restarting of IMF and World Bank aid. But it left large questions about how foreign aid was to be given to Indonesia in the future, and about how financial and judicial institutions can be developed that hold more promise of responsible behavior than those currently in place. ■

AGENCE FRANCE-PRESSE

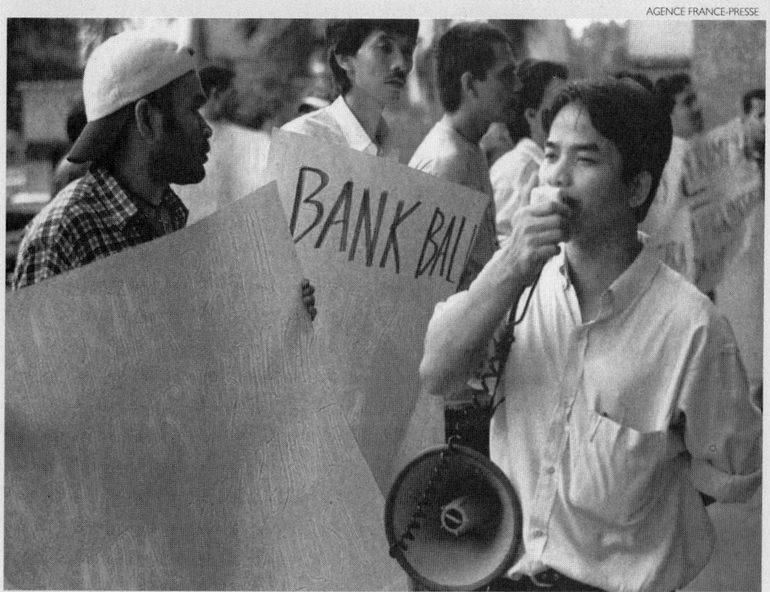

Activists picket headquarters of Bank Bali to protest transfer of $70 million to secure a loan already guaranteed by the government. The transfer was made to a finance company with links to the Golkar party, leading to speculation that it would be used to finance Habibie's run for the presidency.

combat troops, in recognition of the fact that Australia had fought side by side with Americans in every war fought by the U.S. in the past century. At the same time, there was concern in the Pentagon and the Congress that the U.S. was becoming overextended with peacekeeping in far-flung locations. The U.S. compromised: it would contribute 200 noncombat military personnel to help with transportation, communications and intelligence.

In early October, UN Secretary General Kofi Annan took two further steps. He requested the UN High Commissioner for Human Rights to conduct an inquiry into whether atrocities in East Timor called for the creation of an international tribunal, and he requested the Security Council to approve the international organization's taking over responsibility for security in East Timor and for its civil administration, pending independence in two or three years. It was quickly seen that both these initiatives could lead to further issues for the U.S. The rights inquiry could in time lead to requests for U.S. intelligence data bearing on the responsibility of senior Indonesian army generals for atrocities committed by militias. Taking over the administration of East Timor would be the biggest such operation undertaken by the UN since its operations in Cambodia in 1982 and 1983. The main issue for the U.S. was cost. The UN assesses the U.S. 31% of the cost of peacekeeping operations, but Congress has refused to pay more than 25%.

East Timor itself probably will recede from international attention as the immediate threats to human life are brought under control. But the issues it raised are likely to continue to confront the U.S. and the UN.

Military abuses and U.S. relations

At the peak of the East Timor crisis, as the U.S. was increasing the pressure on Indonesia to accept international intervention, Washington announced it was ending military-to-military relations with the Indonesian armed forces. The step was largely symbolic; military-to-military relations were all but nonexistent at that point. However, the U.S. turned only a few days later to the chairman of the U.S. Joint Chiefs of Staff to convey warnings directly by telephone to General Wiranto, the commander of the Indonesian armed forces. General Shelton had testified before Congress at the start of the crisis that contacts between officers of the two militaries were beneficial. These events served to keep alive the long-term debate in the U.S. over military ties with Indonesia.

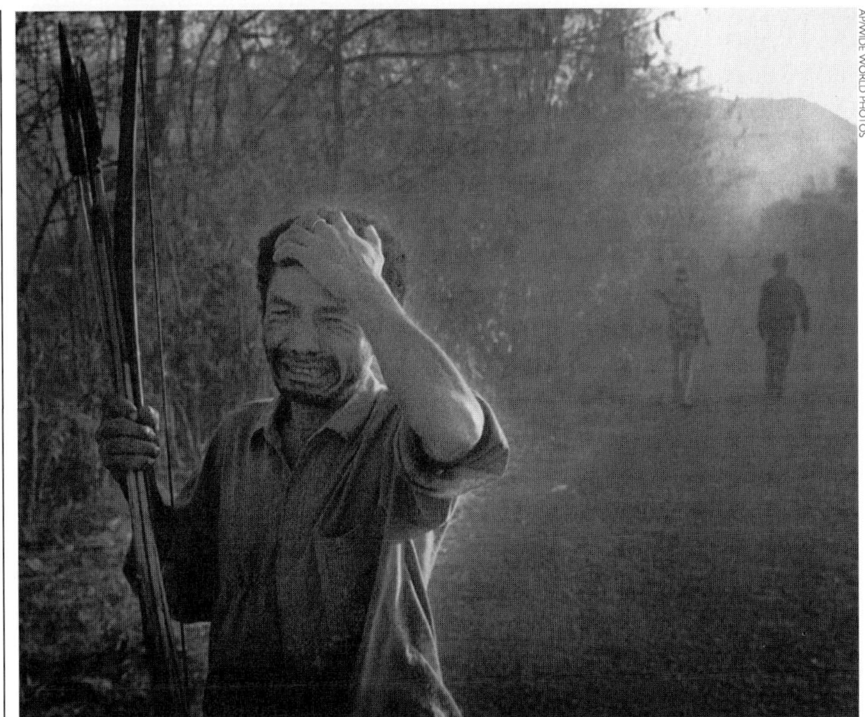

APWIDE WORLD PHOTOS

A VILLAGER *in East Timor, armed with spears and a bow, cries after anti-independence militiamen burned down his house in Memo village, outside the provincial capital of Dili. The entire town of Memo was destroyed, leaving at least two people dead, as violence threatened a UN-sponsored vote on autonomy for the former Portuguese colony.*

In the cold-war atmosphere of the 1950s and 1960s, the U.S. looked on the armed forces of Indonesia as a bulwark against the Communist tide that was threatening Southeast Asia. Large numbers of Indonesian army officers were trained in U.S. military institutions at U.S. expense. This strategy seemed to pay off when the army emerged in 1965 as the victor over the Communist party of Indonesia in the contest to succeed Sukarno, the country's first president. General, later president, Suharto came to power on a wave of popular support for the Indonesian army as a political force. The army solidified its U.S. support by turning to a group of U.S.-trained economists to redirect national policy away from the inward-looking socialism of the early postindependence years and in the direction of an outward-looking, market-oriented economic system.

The invasion of East Timor in 1975 did not greatly change this situation. A small minority of members of Congress expressed concern about the Indonesian invasion of the tiny territory, but its numbers were not sufficient to affect policy. Significant reinforcements were acquired after a massacre occurred at the funeral of a young independence activist in Dili in 1991. An American journalist who was present and who was beaten by Indonesian security personnel became an implacable critic. Congressional opposition to Indonesia's military grew, and year by year the Congress whittled down the transfer of weapons and technology. By the time relations were severed in September 1999, there was little left. One of the last events in planning at the cut-off was to have been a joint seminar in Hawaii, requested by the Indonesians, to hear how the U.S. armed forces had recovered their self-respect after their defeat in Vietnam.

That the Indonesian army had lost its own self-respect is an understatement. Two or three years ago, the conventional wisdom still was that the Indonesian army was the one institution that could hold Indonesia together, and the one institution that could assure a smooth transition from Suharto to the next leader of the country. Neither of these elements of

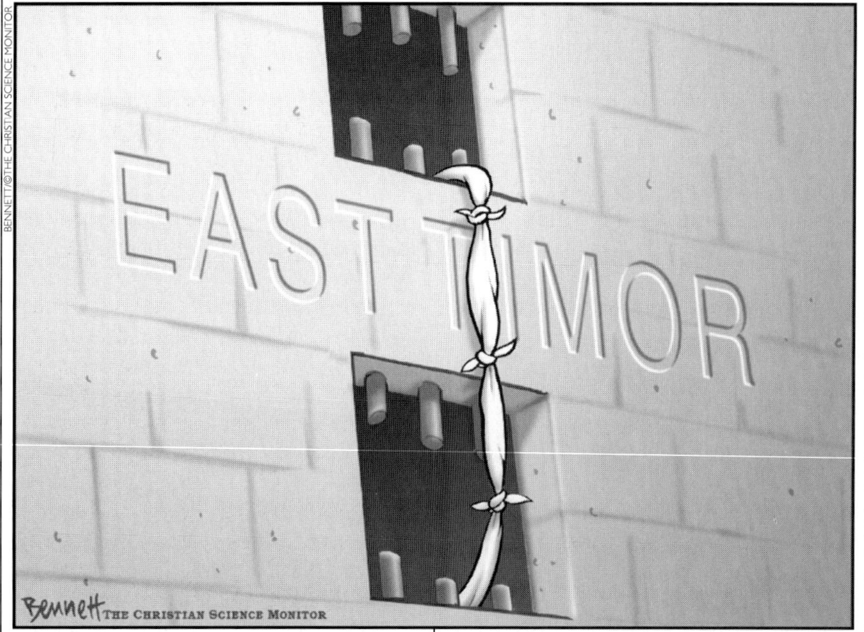

BENNETT/©THE CHRISTIAN SCIENCE MONITOR

conventional wisdom turned out to be reliable. By the late 1990s the leadership ranks of the army were in the hands of men who were selected in terms of their personal loyalty to Suharto. When Suharto's hold on power became precarious, factions within this politicized leadership struggled for control of the army itself, and this struggle took precedence over the management of the transition in the office of the president. Thus the tragedy of rioting, looting, burning and raping that cost 1,000 lives as Suharto fell in May 1998.

With the fall of Suharto, it became clear that the Indonesian army had no idea of what to do about the widening problem of law and order around the country. On the contrary, the army itself was increasingly the source of the breakdown in law and order. The rapid growth of the economy in recent decades had permitted many grievances to be papered over, and the collapse of the economy was leading many groups with a grievance to take the law into their own hands. The answer to violence was a credible government that would dispense social justice. But the army's answer to every problem was to send troops that did not seem able to do much except shoot. Army violence became increasingly frequent as the challenges to public order took on an increasingly political character. Civilian opinion turned against the army, especially after a series of fatal firings on unarmed university students demonstrating in Jakarta. Meeting in late 1998 to write the rules for elections to replace Suharto, the country's highest legislative body stripped the army of half its appointed seats in the Parliament, and leaders of the major political parties agreed that the practice should end altogether in 2004. The Indonesian army became an increasingly dangerous organization, still well provided with the means of violence, but deeply divided about when and where to use them.

Reform within the army

One element in the army found it at fault for permitting itself to become loyal to the interests of President Suharto rather than to the nation. A reform movement within the army aimed to bring about changes that were intended to create a new foundation for amicable civil-military relations. The army would remove itself from responsibility for internal security. The police, separated from the armed forces, would be responsible for internal security, and the army would redirect itself to defense against potential external attack. But warfare was changing. External attack was no longer aimed at taking and holding land. The Indonesian navy and air force were in need of massive modernization, and it was not clear where the money for that could possibly be found in the wake of the economic crisis.

The reformers also proposed that the army remove itself from day-to-day politics. The thousands of military officers in civilian government posts were ordered to choose a military or civilian career; after a suitable period, they would no longer be able to pursue both. But this program of detachment from day-to-day affairs did not deal with the parallel territorial system of the armed forces, which placed military personnel at every administrative level down to that of the village—a system that made for massive political surveillance. So long as this territorial system remained in place, it was hard to see how the armed forces could possibly remove themselves from interfering in everyday political affairs.

Meanwhile a hard-line element in the army was attempting to take the political initiative from civilian politicians by way of forceful action of their own. The creation and arming of the militias in East Timor was the first priority. Winning the referendum in East Timor by way of threat and intimidation would have taught the civilian politicians the cost of failing to consult the armed forces in regard to a matter in which they felt there was a major national security interest. The scorched earth policy that followed the vote for independence might have been designed to "teach a lesson" to the Acehnese and other separatist-minded provincial populations. But there was as well a suspicion of sheer revenge against the people of East Timor for their having had the temerity to vote against a continuation of the status quo.

The army also pushed very hard in the lame-duck Parliament, and on its last day in session obtained passage of a bill that provided easier terms for the declaration of martial law. Students and others protested vigorously against this action, and the army reacted with equal vigor, leaving 11 dead and hundreds wounded. In an effort to calm the public, President Habibie said he would not sign the martial law bill for the time being. But he did not say he would not sign it in due course. Moreover, at just about this time, General Wiranto permitted an effort to be made to promote his candidacy for vice-president, paired on a ticket with Habibie as candidate for president.

At the end of September, U.S. Defense Secretary William S. Cohen visited Jakarta and read the riot act to General Wiranto. The U.S. was concerned that the militias were still intent on destabilizing East Timor from safe havens in West Timor. On his way from their meeting, at the front doorstep to Wiranto's home, Cohen handed out a statement that consisted of an extraordinary dressing down of the commanding officer of the armed forces of another country. Cohen's statement said:

"I told General Wiranto that the military is at a critical turning point.

"If it supports the government's policy and it contributes to a peaceful solution in East Timor, investigates and punishes those guilty of improper behavior, disarms the militia in West Timor and prevents them from destabilizing East Timor, they will be acting in a manner consistent with Indonesia's national interest and international obligations.

"If on the other hand they permit or participate, openly or behind the scenes, in further aiding and abetting violence in East Timor, they will do severe damage to the country they are sworn to defend.

"I urged General Wiranto to make the right choice."

Cohen also said that the U.S. would not consider restoring normal military-to-military contacts until the Indonesian armed forces reform their ways. "The military must show restraint and respect for human rights throughout Indonesia," he said. "It must be clear that the military operates under civilian control."

That seemed to resolve the issue of U.S. policy on military ties with Indonesia for the time being. But fundamental changes afoot in Indonesia have the capacity to test the U.S. in the future. Indonesia has a new government, the result of a peaceful process that the U.S. has applauded. General Wiranto has been kicked upstairs. The new minister of defense is a civilian, a respected academic. And the new government faces a powerful independence movement in Aceh, a province that has been an integral part of Indonesia. The U.S. has said through several officials from the President on down that it supports the geographic integrity of Indonesia. This is clearly in the interest of regional stability in Southeast Asia. And the case of Aceh is one in which the army has been a major contributor through its own brutality. A political solution is clearly required.

Still, it is hard to see how Indonesia's integrity can be assured in the absence of strong Indonesian armed services. And the U.S. has the capacity to strengthen or weaken the Indonesian armed services by its policies, including those applied to military sales. Complicating factors include congressional efforts to set the terms for any resumption in military ties in the wake of the East Timor debacle, and the availability of other sources of supply, including the People's Republic of China. The U.S. also will want to hold out the possibility of some benefits being made available to the Indonesian armed forces as an incentive to continue their current neutrality in Indonesia's domestic politics. So this too remains on the agenda.

U.S. policy options

There are currently a number of policy options for the U.S. to consider in the light of recent experience in Indonesia:

❑ **1. The Departments of State and Defense should increase their resources for monitoring developments in Indonesia and maintaining a dialogue with leaders of this consequential nation-state.**

Pro: The U.S. has a major stake in the outcome of Indonesia's transition to a more democratic political system and a more open, transparent economy. The first requirement for U.S. leadership is to have adequate human resources. Indonesia's large population, its position in Southeast Asia, and its role as the largest Muslim population in the world, more than justify the modest investment this would involve.

Con: The U.S. cannot keep close track of all the countries around the world. It is enough to focus on those it can't ignore, and it must look to international organizations to deal with the rest.

❑ **2. The U.S. should take a strong pro-active position in responding to President Wahid's appeal for economic and political help.**

Pro: The U.S. has played a critical role at key points in Indonesia's transition since the emerging markets financial crisis began in 1997. Now a new civilian government is in place that meets all reasonable American expectations. The U.S. should be quick to lend its support. Failure of the Indonesian state would be far more costly than any actions that would help avoid it.

Con: The U.S. is overextended already in helping with the problems left behind by failed states like Yugoslavia and the U.S.S.R. It should be wary of open-ended commitments to help rescue other countries that might be harmed by the forces of globalization.

❑ **3. The U.S. should maintain a continuing dialogue with the leadership of the armed forces of Indonesia and tie any response to requests for support to progress in implementing reform within Indonesia.**

Pro: The Indonesian armed forces are still a significant political actor and the U.S. has an interest in their continued acceptance of civilian control. It is far better to encourage internal reform than to have to deal with the possible further consequences of an army out of control.

Con: The Indonesian armed forces have been responsible for too many of the country's present difficulties. Nothing the U.S. can say or do will change their behavior. It is better to wait until they have demonstrated conclusively that they have reformed themselves.

❑ **4. The U.S. should encourage continued dialogue with other members of the UN Security Council regarding issues of humanitarian intervention.**

Pro: The experience with East Timor demonstrated that the international community cannot ignore demands for humanitarian intervention—and that it has not yet found an optimal mode of response. Whatever one makes of Kofi Annan's thoughts on the subject, it's clear that the UN needs to find a better way.

Con: The UN cannot play the world's policeman any more than the U.S. can. Humanitarian intervention is an issue that could seriously damage the ability of the UN to function in other areas where it already has some credibility. These politically sensitive cases are better handled within the regions concerned.

❑ **5. The U.S. should encourage a review of the mandate of the IMF in regard to the quality of governance in assisted nations.**

Pro: The issue of financial corruption in emerging markets is not going to go away, and the future of the IMF itself depends on confidence that its funds will be used as intended. There is no easy answer to this issue, but the IMF needs a better means of dealing with it.

Con: The IMF should stick to its current position. It is empowered and staffed to deal with monetary issues, and it should remain focused on this established terrain. ■

Opinion Ballots are on pages 41–42

DISCUSSION QUESTIONS

1. Could the East Timor case have been better handled by the Indonesians?

2. Could and should the East Timor case have been better managed by the UN? Should the UN insist in future on placing an international peacekeeping force on the scene before sponsoring a referendum on self-determination?

3. How could the case have been better dealt with by the U.S.? Was its compromise an optimal response?

4. Is it a given that corruption is endemic to countries that need the IMF's help? Should the IMF have a policy on governance in the countries it assists?

5. How should the U.S. respond to a new and reforming civilian government like that of Abdurrahman Wahid and his popular vice-president, Ms. Megawati, daughter of Sukarno, Indonesia's first president? How far should the U.S. be prepared to go in helping the world's fourth most populous nation, and its most populous Muslim nation, chart its future democratic course? And what does the answer say about the future leadership of the U.S. in world affairs?

READINGS AND RESOURCES

Albright, Madeleine K., "Indonesia, the United States and Democracy." **U.S. Department of State Dispatch,** March 1999, pp. 5–8.*

Baker, Richard W., Ramage, Douglas E., and Kristiadi, J., eds., **Indonesia: The Challenge of Change.** New York, St. Martin's Press, 1999. 327 pp. $55.00. Indonesian and American specialists examine the impact of economic growth on major Indonesian institutions and the reactions of Indonesian society in a time of political, economic and social change.

Bresnan, John, "Indonesia," in **The Pivotal States: A New Framework for U.S. Policy in the Developing World.** New York, W.W. Norton, 1998. pp.15–39. $35.00. Describes the problems the U.S. experienced in applying its foreign policies to the specific case of Indonesia as the crisis loomed. The case is a prime example of the challenges the U.S. faces in dealing with states that are important, even very important, but perhaps not vital to national security.

Kingsbury, Damien, **The Politics of Indonesia.** New York, Oxford University Press, 1999. 286 pp. $19.95. A thorough analysis of the country's main political issues, themes and institutions and the political development of the country from colonial times through the present.

McBeth, John, and Murphy, Dan, "Indonesia: Balancing Act." **Far Eastern Economic Review,** Nov. 4, 1999, pp. 18–21. Examines the Cabinet of newly elected President Wahid and prospects for economic reform.

Paris, Jonathan, and Schwarz, Adam, eds., **The Politics of Post-Suharto Indonesia.** New York, Council on Foreign Relations, 1999. 150 pp. $17.95. In the words of one reviewer, this symposium volume "vividly captures the dynamics of the financial and political crisis that led to Suharto's fall from power."

Schwarz, Adam, **A Nation in Waiting: Indonesia's Search for Stability.** Boulder, CO, Westview Press, 1999. 552 pp. $28.00 (paper). A fine introduction to the recent, past and current problems of Indonesia by a skilled correspondent formerly resident in Jakarta. Especially strong in its analysis of how and why politics intrudes on the domain of economics in a real world situation.

THE ASIA FOUNDATION, 465 California St., 14th fl., San Francisco, CA 94104; (415) 982-4640; Fax (415) 392-8863. ■ A private, nonprofit, nongovernmental organization that seeks to advance the mutual interests of the U.S. and the Asia-Pacific region. **www.asiafoundation.org**

ASIASOURCE, 725 Park Ave., New York, NY 10021; (212) 288-6400; Fax (212) 517-8315 ■ Important new on-line information service from the Asia Society. Includes links to top news stories and latest commentary by topic, keyword, individual and country. **www.asiasource.org**

ASSOCIATION FOR ASIAN STUDIES, 1021 East Huron St., Ann Arbor, MI 48104; (734) 665-2490; Fax (734) 665-3801. ■ A scholarly, nonpolitical, nonprofit professional association open to all persons interested in Asia. **www.aasianst.org**

EAST ASIA INSTITUTE, Columbia University, Mail Code 3333, 420 West 118th St., New York, NY 10027; (212) 854-2592; Fax (212) 749-1497. ■ Sponsors Transition Indonesia, an unusual project bringing together American, Japanese and Australian expertise on Indonesia in a search for common ground. Reports are available on request.

EAST-WEST CENTER (EWC), 1601 East-West Rd., Honolulu, HI 96848-1601; (808) 944-7111; Fax (808) 944-7376. ■ Aims to promote cooperation and understanding among the peoples of Asia, the Pacific and the U.S. The EWC publishes a quarterly newsletter, **The Observer,** and has an extensive list of publications. **www.ewc.hawaii.edu**

NATIONAL BUREAU OF ASIAN RESEARCH (NBR), 4518 University Way, NE, Suite 300, Seattle, WA 98105; (206) 632-7370; Fax (206) 632-7487. ■ Conducts advanced research on policy-relevant issues in Asia. **www.nbr.org**

You can find links to this document and additional readings on our website at* **www.fpa.org/program.html

OPINION BALLOTS

Please feel free to xerox opinion ballots, *but be sure to submit only one ballot per person. To have your vote counted, mail ballots by June 30, 2000. Send ballots to:*

FOREIGN POLICY ASSOCIATION, 470 PARK AVENUE SOUTH, NEW YORK, NY 10016-6819

TOPIC 3 Indonesia

ISSUE A. Do you agree or disagree with the following statements?

	AGREE	DISAGREE
1. The military is too influential in Indonesian politics.	❑	❑
2. For all its size, Indonesia is a country of little strategic interest to the U.S.	❑	❑
3. Human-rights abuses in East Timor warranted a more vigorous response from the U.S.	❑	❑
4. The financial woes of Indonesia pose a serious hazard for the U.S.	❑	❑
5. Secretary of Defense Cohen did the right thing “reading the riot act” to the Indonesian military.	❑	❑
6. Corruption is too deeply entrenched in Indonesia for that country to get its house in order any time soon.	❑	❑
7. The U.S. owes a big debt to Australia for taking the lead in peacekeeping in East Timor.	❑	❑

Your zip code: ____ ____ ____ ____ ____

Date: / /2000 *Ballot continues on reverse side...*

TOPIC 3 Indonesia

ISSUE A. Do you agree or disagree with the following statements?

	AGREE	DISAGREE
1. The military is too influential in Indonesian politics.	❑	❑
2. For all its size, Indonesia is a country of little strategic interest to the U.S.	❑	❑
3. Human-rights abuses in East Timor warranted a more vigorous response from the U.S.	❑	❑
4. The financial woes of Indonesia pose a serious hazard for the U.S.	❑	❑
5. Secretary of Defense Cohen did the right thing “reading the riot act” to the Indonesian military.	❑	❑
6. Corruption is too deeply entrenched in Indonesia for that country to get its house in order any time soon.	❑	❑
7. The U.S. owes a big debt to Australia for taking the lead in peacekeeping in East Timor.	❑	❑

Your zip code: ____ ____ ____ ____ ____

Date: / /2000 *Ballot continues on reverse side...*

TOPIC 4 The Military

ISSUE A. Compared with what it is now spending on national defense, in the future the U.S. should:

___ **1.** Spend more on national defense

___ **2.** Spend less on national defense

___ **3** Spend the same amount on national defense

ISSUE B. Should the next Administration give greater weight to the Powell doctrine or the Clinton doctrine?

___ **1.** The Powell doctrine

___ **2.** The Clinton doctrine

Your zip code: ____ ____ ____ ____ ____

Date: / /2000 *Ballot continues on reverse side...*

TOPIC 4 The Military

ISSUE A. Compared with what it is now spending on national defense, in the future the U.S. should:

___ **1.** Spend more on national defense

___ **2.** Spend less on national defense

___ **3** Spend the same amount on national defense

ISSUE B. Should the next Administration give greater weight to the Powell doctrine or the Clinton doctrine?

___ **1.** The Powell doctrine

___ **2.** The Clinton doctrine

Your zip code: ____ ____ ____ ____ ____

Date: / /2000 *Ballot continues on reverse side...*

OPINION BALLOTS

A. *How many years have you participated in the* GREAT DECISIONS *program (that is, attended one or more discussion sessions)?*
❑ **1.** This is the first year I have participated.
❑ **2.** I participated in one previous year.
❑ **3.** I participated in more than one previous year.

B. *What is your age?* ❑ **1.** 17 or under ❑ **2.** 18 to 30 ❑ **3.** 31 to 45 ❑ **4.** 46 to 60 ❑ **5.** 61 or over

C. *Your sex?* ❑ **1.** Female ❑ **2.** Male

D. *Have you been abroad during the last two years?*
❑ **1.** Yes ❑ **2.** No

E. *Do you know, or are you learning, a foreign language?*
❑ **1.** Yes ❑ **2.** No

F. *What is the highest level of formal education you have completed?*
❑ **1.** Some high school ❑ **2.** High school degree
❑ **3.** Some college ❑ **4.** College graduate
❑ **5.** Advanced degree

G. *How often are you asked for your opinion on foreign policy matters?*
❑ **1.** Often ❑ **2.** Sometimes ❑ **3.** Hardly ever

H. *How many* ***hours,*** *on average, do you spend reading one* GREAT DECISIONS *chapter?*
❑ **1.** Less than 1 hr. ❑ **2.** 1–2 hrs.
❑ **3.** 3–4 hrs. ❑ **4.** More than 4 hrs.

I. *Do you have access to the Internet (check all that apply)?*
❑ **1.** Yes, at home. ❑ **2.** Yes, at work. ❑ **3.** Yes, at school.
❑ **4.** Yes, at the library or Internet café. ❑ **5.** No.

J. *Would you say you have or have not changed your opinion in a fairly significant way as a result of taking part in the* GREAT DECISIONS *program?*
❑ **1.** Have ❑ **2.** Have not ❑ **3.** Uncertain

ISSUE C. Would you support or oppose the use of U.S. troops in the event that:

	SUPPORT	OPPOSE
1. North Korea invaded South Korea	❑	❑
2. Iraq invaded Saudi Arabia	❑	❑
3. Mainland China invaded Taiwan	❑	❑
4. Yugoslavia invaded one of its neighbors	❑	❑

ISSUE D. Do you agree or disagree with the following statements?

	AGREE	DISAGREE
1. Military power is obsolete in the age of globalization.	❑	❑
2. The U.S. should use its unrivaled military power to establish a "Pax Americana."	❑	❑
3. It no longer makes sense for the U.S. to maintain a two-war strategy.	❑	❑
4. Humanitarian intervention is not a proper role for the U.S. military.	❑	❑

Other, or comment: ______________________

____

____

A. *How many years have you participated in the* GREAT DECISIONS *program (that is, attended one or more discussion sessions)?*
❑ **1.** This is the first year I have participated.
❑ **2.** I participated in one previous year.
❑ **3.** I participated in more than one previous year.

B. *What is your age?* ❑ **1.** 17 or under ❑ **2.** 18 to 30 ❑ **3.** 31 to 45 ❑ **4.** 46 to 60 ❑ **5.** 61 or over

C. *Your sex?* ❑ **1.** Female ❑ **2.** Male

D. *Have you been abroad during the last two years?*
❑ **1.** Yes ❑ **2.** No

E. *Do you know, or are you learning, a foreign language?*
❑ **1.** Yes ❑ **2.** No

F. *What is the highest level of formal education you have completed?*
❑ **1.** Some high school ❑ **2.** High school degree
❑ **3.** Some college ❑ **4.** College graduate
❑ **5.** Advanced degree

G. *How often are you asked for your opinion on foreign policy matters?*
❑ **1.** Often ❑ **2.** Sometimes ❑ **3.** Hardly ever

H. *How many* ***hours,*** *on average, do you spend reading one* GREAT DECISIONS *chapter?*
❑ **1.** Less than 1 hr. ❑ **2.** 1–2 hrs.
❑ **3.** 3–4 hrs. ❑ **4.** More than 4 hrs.

I. *Do you have access to the Internet (check all that apply)?*
❑ **1.** Yes, at home. ❑ **2.** Yes, at work. ❑ **3.** Yes, at school.
❑ **4.** Yes, at the library or Internet café. ❑ **5.** No.

J. *Would you say you have or have not changed your opinion in a fairly significant way as a result of taking part in the* GREAT DECISIONS *program?*
❑ **1.** Have ❑ **2.** Have not ❑ **3.** Uncertain

ISSUE C. Would you support or oppose the use of U.S. troops in the event that:

	SUPPORT	OPPOSE
1. North Korea invaded South Korea	❑	❑
2. Iraq invaded Saudi Arabia	❑	❑
3. Mainland China invaded Taiwan	❑	❑
4. Yugoslavia invaded one of its neighbors	❑	❑

ISSUE D. Do you agree or disagree with the following statements?

	AGREE	DISAGREE
1. Military power is obsolete in the age of globalization.	❑	❑
2. The U.S. should use its unrivaled military power to establish a "Pax Americana."	❑	❑
3. It no longer makes sense for the U.S. to maintain a two-war strategy.	❑	❑
4. Humanitarian intervention is not a proper role for the U.S. military.	❑	❑

Other, or comment: ______________________

____

____

The military: what role in U.S. foreign policy?

How large an armed force should the U.S. maintain, and how should it use that force? Will military power be obsolete in the 21st century?

by Lawrence J. Korb

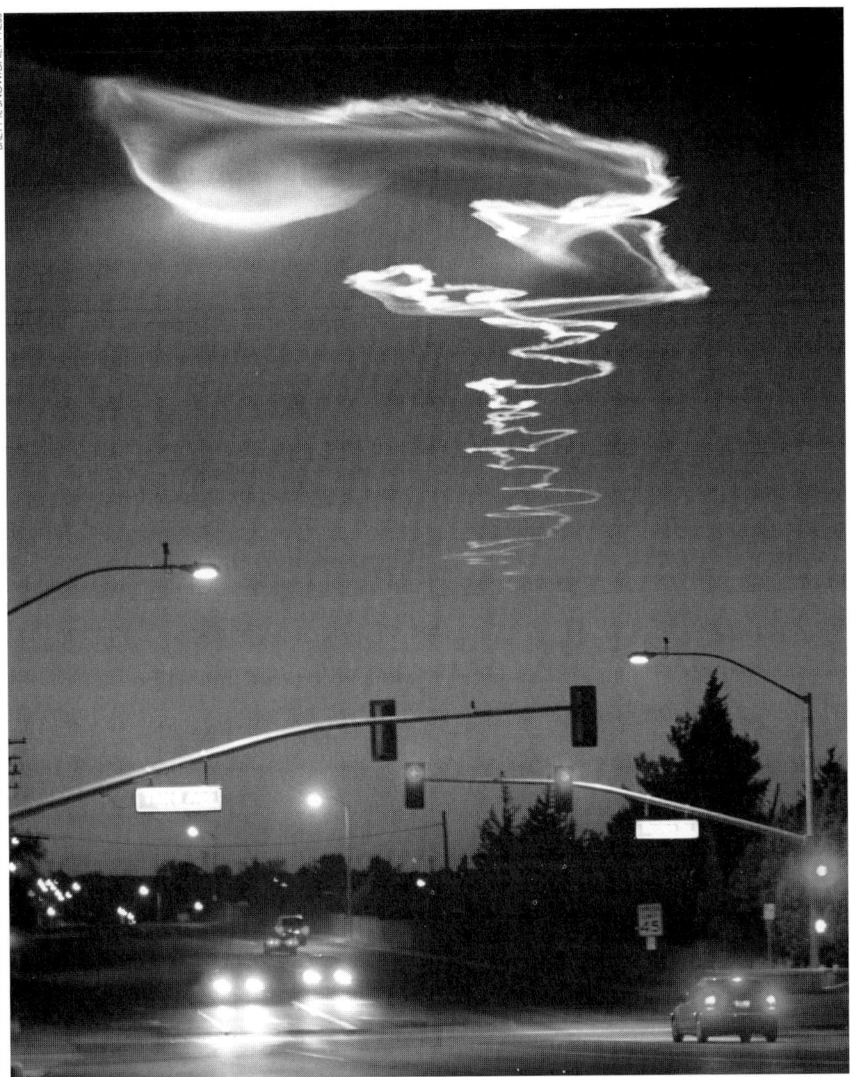

BRETT K. SNOW/DAILY PRESS

A MINUTEMAN MISSILE *leaves a trail in the evening sky. The missile was destroyed by an interceptor in the air over the Pacific Ocean in the first successful test of a national missile defense system.*

During the Cold War, the role of the American military in U.S. foreign policy was quite clear. The basic aim of U.S. foreign policy was to contain Soviet Communist expansion through diplomacy backed by force or containment through deterrence. As former Secretary of Defense William J. Perry and former Assistant Secretary of Defense Ashton Carter note, this policy was easy to understand but difficult to implement. Or, as Phillip Zelikow, a Bush Administration national security official, put it, "The doing might have been tough, but the choosing was easy."

Implementation of this strategy of containment through deterrence was costly to the U.S. in terms of both blood and treasure. It required the U.S. military to fight two major land wars, in Korea (1950–53) and Vietnam (1965–75), that resulted in the deaths of some 100,000 American men and women. The U.S. also employed military force in a number of smaller conflicts like Lebanon in 1958 and 1982, the Dominican Republic in 1965, Grenada in 1983 and Panama in 1989. In addition, containment required the U.S. to deploy some 500,000 servicemen and women outside the U.S. on a continuous basis and in a high state of readiness. To prevent the Soviet Union or its allies from expanding their power and influence, 30 million Americans served on active duty between 1950 and 1990, maintaining a force that averaged 2.5 million. In Europe alone, the U.S. military kept about 300,000 people prepared to respond, with its North Atlantic Treaty Organization (NATO) allies, to a Soviet blitzkrieg attack in a matter of hours. Maintaining this high state of readiness resulted in the deaths of an average of three members of the military a day for 40 years, or 40,000 men and women.

Containment through deterrence was also costly in monetary terms. Measured in today's dollars, the U.S. spent about $15 trillion, or 8% of its economic output, on its military from

LAWRENCE J. KORB *is the director of studies at the Council on Foreign Relations. Before joining the Council, he was the director of the Center for Public Policy Education and a senior fellow in the Foreign Policy Studies Program at the Brookings Institution. He has written widely on defense issues and was assistant secretary of defense from 1981 to 1985.*

1950 through 1990. (The Korea and Vietnam conflicts alone cost over $1 trillion each.) About one third of that total amount, or $5 trillion, was spent on building, deploying and maintaining sufficient strategic nuclear weapons to deter the Soviet Union from using or threatening to use its nuclear arsenal against the U.S. and its allies. By the mid-1980s, the U.S. had lined up nearly 25,000 strategic nuclear weapons against the Soviets' 20,000. In addition the U.S. and U.S.S.R. each had more than 30,000 nonstrategic or tactical nuclear weapons in their inventories.

Since the U.S. had never maintained a large standing military in peacetime prior to the cold war, the issue of how large a military the U.S. should maintain was bound to arise once the Soviet Union and the Soviet empire collapsed. To answer this question in turn required asking what role the U.S. wished to play in the international system and how military power would help it fulfill that role.

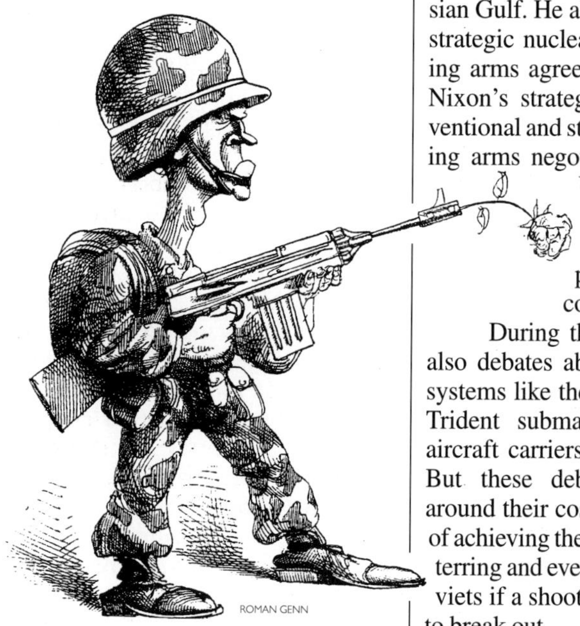

To be sure, there were controversies over the appropriate role of the military in implementing foreign policy during the cold war. But these disputes usually revolved around the best military means to achieve deterrence. President Dwight D. Eisenhower (1953–61), the former general, put his emphasis on nuclear weapons and adopted a policy of massive retaliation, which stated that the U.S. would respond with overwhelming military force, up to and including nuclear weapons, and at a time and place of its choosing, to any attack on American interests. Thus Eisenhower spent most of his defense budget on long-range bombers and missiles and comparatively little on conventional or nonnuclear forces, particularly ground forces. President John F. Kennedy (1961–63) adopted a policy of flexible response and built up both conventional and nuclear forces, from the Army's special forces (Green Berets) to intercontinental ballistic missiles (Minuteman and Polaris). He wanted conventional forces capable of fighting two major wars and one smaller conflict simultaneously. After the tragedy of Vietnam, however, President Richard M. Nixon (1969–74) resolved to fight no more land wars in Asia and configured conventional forces to be able to fight only one and a half wars, specifically in Europe and the Persian Gulf. He also slowed the growth of strategic nuclear weapons by negotiating arms agreements with the Soviets. Nixon's strategy for configuring conventional and strategic forces and pursuing arms negotiations with the Soviet Union was essentially adopted by his successors and remained in place until the end of the cold war in late 1991.

During the cold war, there were also debates about particular weapons systems like the B-1 and B-2 bombers, Trident submarines, nuclear-powered aircraft carriers and main battle tanks. But these debates usually revolved around their cost-effectiveness in terms of achieving the agreed-upon goal of deterring and eventually defeating the Soviets if a shooting war with them were to break out.

The end of the cold war came so suddenly and unexpectedly that the national security establishment was caught unaware. There was very little thought given to the goals of post-cold-war U.S. foreign policy, let alone what role the military should play. In other words, there was no contingency planning for the U.S. military in a world without a Soviet military threat.

Very quickly, however, three possibilities began to emerge. One school of thought assumed that the U.S. military would return to its pre–World War II role. For example, on January 25, 1989, former Senator John G. Tower, who had been chairman of the Senate Armed Services Committee and an architect of the massive Reagan defense buildup, told the committee that if his nomination as President George Bush's secretary of defense were confirmed, he would support an arms reduction once the Soviet threat diminished. "If there were no [Soviet] threat we'd be spending enormously less than we spend now. We'd be maintaining the kind of Army we had in 1938 [which was] about half the size of what the Marine Corps is now."

The U.S. Army vs. the Salvation Army

While Tower might have been branded an isolationist, that was not the case. Proponents of his view, which included people from all parts of the political spectrum, felt that the U.S. did indeed need to remain involved in the world. However, they felt that the post-cold-war era would be characterized by cooperation and concert, rather than competition and conflict. Moreover, without a large military threat to its vital interests, the U.S. could rely on diplomacy or its economic power to carry out its foreign policy objectives. Many of those who came to embrace the Tower view felt in fact that, in the post-cold-war world, economic power would become more important than military power. Military alliances like NATO, the Southeast Asia Treaty Organization, the Central Treaty Organization and Anzus (Australia, New Zealand, U.S.) would give way to economic organizations like the Group of Seven leading industrialized nations, the Asia-Pacific Economic Cooperation, the Association of Southeast Asian Nations, the European Union and the General Agreement on Tariffs and Trade. And real global power and influence would result more from the size of a nation's economy and trade deficits than from the size of its nuclear and conventional arsenals.

A second school of thought took the opposite view. Its devotees argued that the collapse of the Soviet Union left the U.S. in the fortunate position of being the world's only military superpower and the U.S. should use that power to create, in Bush's words, "a new world order," inviting nations to embrace the American ideal of liberal democratic capitalism. Proponents of this school, including Robert Kagan of the Carnegie

Endowment and William Kristol, editor of *The Weekly Standard,* argued that defense spending and military forces should remain at the historically high levels that they had reached during the Reagan years and that the U.S. should use its military force against those who challenged the new American hegemony and to deter potential rivals like China. Just as the 19th century was a "Pax Britannica," the 21st century would be a "Pax Americana."

As it often does, the U.S. political system rejected both as too extreme. The U.S. would not downsize its military the way it did in the period between World Wars I and II, when its Army was ranked 19th largest in the world, between Portugal and Romania, and one tenth the size of Germany's. Nor would the U.S. become the world's policeman, seeking to impose American values around the globe. The U.S., despite its comparative advantages in economic and military power, was viewed as not having enough strength and power to play such a role for an extended period. Eventually, the U.S. would fall victim to what the Yale historian Paul M. Kennedy has called imperial overstretch. (For example, in the late 19th century, Britain was forced to send its troops into Sudan because Britain's strategic interests rested on its empire in India, and access to India required a secure Suez Canal, which required a secure Egypt, which required a secure Sudan.) Nor was there any great enthusiasm on the part of the American public for such a role. Indeed, a U.S. public opinion survey in November 1998 by the Chicago Council on Foreign Relations indicated that 66% of respondents opposed the use of American troops if North Korea invaded the South, 68% percent were opposed to joining Taiwan's war against China, and only 52% supported U.S. ground action to defend Saudi Arabia against an Iraqi invasion.

A consensus emerged that while economic power would indeed be more important in the post-cold-war world, military power would still be vital to safeguarding U.S. interests. Therefore, the U.S. needed to maintain a strong military able to back U.S. diplomacy and to maintain, when needed, stability in this period of globalization.

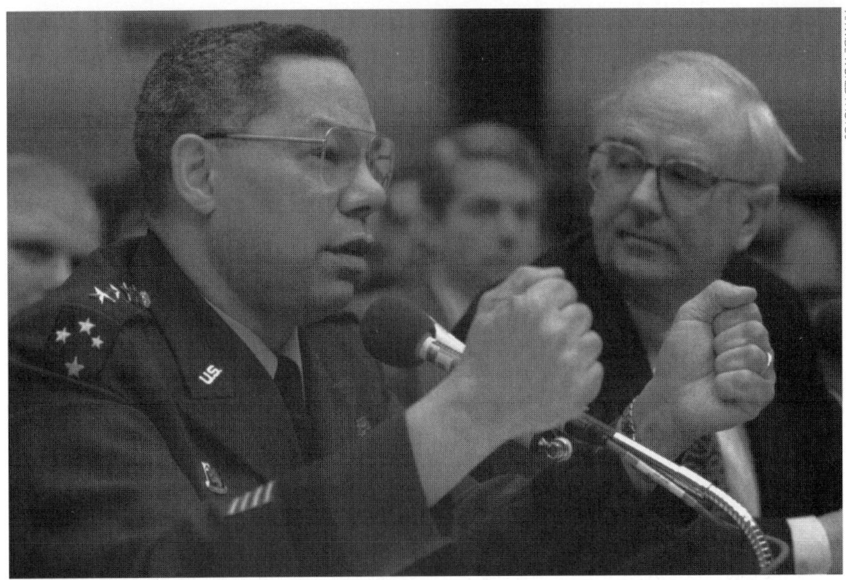

APWIDE WORLD PHOTOS

GENERAL COLIN POWELL *(left, then Chairman of the Joint Chiefs of Staff) and Les Aspin (then Secretary of Defense), appeared before the Defense Base Closure and Realignment Commission in 1993. Powell testified that, even with the proposed closures, the military would be able to operate effectively.*

As *The New York Times* Foreign Affairs columnist Thomas L. Friedman has pointed out, globalization depends upon striking three balances in the international system. Not only must there be a balance between states and "supermarkets" (the huge global stock and bond markets), but also between states and states (the traditional balance) and between states and "superpowered individuals" (like the terrorist Osama bin Laden, a Saudi millionaire with his own global network). As the nation that benefits most from globalization, the U.S. has a vital interest in ensuring the stability of this system. And while the U.S. military cannot do much about controlling supermarkets, it can play an important role in maintaining the traditional state-to-state balance and the balance between the state and the superpowered individuals.

But even this consensus on a third way left unanswered a number of questions, among them, how large a military force was necessary as a backdrop for diplomacy in maintaining these balances in the global system, and under what circumstances the U.S. should intervene militarily.

The first to tackle these questions was a military man, General Colin L. Powell, chairman of the Joint Chiefs of Staff from 1989 to 1994. Powell, who had been President Ronald W. Reagan's last national security adviser before moving to the Joint Chiefs of Staff, knew from that experience that the Soviet Union was already on its last legs. He feared that when the Soviet threat collapsed, the rationale for a large standing U.S. military would be undercut and the Tower view might indeed be adopted. In Powell's mind there would be a stampede by members of Congress to start shifting money to such things as schools or housing or crime prevention. Powell also knew that, without a Soviet threat, the U.S. military would have to be smaller. There would be very little political support for a cold-war-size military in a post-cold-war world. And without an overarching strategy to guide the reductions, the Pentagon's political enemies would come after it with a chain saw.

Powell was also aware that abstract concepts like "maintaining stability, preventing chaos in the international arena, or establishing a new world order" would not resonate politically as justification for having a significant military force in the post-cold-war period. Finally, Powell did not wish to see the U.S. military diverted into such nonmilitary tasks as peacekeeping and nation-building. In his view, and that of his colleagues, the U.S. military existed to deter potential adversaries and to fight and win the nation's wars. And as he took office, in 1989—before the collapse of the Soviet Union—he began planning for what he called the post-cold-war "Base Force."

Powell's action was a reversal of the normal procedure in the executive

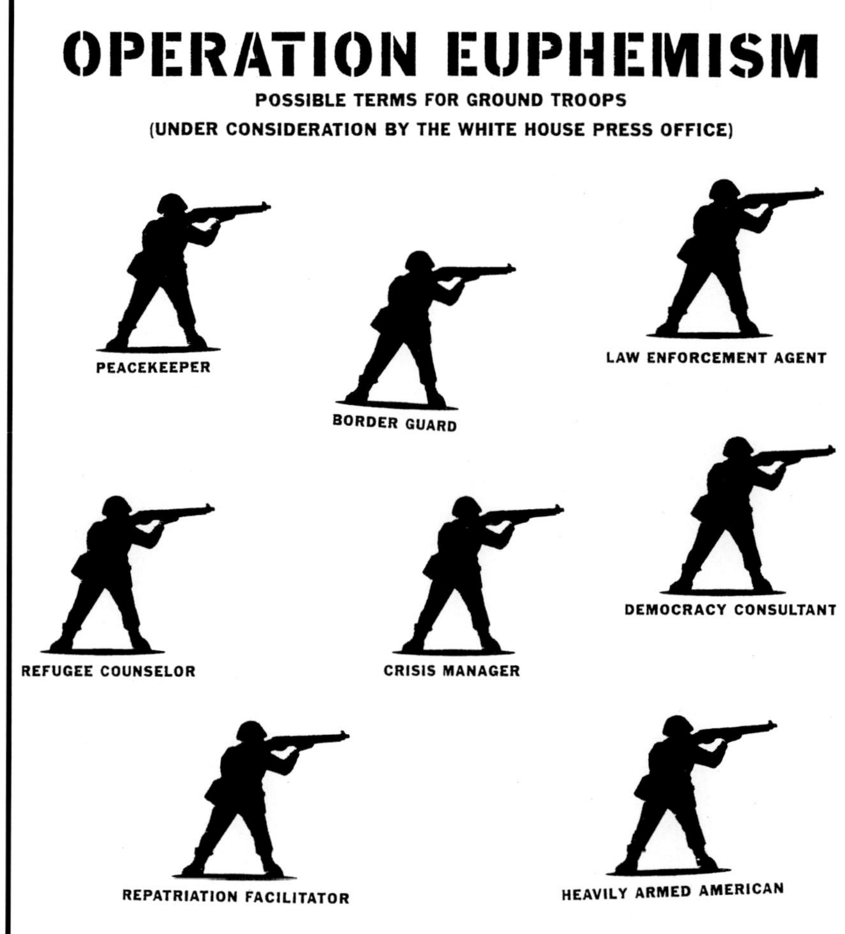
OPERATION EUPHEMISM
POSSIBLE TERMS FOR GROUND TROOPS
(UNDER CONSIDERATION BY THE WHITE HOUSE PRESS OFFICE)
PEACEKEEPER
BORDER GUARD
LAW ENFORCEMENT AGENT
REFUGEE COUNSELOR
CRISIS MANAGER
DEMOCRACY CONSULTANT
REPATRIATION FACILITATOR
HEAVILY ARMED AMERICAN

branch. Usually the secretary of defense and his staff or the national security adviser and his staff would develop the policy and strategy and leave it to the military to execute it. Unlike Powell, his civilian bosses, Secretary of Defense Dick Cheney and National Security Adviser Brent Scowcroft, did not believe the collapse of the Soviet Union was imminent in 1989, or 1990 for that matter. In fact, even after the fall of the Berlin Wall in late 1989 Cheney recommended that the 1990–95 military budget be cut by only 10%.

Powell's Base Force envisioned a military about 75% of the size and cost of the military that existed when he took office. According to the timetable Powell presented to his superiors, the Pentagon would reduce its force structure and budget by 5% a year each year between 1990 and 1995. By 1995, Powell's plan would have reduced the total force of uniformed military personnel from 3.3 million (2.1 million active and 1.2 million guard and reserve) to 2.6 million (1.6 million active and 0.9 million guard and reserve). The Base Force reductions in personnel would result in parallel cuts in the number of ground divisions, ships and tactical air wings. However, the essentials of the U.S. military would remain the same, if somewhat smaller.

The Base Force represented a change in the way the U.S. rationalized its force structure. In the post-cold-war world, with no Soviet military threat, the U.S. would shift from a threat-based force to a threat- and "capability-based" force. According to Powell, while the U.S. military might no longer have a specific airlift requirement to move millions of tons of supplies and equipment to Europe to deal with a massive Soviet and Eastern Europe invasion, the U.S. military still needed to be able to move large amounts of material to several places around the world. Similarly, while the U.S. might no longer face the Red Army on the plains of Germany, the nation needed to be able to project power other places around the globe.

Powell's Base Force would be capable of performing four basic missions: first, to fight across the Atlantic; second, to fight across the Pacific; third, to have a contingency force in the U.S. that could be deployed rapidly to hot spots, as done in Panama in 1989; and finally, to possess a sufficient nuclear force to deter nuclear adversaries.

Powell dealt with the question of a specific enemy by arguing that his Base Force needed to be capable of waging war by itself, that is, without allies, against what later became known as rogue or outlaw states. According to Powell, the threat from the Soviet Union had been replaced by something quite different: demons and dangers of a regional nature, which the U.S. armed forces might have to go fight.

Rogue states are hostile Third World countries with comparatively large military forces and weapons of mass destruction. According to those who so characterize them, these states harbor aggressive intentions against their less powerful neighbors, oppose the spread of democracy and are guilty of circumventing international limits on nuclear, biological and chemical proliferation.

When he took over as chairman of the Joint Chiefs of Staff in 1989, Powell identified six rogue states that, in his view, posed a military threat to U.S. interests: Iran, Iraq, Syria, Libya, Cuba and North Korea. Powell argued that U.S. forces could not be sized to defeat just one, because that might tempt another potential aggressor to move in knowing all U.S. forces were committed elsewhere. (For example, if U.S. forces were all at war against Iran or Iraq in the Persian Gulf, North Korea might be tempted to cross the 38th parallel.) Powell thus complemented his doctrine with a two-war strategy, saying the military should be structured to handle two major regional conflicts simultaneously. Finally, the U.S. had to assume that its allies would not automatically come to the aid of the U.S. in the Persian Gulf or the Korean Peninsula. In Powell's view, a two-conflict strategy, assuming no allied support, justified a force that was about 75% the size maintained during the cold war.

Powell also had strong ideas about the circumstances in which U.S. military forces should be committed. The chairman argued, in what became known as the Powell Doctrine, that the

U.S. military should be sent into battle only when three conditions were met: U.S. political objectives were clear and measurable; the country was prepared to use overwhelming force quickly and decisively to advance that objective; and military forces would be withdrawn when that objective was accomplished, requiring political leaders to have an exit strategy. Powell and his military colleagues did not wish to see the U.S. become involved in more Vietnams (1965–75) or Lebanons (1982–83), where objectives were unclear and the military fought with one hand tied behind its back. ■

Powell meets Clinton

BEFORE POWELL'S five-year plan for downsizing the military could be completed, President Bill Clinton took office. The new Administration had some problems with Powell's vision. First, it felt that the Base Force was not a real post-cold-war force but a "cold-war-lite force," that is, simply a smaller version of the force that won the cold war. Second, it argued that the Base Force was too expensive. (In his 1992 campaign, Clinton had pledged to cut the Pentagon's five-year plan by at least $60 billion.) Third, in the view of Clinton and his colleagues, Powell had overestimated the threat posed by the rogue states. (For example, Powell had postulated that the North Korean military was more effective than that of South Korea and on a par with that of the U.S.) Yet the Base Force proposal failed to anticipate such threats to world peace and security as Somalia, Bosnia and Haiti. Military interventions in these areas were called peacekeeping by the international community or operations other than war by the U.S. military, raising questions about the Pentagon's role in carrying them out.

Accordingly, in 1993 the Clinton Administration conducted its own review of the role and structure of the U.S. military. Clinton's first secretary of defense, the late Les Aspin, led this so-called Bottom Up Review, a sweeping, start-from-scratch assessment of the Pentagon's programs and powers that would shape defense policy in the post-cold-war, post-Soviet world.

As a result of his analysis, Aspin argued that the Base Force could be reduced by about 5% to 2.35 million uniformed personnel (1.5 active and 0.9 million reserve) and that military spending could be cut by another $120 billion or 9% over the 1993–97 period. Aspin attempted to rationalize this smaller force and free up some forces for peacekeeping by modifying the two-war strategy, and by making a more realistic assessment of the threats posed by such rogue states as Iraq, Iran and North Korea. But this position was adamantly opposed by the Joint Chiefs, and when word of Aspin's analysis was leaked to the media, Clinton, who felt himself vulnerable on military issues, reaffirmed the threat assessment and the two-war strategy and promised no further reductions in military spending. Indeed, by the end of his first Administration, Clinton was spending more on defense than Nixon had spent by the end his first term.

Starting with the last days of the Bush Administration, when the military was stationed in the Persian Gulf area permanently and troops were sent to Somalia to feed the populace, the U.S. military began to be deployed with increasing frequency and became the preferred instrument for implementing U.S. foreign policy. According to some estimates, the U.S. military has been used for unexpected contingencies about once every nine weeks since the end of the cold war. These missions have ranged from traditional military operations (Korea, Kuwait, Taiwan) to humanitarian relief (Central America) and peacekeeping functions (Somalia, Haiti, Rwanda, Bosnia and Kosovo).

The increasing use of the military in operations other than war has been justified by what has become known as the Clinton Doctrine. In a speech to NATO troops in Macedonia in June 1999, Clinton said, "Whether you live in Africa, or Central Europe, or any other place, if somebody comes after civilians and tries to kill them en masse because of their race, their ethnic background, or their religion, and it's within our power to stop it, we will stop it. We should not countenance genocide or ethnic cleansing anywhere in the world...." In that same speech the President also

AP/WIDE WORLD PHOTOS

PRESIDENT CLINTON *salutes attendees of the 100th anniversary convention of the Veterans of Foreign Wars (VFW) in August 1999. At right is John Smart, VFW Senior Vice Commander in Chief.*

DRAWING BY HARLEY L. SCHWADRON

expressed regret that the U.S. acted too slowly to stop ethnic slaughter in Bosnia and did nothing to halt genocide in Rwanda.

The difference between the Clinton and the Powell doctrines was clearly demonstrated during the early days of the Administration. In response to constant calls from the Clinton foreign policy team to "do something" to punish the Bosnian Serbs for shelling Sarajevo, Powell's unwelcome message in the spring of 1993 was that the U.S. should not commit military forces until the Administration had a clear political objective. This clearly frustrated the then U.S. ambassador to the United Nations, Madeleine K. Albright, who asked Powell, "What's the point of having this superb military that you are always talking about, if we can't use it?"

In Powell's view, the Serbs, like the North Vietnamese, had matched their political objectives with their military actions, that is, they were prepared to use sufficient military power and endure a large number of casualties to accomplish their goals. And no American President could defend to the American people the heavy sacrifice of lives it would cost to resolve this "baffling conflict." The specter of Lebanon also affected Powell's vision of Bosnia. Whenever the Bosnian issue was brought up, he said, "the shattered bodies of Marines at the Beirut airport were never far from my mind in arguing for caution." There was in fact an unusual similarity between Bosnia and Lebanon: Once the U.S. was involved in Bosnia in a limited fashion, withdrawing without achieving its objectives would be undesirable. Yet, it would be difficult, if not impossible, to achieve a decisive result without use of massive force.

In the view of Powell and the other chiefs, some 400,000 troops would have been necessary to resolve the "unhappy conflict" in Bosnia satisfactorily, with casualties conceivably running into the tens of thousands. Powell felt that no President could sustain the long-term involvement necessary to prevent the two sides from "going at each other's throats all over again."

The Clinton Doctrine has been criticized by Senator John McCain (R-Ariz.), Michael Mandelbaum of the Council on Foreign Relations, and others as foreign policy as social work and for confusing peripheral with central foreign policy concerns. It is also directly at odds with the Powell Doctrine in terms of the role of the military in foreign policy. Under the Clinton Doctrine, the military could be sent into hostile situations without invoking a specific, vital national interest and with only the goal of achieving such open-ended objectives as stopping violence or building democracy. While the Powell Doctrine attempts to draw lessons from the American experiences in Vietnam and Lebanon, the Clinton Doctrine seeks to learn from what occurred in Auschwitz in the 1940s and in Sarajevo in 1914. As U.S. ambassador to the UN Richard C. Holbrooke noted in justifying the military interventions in Bosnia and Kosovo, Europe cannot be peaceful and secure as long as war and ethnic hatred exist within its common boundaries.

Doctrine gap

The differences between the Powell and the Clinton doctrines are profound both for the nation and the military. If foreign policy is to be guided by the precepts of the Powell Doctrine, then the U.S. military should be of sufficient size and structure only to deter current or future threats to vital national security interests and should be employed only when these interests are directly threatened (i.e., in the Persian Gulf, the Korean Peninsula, or the Taiwan Straits.) On the other hand, if guided by the Clinton Doctrine, the U.S. in effect would become a global policeman and caregiver and run the risk of stretching its military thin trying to accomplish virtually impossible goals—restoring democracy in Haiti, for example, or building multiethnic states in the Balkans.

Today the U.S. military finds itself in an untenable position. It is sized and structured to carry out the Powell Doctrine—that is, to wage two major regional conflicts with "heavy" divisions (ground forces equipped with large tanks), nuclear-powered aircraft carriers and sophisticated combat planes—but it is being asked to implement the Clinton Doctrine, which calls for lighter, more agile forces.

This dichotomy has created a number of problems for the military as it attempts to carry out U.S. foreign policy.

To begin with, it has created an investment shortfall. The Pentagon argues that it needs to buy $60 billion worth of new equipment each year in order to replace its aging planes, ships and tanks and maintain its technological edge over any potential rivals who might challenge the U.S. in the next century. The increasing number of deployments have meanwhile forced the military to spend larger than anticipated amounts just operating and maintaining its current force. Thus, between 1995 and 2000 the Pentagon was able to spend only about $45 billion a year on new equipment, a $15 billion, or 25%, shortfall. The average age of equipment is growing rapidly and many systems are being operated beyond their projected life span. For example, three quarters of military aircraft are more than 20 years old.

Second, as the U.S. military gets diverted—with increasing frequency—into operations other than war, it is losing readiness to carry out what it views as its primary task of being able to wage two major regional wars simultaneously. The Army leadership argues that a division that spends the bulk of its time keeping sewage plants open in Kosovo will forgo its ability to engage in tank warfare in the Persian Gulf or on the Korean peninsula. Moreover, these frequent deployments are wearing out equipment and using up ammunition more rapidly than expected; after the Desert Fox operation against Iraq in December 1998 and the 78-day bombardment of Kosovo in spring 1999, the military had nearly exhausted its supply of cruise missiles.

These frequent deployments, as well as confusion about the military's real purpose, are beginning to cause recruiting and retention problems for the armed services. The percentage of high school seniors willing to consider joining the military has dropped from 55% to 35% over the last decade. In 1999 recruitment fell short about 20,000 people, or 10%, below its objectives despite a lowering of standards since the early 1990s and a substantial increase in spending on recruiting, pay and benefits. Similarly, reenlistment rates for critical jobs like pilots continue to fall as the men and women with these skills spend more and more time away from home in what they regard as nonessential tasks. In 1998 only one in 10 eligible carrier-based naval aviators accepted incentive bonuses to remain in the service.

" GEE, I JUST DON'T UNDERSTAND WHY RECRUITMENT IS DOWN! "

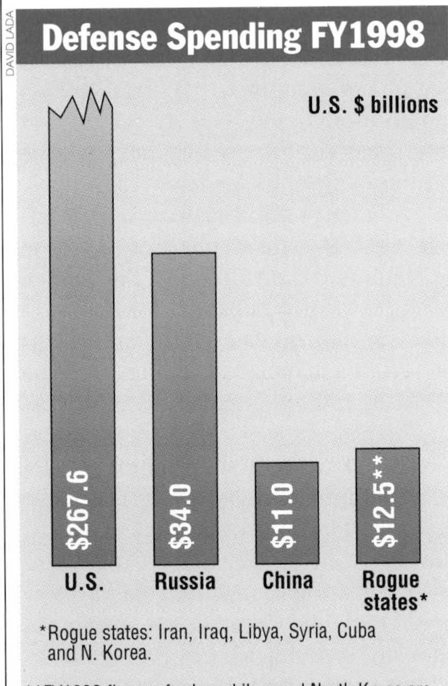

*Rogue states: Iran, Iraq, Libya, Syria, Cuba and N. Korea.

**FY1998 figures for Iraq, Libya and North Korea are estimates. No figure available for Cuba.

Source: IISS, The Military Balance, 1998/1999.

Morale has also been undermined because in operations other than war or humanitarian intervention, the military is seldom able to use all the force it feels is necessary to achieve its objectives. This was visibly demonstrated during the U.S.-led NATO alliance campaign against Yugoslavia in spring 1999. Political leaders not only ruled out a ground invasion but also initially refused to let their aircraft attack strategic targets in Serbia. This allowed President Slobodan Milosevic of Yugoslavia to escalate his suppression and expel nearly one million ethnic Albanians, more than half of the population, from Kosovo. Moreover, fear that casualties might undermine popular support for the war caused leaders to prohibit aircraft from going below 15,000 feet on their bombing runs. This made it very difficult to attack the tanks, armored personnel carriers and artillery pieces of the Serbs and resulted in the military inadvertently killing scores of innocent civilians.

Morale is further eroded when the military is ordered to leave an area before accomplishing its objectives. In August, Clinton announced that all U.S. military forces would be out of Haiti by the end of 1999—five years after 20,000 American troops landed there and some hundred million dollars were spent to restore democracy. The U.S. military left this island in the hands of René Préval who dissolved his Parliament and rules by decree, and, having been restored to power by the U.S., is now the main beneficiary of widespread political corruption. In Yugoslavia, as Michael Mandelbaum has pointed out, after the U.S. intervened in a civil war (between the Serbs and Kosovar Albanians), the military defeated one side (the Serbs) but embraced the Serbs' position (on Kosovo's independence) that had ignited the war in the first place.

There are several ways in which these problems can be alleviated. One is to add more money to the defense budget. In September 1998, after the Joint Chiefs of Staff complained to Congress about their readiness and modernization problems, Clinton added $112 billion, or about 10%, to his own five-year defense plan, primarily to increase readiness and retention in the current force. The Republican-controlled Congress added additional funds for modernization and procurement. Last year alone, military spending rose about $20 billion, or 15%, to about $280 billion. The Joint Chiefs contend, however, that they are at least $50 billion short of their minimum readiness and modernization goals.

But adding significantly more money to the defense budget is virtually impossible. The U.S. already spends more on defense than all of its potential adversaries combined. (China, Russia and all the rogue states together spend only about $100 billion.) Recent additions brought Pentagon spending back to about 90% of its cold-war average and have already forced large reductions in nondefense discretionary spending as the President and Congress attempt to keep the federal budget in balance.

If anything, the Pentagon's money woes will get worse over the next couple of years. The booming economy will force the military to increase the pay and benefits of personnel if it is to remain competitive with the private sector. Moreover, buying the projected number of three new fighter aircraft—the F-22, the F/A-18 E/F and the Joint Strike Fighter—will cost the Pentagon at least $350 billion over the next 15 years.

It is also likely that it will be forced to deploy a National Missile Defense System to protect the U.S. from missiles launched accidentally, by a state like Russia, or deliberately, by a rogue state like North Korea. In the spring of 1999, Congress passed a law stating that the system should be deployed as soon as it is technologically feasible. Clinton has promised to make a deployment decision by June 2000, and the Republican presidential front-runner, Governor George W. Bush, has promised to deploy a national antiballistic missile system as soon as possible. The cost of such a system could range from $20 billion to over $100 billion.

Strategic choices for the military

One way to handle this situation would be to drop the two-war strategy. Indeed, a congressionally appointed group, the National Defense Panel, urged such a step in December 1997. In the panel's view, the two-war strategy is primarily a device for justifying a cold-war-type force structure and prevents the Pentagon from adapting to security threats.

Several Air Force officers, including General Tony McPeak, chief of staff from 1990 to 1994, argued that the chances of two major regional wars occurring simultaneously defy logic and history. After all, they point out, no one "took advantage" of the U.S. when it was bogged down in Korea, Vietnam or the Persian Gulf. Others argue, however, that the U.S. cannot remain a great power if it cannot handle two rogues

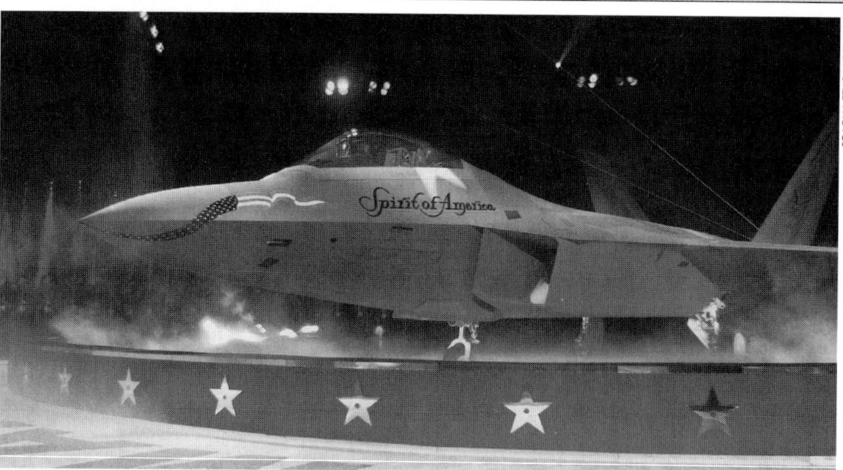

APWIDE WORLD PHOTOS

THE F-22 "RAPTOR," *unveiled in 1997, is destined to replace the F-15 as the Air Force's air dominance fighter.*

simultaneously. The Pentagon's Quadrennial Review of Defense Strategy, completed in May 1997, states that without a two-war capability, U.S. standing as a global power, as the security partner of choice and as leader of the international community would be called into question. Clinton, perhaps taking a lesson from Aspin when he attempted to alter the strategy, shows no inclination to challenge the Pentagon on this issue.

Another solution would be to choose either the Powell or Clinton Doctrine as the basis for planning. The executive and legislative branches, however, are divided on this issue and neither branch has taken its case to the people to obtain a mandate. As the U.S. and its military attempt to accomplish both goals simultaneously, the military sends its forces into Kosovo, Bosnia and Haiti and then attempts to get them out as quickly as possible in order to retrain them expeditiously for their "real" mission. In many cases, the President imposes artificial deadlines on these interventions—one year in Bosnia, six months in Haiti, etc.—even though the missions are open-ended.

Pivotal powers

The U.S. could, of course, depend more on the regional powers for both war fighting and peacekeeping. Samuel Huntington, the Harvard political scientist, refers to these regional powers as pivotal states. Since the Europeans are so much more dependent on Persian Gulf oil, should they not take on a larger role in containing Iran and Iraq? Since problems in the Balkans, or Africa, or Asia, threaten the security of nearby nations more than the U.S., should not the regional actors take the lead?

In practice, this theory has been hard to implement. Some regional actors have proven incapable of handling these situations (Europeans attempted for several years without much success to stop the bloodshed in Bosnia, and it was only when the U.S. moved in that the situation was brought under control. In Kosovo, 70% of the missions were flown by U.S. rather than European pilots. And though Australia took the lead in going into East Timor in fall 1999, it still had to rely on the U.S. military for logistics and intelligence). In some regions, the "pivotal" or strongest state is not accepted as the legitimate policeman by the weakest states, or it is the dominant state that requires policing (e.g., Iran and Iraq). This may be changing in Europe at least. By late 2000, a single foreign and security policy czar will speak for Europe and carry out the military will of its leaders.

Another possibility would be to allow the UN to take over more of these operations. To date the UN has shown itself reasonably capable of peacekeeping when it is invited in after an agreed-on settlement, as it has in Cyprus since 1964. In 1999 the world body had over 12,000 peacekeepers in 16 operations at a cost of $870 million. Though the UN could establish a rapid deployment headquarters and obtain standby authority from the Security Council to mobilize forces, it would need additional tools and member support to become the world's primary peacekeeper.

Yet another way for the U.S. to resolve these tensions would be to support those who are willing to fight for their own interests rather than call in U.S. combat troops. In the early 1990s, for example, the U.S. could have lifted the arms embargo against the Muslims in Bosnia and allowed them to get the weapons they needed to defend themselves from the Serbs. Or, rather than drop 25,000 bombs on Kosovo, the U.S. could have armed the Kosovo Albanians or the Kosovo Liberation Army (KLA) and let them fight for their own independence. This strategy could encourage other countries to support opposing local forces, however, resulting in escalation of the conflict. While supporting local forces would keep the U.S. from being directly involved, it would not guarantee that "our side" would win. Moreover, the failure of these local forces would be seen as a failure of U.S. policy. If the KLA had been defeated by Milosevic and he then completed the ethnic cleansing of Kosovo, what would the U.S. have done?

The U.S. could also try to resolve this situation by relying less on military force and more on diplomacy. But given the amount the U.S. now spends on foreign affairs, funding an enlarged diplomatic role would prove difficult. The fiscal year 2000 foreign affairs budget approved by Congress is $12.7 billion, about $2 billion less than the President requested, nearly $3 billion less than was spent in fiscal year 1999, and $10 billion less than a bipartisan Council on Foreign Relations task force deemed the minimum necessary to conduct an effective foreign affairs policy.

In the post-cold-war period, as the columnist Jim Hoagland pointed out in *The Washington Post,* political leaders in the U.S. refuse to address the political framework that created conflicts like Bosnia and Kosovo. Nor have they shown much imagination in dealing with the Saddam Husseins and Slobodan Milosevics of the world. For example, the U.S. recognizes Milosevic's regime as the legal sovereign authority over Kosovo while simultaneously ensuring he cannot exercise his sovereignty.

The Pentagon could ease the pressure on its forces by reducing its overseas commitments, currently numbering 100,000 in Europe, 100,000 in Asia, 23,000 in the Persian Gulf and 10,000 in the Balkans. But U.S. combat commanders in Europe, Asia and the Persian Gulf are on record as opposing any reduction. In August 1999, General Wesley C. Clark, the supreme allied commander in Europe, agreed that even though the U.S. sees no nation in Europe as an adversary, local instabilities and failed states are more common now than they were during the cold war and the U.S. needs to maintain the current level of forces in Europe for deterrence.

It would be even more difficult to reduce the U.S. military presence in Asia, given the fact that three major crises are erupting in a 4,000-mile arc from South Asia to Taiwan and the Koreas in the East, all with potential impact on U.S. strategic interests. China is threatening military action to punish Taiwan because President Lee Teng-hui called for a dialogue between Taiwan and China on a "state-to-state" basis, implicitly rejecting the one-China policy; North Korea may be preparing to launch a long-range missile capable of attacking Japan and parts of the U.S. with weapons of mass destruction; and India and Pakistan, both of which exploded nuclear weapons in May 1998, fought in Kashmir in spring and summer 1999.

In August 1999, General Anthony Zinni, head of the Central Command, which controls U.S. forces in the Persian Gulf, argued that because of Iraq's continuing refusal to allow UN inspectors into the country and the challenges that Iraq has made to U.S. and British air patrols over northern and southern Iraq since last December, he could not agree to any pullback of the 14,000 sailors, 5,800 Air Force personnel and 3,000 soldiers currently deployed in the Persian Gulf.

Finally, U.S. forces in Bosnia have been reduced from 30,000 in 1995 to about 6,000 today. And the 4,000 U.S. troops deployed to Kosovo now number fewer than their British and French counterparts.

Another way to free up more resources would be to reduce the nuclear weapons stockpile. The military spends about $35 billion a year, or nearly 13% of its entire budget, to maintain 7,500 strategic nuclear weapons and land- and sea-based intercontinental ballistic missiles. Many analysts, including several retired military officers, have urged the Pentagon to reduce that number substantially or even eliminate it altogether. Among them are Admiral Stansfield Turner, former head of the Central Intelligence Agency, General Lee Butler, former head of the Strategic Air Command, and General Charles Horner, former head of the Space Command and Commander of the Air Force in the Persian Gulf war. Reducing the number of strategic nuclear weapons to 1,000, for example, could free up more than $10 billion annually.

PHOTO BY CAMERA ONE

GENERAL WESLEY K. CLARK, *Supreme Allied Commander Europe, addresses the Foreign Policy Association in September 1999.*

However, Congress has ordered the Pentagon not to reduce the number below 7,500 until the Russian legislators ratify START II, which would limit the U.S. and Russian arsenals to no more than 3,500 warheads. Given the refusal of the Senate to ratify the Comprehensive Test Ban Treaty signed by the President in 1996, it is unlikely that the Congress would allow the Pentagon to make drastic reductions in the number of strategic nuclear warheads even if the Pentagon should desire to do so.

The next step

The tension between the Powell and Clinton doctrines, along with its impact on the military, is shaping up as a campaign issue. Since the end of the cold war, the American people have allowed the politicians and experts to debate this issue without voters' input. The next Administration will be able to use the military more effectively in carrying out its foreign policy if the new President has the "advice and consent" of the citizens. ■

Opinion Ballots are on pages 41–42

DISCUSSION QUESTIONS

1. Is economic power more important than military power in the post-cold-war world? Has globalization made military power obsolete?

2. Should the U.S. use its unrivaled military power to establish a "Pax Americana"? Why would Americans not support such a policy?

3. Does it still make sense for the U.S.to maintain the two-war strategy? Can it still maintain its standing as a global power if it drops the two-war strategy?

4. Are humanitarian interventions really social work? Do they risk turning the U.S. Army into the Salvation Army?

5. Should the next Administration emphasize the Clinton or Powell doctrine? Should the next Administration spend part of the budget surplus on the military?

6. What can the U.S. do to enhance the ability of its allies and the UN to handle humanitarian causes? Should the U.S. play a lead role?

READINGS AND RESOURCES

Callahan, David, **Unwinnable Wars: American Power and Ethnic Conflict.** New York, Hill and Wang, 1998. 288 pp. $13.00 (paper). A thorough history of ethnic conflicts before and after the fall of communism.

Cohen, William S., **Report of the Quadrennial Defense Review.** Department of Defense, May 1997. The secretary of defense discusses why the U.S. military must be capable of shaping the international environment, responding to crises and preparing for future conflicts.*

Fromkin, David, **Kosovo Crossing: American Ideals Meet Reality on the Balkan Battlefields.** New York, The Free Press, 1999. 176 pp. $21.00. Examines U.S. involvement in Kosovo and addresses the question of whether or not the U.S. should go to war in pursuit of humanitarian ideals.

Hillen, John, ed., **Future Visions for U.S. Defense Policy.** New York, Council on Foreign Relations, 1998. 81 pp. $10.00 (paper). Offers four alternatives for the U.S. to deal with the wide range of threats and uncertainties that characterize the current international system.

Klare, Michael, **Rogue States and Nuclear Outlaws: America's Search for a New Foreign Policy.** New York, Hill and Wang, 1996. 291 pp. $12.00 (paper). The first full-scale critical analysis of the dramatic shift in American strategic thinking from the threat posed by the Soviet Union to that of the rogue states.

Mandelbaum, Michael, "A Perfect Failure: NATO's War against Yugoslavia," **Foreign Affairs,** Sept./Oct. 1999, pp. 2–8. A discussion of why the war in Kosovo was just the opposite of what NATO intended.

O'Hanlon, Michael, **How to Be a Cheap Hawk: The 1999 and 2000 Defense Budgets.** Washington, DC, Brookings Institution, 1998. 140 pp. $16.95 (paper). While agreeing with much in the strategic policies of the Clinton Administration, the author challenges their affordability, the two-war strategy and the plans for modernizing weaponry.

Powell, Colin, **My American Journey: An Autobiography.** New York, Random House, 1995. 656 pp. $25.95. A moving autobiography of a man who rose from the streets of Harlem to the highest positions in the national security establishment. Gives behind-the-scenes portraits of decisionmaking in the Reagan, Bush and Clinton Administrations.

CENTER FOR STRATEGIC AND INTERNATIONAL STUDIES (CSIS), 1800 K St., NW, Suite 400, Washington, DC 20006; (202) 887-0200; Fax (202) 775-3199. ■ A public-policy research institute committed to advancing the understanding of global issues in the areas of international security, politics, economics and business. Publications relating to national security are available on the CSIS website. **www.csis.org**

DEFENSE TECHNICAL INFORMATION CENTER (DTIC), 8725 John J. Kingman Rd., Suite 0944, Ft. Belvoir, VA 22060-6218; (800) 225-3842. ■ The central Department of Defense facility for providing access to and exchange of scientific and technical information in the area of security studies. DTIC provides information on records of planned, ongoing or completed defense-related research, technical reports and independent research and development summaries. **www.dtic.mil**

DEPARTMENT OF DEFENSE, OASD(PA)/DPC, 1400 Defense Pentagon, Rm. 1E757, Washington, DC 20301-1400; (703) 697-5737. ■ Provides official, timely and accurate information about defense policies, organizations, functions and operations. **www.defenselink.mil**

INSTITUTE ON GLOBAL CONFLICT AND COOPERATION (IGCC), University of California, 9500 Gilman Dr., Mail Code 0518, La Jolla, CA 92093-0518; (858) 534-3352; Fax (858) 534-7655. ■ A nonprofit institute that coordinates research on military strategy and the definitions of security. **www-igcc.ucsd.edu**

You can find links to this document and additional readings on our website at* **www.fpa.org/program.html

The Middle East at the millennium

Tensions are easing in the Middle East, as old conflicts seem on their way to settlement. What role should the U.S. play there in the future?

by Lawrence G. Potter

AGENCE FRANCE-PRESSE

ELECTION POSTERS *of Benjamin Netanyahu, right, and Ehud Barak, torn from a wall in Tel Aviv.*

THE YEAR 2000 HOLDS no special magic for Middle Easterners, many of whom do not reckon time from the birth of Christ, as does the Gregorian calendar. Islamic calendars are based on the flight (*hijra*) of the Prophet Muhammad from Mecca to Medina in A.D. 622. For Arab Muslims, who use the lunar calendar, the year is 1420; for Persian Muslims, who employ a solar calendar, it is 1378. In the Hebrew or Jewish calendar, which reckons time from the year of creation, it is 5760. However time is counted, though, it is an appropriate moment to take stock of how the Middle East has fared in this century, of some key issues today and of the prospects ahead.

LAWRENCE G. POTTER, *a longtime contributor to* GREAT DECISIONS, *holds a Ph.D. in history from Columbia University, where he is currently teaching. He also serves as deputy director of Gulf/2000, a research and documentation project on the Persian Gulf states.*

The end of the century is a period of hope in the Middle East. One of the most intractable conflicts of the past half century, that between Palestinians and Israelis, appears to be in the process of resolution. And after a bitter 15-year armed struggle with the Turkish government, Kurds are now seeking political reconciliation and may forgo their desire for statehood. Following decades in which the leadership of Middle Eastern states seemed frozen in place, a transition of power has begun. In 1999, new monarchs were installed in Bahrain, Jordan and Morocco, following a leadership change in Qatar in 1995. With the new, younger leaders, issues of the past have begun to be eclipsed by the concerns of a new generation. In Iran, the election of President Mohammad Khatami in 1997 was a dramatic acknowledgment that the forces pressing for reform would not be denied.

A Reuters dispatch of July 1999 comments, "Were it not for the durability of Iraqi president Saddam Hussein the Middle East might soon become a rogue-free zone in European eyes." Even Libya's mercurial leader, Colonel Muammar Qaddafi, in power for 30 years, has mellowed. In 1999 he handed over for trial two suspects implicated in the bombing of a Pan American airliner over Lockerbie, Scotland, in 1988. In return, Britain has restored diplomatic relations with Libya, and United Nations sanctions, which cut off air travel to the country, have now been dropped.

A key event fueling optimism in the Middle East, and driving a renewed U.S. commitment to the peace process, was the election of Ehud Barak as prime minister of Israel in May 1999. Moving at a speed that surprised observers, Barak agreed with Palestinian leader Yasir Arafat to conclude a basic framework for a settlement by February 2000, with a final agreement to be signed by September 2000. This would include sensitive "final status" issues, such as the question of Palestinian statehood, sovereignty over Jerusalem, the disposition of Israeli settlements and the return of Palestinian refugees who fled after the creation of the state of Israel in 1948. Barak has the support of most Israelis to reinvigorate the peace process and comes to office at a time when the other key players are ready to settle: Syrian President Hafez al-Assad, 69, and Arafat, 70, are both ailing and want to secure a settlement before they die. "We are at the moment of truth," according to Barak. "Our generation must find a way to solve this conflict."

Key to any peace agreement will be the U.S. role. President Bill Clinton and American diplomats sense the opportunity for a diplomatic breakthrough before he leaves office, and the political calendar is now driving the negotiations. According to one of the President's top foreign policy advisers, "This is one of his legacy issues. Along with Ireland, and getting China relations back on course, the Middle East is what he wants to be remembered for."

Thanks to new communication tech-

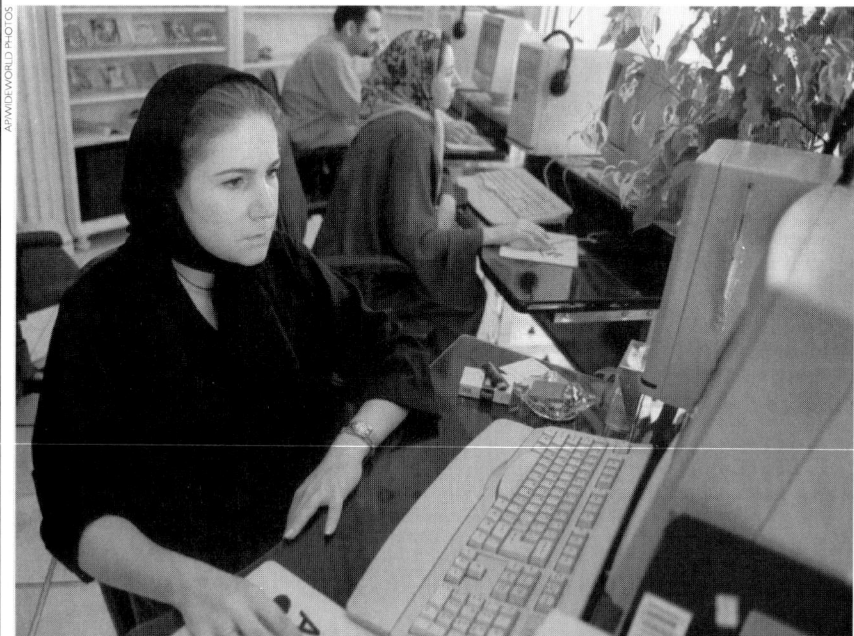

AP/WIDEWORLD PHOTOS

A STUDENT AT AZAD UNIVERSITY, *Tehran, Iran, uses the Internet to research her project at one of the Internet cafés, which have recently opened in Tehran.*

nologies such as the Internet, satellite television and fax machines, there is now a much greater flow of information to the Middle East, leading to increased pressure for political reform and democratization. Governments that have long held a monopoly on information can no longer prevent their citizens from learning more about their own country and the outside world. The Al-Jazeera satellite-television channel, for example, which has been broadcasting from Qatar for the last three years, has infuriated practically every Arab state by fearlessly broadcasting opinions on previously taboo topics such as human rights, corruption and religion. Internet use has spread rapidly, except in Syria and Iraq. The United Arab Emirates (UAE) and Egypt have the largest numbers of Internet users in the Arab world; and Internet cafés have sprouted in places such as the capital cities of Tehran (Iran) and Riyadh (Saudi Arabia).

There are also reasons for pessimism about the region's future. Almost a decade after Desert Storm, the military operation in which a U.S.-led coalition liberated Kuwait from Iraqi occupation, President Saddam Hussein remains in power in Iraq and there is a sense of unfinished business in the Persian Gulf. Kuwait and Saudi Arabia remain wary of Iraqi intentions, and the states of the Arabian peninsula also seek to prevent Iran from exercising hegemony in the Gulf region. Long-simmering territorial disputes, such as between Iran and Iraq over the location of their common border, or between Iran and the UAE over the sovereignty of Abu Musa and the Tunb Islands in the middle of the Persian Gulf, periodically threaten to reignite.

Since the allied victory in 1991, the U.S. has been the dominant external power in the Gulf region and protector of the small monarchies of the Gulf Cooperation Council (GCC)—Kuwait, Saudi Arabia, Bahrain, Qatar, the UAE and Oman—from intimidation by their two larger neighbors, Iraq and Iran. The exclusion of these two major powers from regional affairs is increasingly untenable, and the U.S. presence is also a potential source of instability for Arab friends. Should Saddam Hussein's government be replaced and the power struggle in Iran resolved in favor of the reformers, erstwhile allies may politely invite the U.S. to revert to its former "over-the-horizon" role.

There has been a notable warming of ties between Iran and Saudi Arabia, easing tensions in the Gulf. Iraq's rapprochement with its Arab neighbors is also under way. Last September in Cairo, the Egyptian capital, it chaired a meeting of the Arab League, a 22-member organization founded in 1945, for the first time since the Gulf war. Iraq has gained growing sympathy from other Arab states due to the devastation wrought by almost 10 years of UN sanctions.

A peace settlement in 2000 would finally enable governments to focus on other key concerns, such as economic development and regional integration, the population explosion and the shortage of water. The regional economy is highly dependent upon the price of oil, which has been on a roller coaster recently. In early 1999, crude oil averaged $11 a barrel, but by late November it had risen to over $25, the highest level since the Gulf war. The question is whether these prices are sustainable, due to uncertainty over future global demand, increased supply from non-OPEC (Organization of Petroleum Exporting Countries) producers, and doubts whether OPEC members will maintain production cuts imposed in March 1999. All the wealthy oil-producing Persian Gulf states have been running deficits for the past decade and show little willingness to undertake the structural economic reforms that all agree are needed.

Tradition and transformation

At the turn of the millennium in the Middle East, the region is still dealing with problems arising from the dissolution of the Ottoman Empire after World War I. The major regional states, Iran, Turkey and Egypt, have long histories and secure national identities. This is not the case for some of the Persian Gulf monarchies or new states created in the wake of war by outside powers, such as Iraq, Jordan and Lebanon. Their governments have worked hard to promote a sense of national identity, even as older ethnic, religious and linguistic ties created transnational loyalties.

The state system is secure today in the Middle East and has managed to contain forces such as pan-Arabism and Islamic revival. The state is the major employer in many countries and has a pervasive presence, in sharp contrast to the premodern period. Political borders are generally respected, if occasionally contested. If, as a result of its invasion, Iraq had been allowed to absorb Kuwait, it would have thrown into doubt all the borders artificially imposed. One of the most notable achievements of the past half century is the widespread acceptance of Israel as a regional state.

The threat of political Islam has declined markedly, and throughout the region national interest rather than ideology drives agendas. Governments in Egypt and Algeria have brought a potent Islamic opposition under control, and Islamists in countries such as Jordan and Kuwait are running for office. Islamic groups in places like Lebanon are organizing schools and charitable organizations, and they have also helped with disaster relief. The most notable fact, considering the exaggerated fears of the late 1970s and early 1980s, is that the Iranian revolution did not spread. Suspicions of Iranian intentions in the Gulf region may linger, but Iran is no longer trying to export its revolution, which holds little attraction for neighboring states in any case. Violent acts such as the assassination of pro-Western leaders like Anwar Sadat of Egypt in 1981 or the storming of the Grand Mosque in Mecca by anti-government militants have not been repeated. They did not lead to significant policy changes, but rather triggered state repression.

After the Gulf war an Islamic opposition arose in Saudi Arabia, which criticized the royal family for corruption, lack of piety and consorting with Westerners. In 1991 and 1992, Islamic clerics (*ulama*) presented unprecedented petitions to the government demanding reforms that would seriously circumscribe its power. So far this opposition has been more an annoyance than a threat. Terrorist incidents blamed on Islamists, however, such as the bombing of a U.S. military housing complex in Dhahran, Saudi Arabia, in June 1996 and an American military training mission in Riyadh in November 1995, caused widespread alarm. By a mixture of cooptation and force the government has gotten the Islamic opposition under control, and in the summer of 1999 it released two leading clerical dissidents jailed in 1994, after they signed an apology.

Century's end

Some outside observers are disappointed that more progress has not been made. "In the last half of the 20th century...the Middle East was often regarded as a synonym for trouble and hopelessness," according to Martin Indyk, assistant secretary for Near East Affairs at the State Department. What has led to so much upheaval in the region? Why have there been so many wars, so much poverty and illiteracy, lack of democracy and abuse of human rights? Political leaders are very much to blame, in the opinion of William Quandt, an American foreign policy adviser during the Carter Administration:

> When all the excuses are made...many of the problems of the Middle East today are the result of decisions made by leaders who could have acted otherwise....[The source of the region's unhappiness] does not lie with its culture, with the structure of its society, or with its economic potential but with its politicians. In short, those who have acquired power often have used it poorly on behalf of their peoples. If the next century is to be different in fundamental ways from the present one, this core political deficit will have to be overcome.

The succession

If indeed there has been a deficiency in political leadership and a retardation of the political process, what are the prospects for improvement? Until recently, the Middle East has been notable for the longevity of its leaders. Muammar al-Qaddafi seized power in Libya in 1969, Hafez al-Assad in Syria in 1970, and Saddam Hussein has been at the top level of the Iraqi government since 1968. Palestinian Liberation Organization leader Yasir Arafat has held his position since 1969, and Hosni Mubarak has led Egypt since 1981. In Saudi Arabia, King Fahd has ruled since 1982, although there has been an effective transfer of power to the Crown Prince, Abdullah, with the king's growing incapacitation. The transition to power now under way throughout the region will result in a new lineup of political leadership in the near future.

The year 1999 was not kind to Middle Eastern rulers. The death in February of King Hussein of Jordan, after nearly 47 years in power, shook the region and reminded other longtime leaders of their own mortality. The new king of Jordan, Hussein's son Abdullah, 37, is regarded as a pro-Western modernizer. In March, Shaikh Isa of Bahrain, who had ruled for 38 years, died, and power passed to his son, Shaikh Hamad bin Isa al-Khalifa, 49. In July, King Hassan II of Morocco, who had ruled for 38 years, died, and power passed to his son, King Mohammed VI, age 36.

In contrast to the smooth succession in the Arab monarchies, succession in republics may be more problematic. In Iraq and Syria, where there are no royal families, the leaders are trying to establish dynasties anyway. In Syria, President Assad is grooming his son Bashar, a 34-year-old opthamologist, to succeed

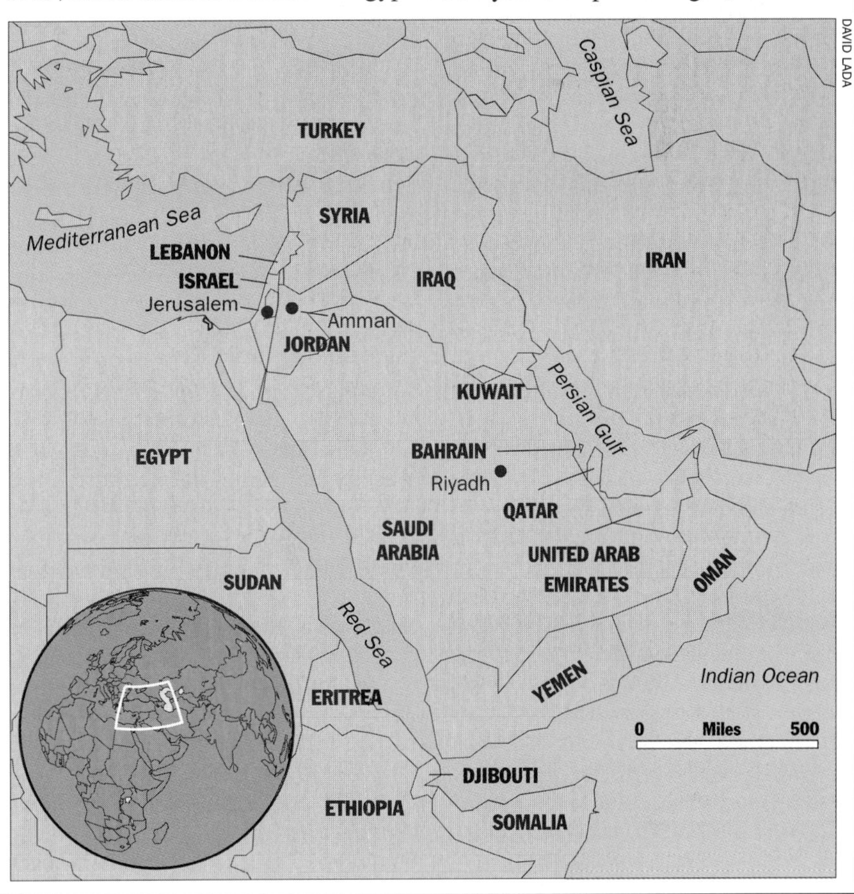

him. In Iraq, Saddam Hussein has been positioning his youngest son, Qusay, to assume presidential powers in an emergency.

Although numerous vested interests stand in the path of real change, many expect the new leaders to be more liberal and Western-oriented than their predecessors. The model for this is Shaikh Hamad bin Khalifa al-Thani, 49, of Qatar. The first member of his generation to achieve power in the Gulf, Shaikh Hamad has instituted dramatic policies, such as opening ties with Israel and allowing women to participate in local politics.

This transition to power of younger pro-West monarchs in some Arab countries, coupled with the election of Barak, 57, in Israel, and Khatami, 53, in Iran, heralds progress. In the new Middle East, expectations for change run high and governments will have to respond. ■

The peace process: back on track?

THE REINVIGORATION of the peace process is largely due to the determination of Prime Minister Barak to seize a historic opportunity and push rapidly for a final settlement. The basis for an eventual accord has long been apparent and was embodied in UN Security Council Resolution 242 of November 1967. This resolution, which called for an exchange of land for peace, followed the six-day war between Israel and its Arab adversaries in June 1967. This war was a political turning point in the Middle East, and in it Israel captured the West Bank (including East Jerusalem) from Jordan; the Gaza Strip and Sinai from Egypt; and the Golan Heights from Syria. Under the resolution, Israel would give up "territories" it had captured in the war in return for recognition by its Arab neighbors of the right to live in peace within secure boundaries. Arabs argue that *all* the territories should be relinquished whereas many Israelis insist that parts of the West Bank (referred to by some by the Biblical names Judea and Samaria) should be retained on the grounds of historic right, or, in the case of the Golan Heights, national security.

U.S. diplomacy has been crucial to peace in the Middle East. At Camp David, Maryland, in 1978, President Jimmy Carter persuaded Israeli Prime Minister Menachem Begin and Egyptian President Sadat to sign two key agreements: one provided for Israeli withdrawal from Sinai and an Israeli-Egyptian peace treaty; the other was a framework for Palestinian autonomy in the West Bank and Gaza Strip that left the future of the area unresolved.

In the decade after Camp David, the Reagan Administration (1981–89), concerned with instability in the Persian Gulf due to war between Iran and Iraq, put the Arab-Israeli dispute on the back burner. Iraq's occupation of Kuwait in August 1990, and the subsequent victory by the U.S.-led coalition, kept world attention focused on the Persian Gulf. However, issues in the Gulf and Israel were linked, as Saddam Hussein tried to make clear by Iraq's provocative missile attacks on Israeli territory.

The Oslo process

In 1993, the Clinton Administration took office. The new U.S. President was noted for his sympathy for Israel and his readiness to work closely with Prime Minister Yitzhak Rabin and Foreign Minister Shimon Peres, whose Labor party was willing to make territorial compromise in return for peace. Secret Norwegian-mediated negotiations in Oslo, Norway, led to a landmark agreement in September 1993. The Declaration of Principles on Interim Self-Government Arrangements was signed with great fanfare by Clinton, Arafat and Rabin at the White House on September 13. The declaration called for a five-year period of limited autonomy for Palestinians in the occupied territories and, after local elections, negotiations for a permanent settlement.

The accords led to an upsurge of optimism as the two adversaries recognized each other's existence and pledged to negotiate their future relations rather than fight over them. President Clinton continued to work closely with Rabin until his assassination by a young Jewish right-wing extremist on November 4, 1995, and with his successor, Peres, until May 1996. Under the government of Benjamin Netanyahu (1996–99), however, U.S.-Israeli relations were testy as the new prime minister tried to evade implementing provisions of the Oslo accords. Due to the lack of trust between the Netanyahu government and the Palestinian Authority (PA), which governs the areas that have been returned to the Palestinians and is led by Arafat, the U.S. expanded its diplomatic efforts to break the stalemate.

The Oslo accords, which have been criticized by some for not dealing with the hard issues, especially Palestinian statehood, have been subject to continuous renegotiation as original timetables for implementation could not be met. The next milestone was the Wye River Memorandum, signed in Washington on October 23, 1998, by Netanyahu and Arafat, with the active intervention of Clinton and King Hussein. This agreement called for a further withdrawal of Israeli troops from the West Bank in return for the PA's commitment to take stronger security measures and crack down on terrorism.

However, many disputes arose between the parties over security issues (especially regarding Israeli settlements and the redeployment of Israeli troops in the West Bank), and the type of authority the PA can exercise in its area. The Netanyahu government ultimately turned over a further 2% of West Bank territory (as opposed to 13% called for in the accord), before halting its implementation.

Negotiations resume

The latest peace accord, reached in September 1999, commits the Israelis and Palestinians to negotiate a conceptual framework for a permanent settlement by February 15, 2000, with a final peace agreement to be reached by September 2000. During this time, Israel has, in effect, promised not to build any new settlements, and the Palestinians have promised not to declare independence. Additional provisions call for further troop withdrawals, which would leave 40% of the West Bank under full or partial Palestinian control, the construction of a seaport in Gaza, opening safe-passage routes to connect the West Bank and Gaza, and the release of 350 Palestinian prisoners.

Implementation has moved forward, but not without delay. Skepticism remains that the ambitious timetable can be met. Israel completed its first of three troop withdrawals ahead of schedule. The opening in October of a safe-passage route—a 28-mile highway between the Gaza Strip and the West Bank—was an important step in improving the job prospects for a million poor Gazans. Barak has authorized the expansion of some settlements on the West Bank over Palestinian protests, but he has also dismantled a few minor unauthorized settlements, which is symbolically important.

Both the Israeli and Palestinian leaderships feel that they have a limited time frame to negotiate. In order to achieve peace, Barak assembled a wide coalition that may not hold together. Arafat has the prestige to conclude a settlement, although he has been widely criticized by other Palestinians for his autocratic exercise of power and for the corruption, inefficiency and human-rights violations of the PA.

Final-status talks

Observers are doubtful that the most critical issues that have long divided Israelis and Palestinians can be resolved within one year. These include:

RANAN LURIE CARTOONEWS SYNDICATE, N.Y., N.Y.

■ **Palestinian statehood.** This is the key demand of Arafat, for which he may make concessions on other issues. Many Israelis are reconciled to this eventuality, as long as there are security constraints so a new state would not present a military threat to Israel. Palestinians argue that they alone should be entitled to determine the internal structure of their state.

■ **Jerusalem.** Since the capture of the eastern portion of the city from Jordan in the 1967 war, Israeli governments have insisted that a united Jerusalem must remain under its sovereignty. Palestinians have responded with equal force that East Jerusalem is an Arab city and must be the capital of their state. For Muslims, Jerusalem (*Al-Quds* in Arabic) is the holiest city next to Mecca and Medina. One proposed way out of this problem would be to designate as the Palestinian capital the Arab suburb of Abu Dis, on the eastern outskirts of Jerusalem.

Israel's Arab neighbors

While Israel can grant the Palestinians what they want, namely statehood, only neighboring Arab states can give Israel what it yearns for, a secure peace and regional acceptance, including the exchange of diplomats and an end to the economic boycott. So far Israel has concluded peace treaties with Egypt (1979) and Jordan (1994). But the "cold peace," an unwillingness to develop economic and people-to-people ties fully, especially in the case of Egypt, has affected Israeli willingness to take further risks. The remaining frontline state, technically still at war with Israel, is Syria. Once an Israeli-Syrian agreement is reached, normalization with Lebanon is likely to follow. What are the key concerns of the negotiators?

Syria. In return for a peace treaty, Syria insists on a full withdrawal from the Golan Heights to the line that existed before the 1967 war, meaning to the Sea of Galilee; Israel so far has been unwilling to do so. Israelis love this beautiful, fertile plateau and have long been told it is vital to their security. But it is not considered part of Palestine or the Land of Israel, and most Israelis expect it to be given up in negotiations.

The Syrian government appears serious about peace and Assad would like a peace settlement to be a legacy to pass on to his son. Syria also looks forward to the financial benefits that the U.S. would probably provide in the context of a peace treaty. The government has told dissident Palestinian groups operating from Damascus, the Syrian capital, to discontinue their armed struggle and retreat to the political arena. Talks with Israel were suspended in 1996 and by late 1999 Syria and Israel still had not entered into substantive negotiations. Observers now fear that a succession crisis in Syria could derail the negotiations.

Lebanon. Israel's northern neighbor has been a reluctant participant in the Israeli-Palestinian struggle since the first wave of Palestinian refugees arrived in 1948. When Lebanon took in many Palestinians forced out of Jordan in 1970, the fragile internal political balance broke down. Arafat set up a virtual state-within-a-state for Palestinians, which Israel destroyed in 1982. Since that time, Israel has controlled a strip of territory in the south to protect settlements in northern Israel from terrorist activity, while Syria maintains 35,000 troops in eastern Lebanon. Syria has felt entitled to intervene in Lebanese affairs, both on historical grounds and because developments in Lebanon affect Syrian national security. Syria also is the main supporter of the paramilitary group Hizbullah, which has harassed Israeli troops in the south. In the context of a settlement, Syria would be expected to rein them in.

During the election campaign, Barak promised to withdraw Israeli troops from Lebanon within a year, by the summer of 2000. Already Israel has scaled back troop deployments to hold down casualties. This is a policy that most Israelis favor; since 1982 Israel has lost hundreds of soldiers here, seemingly to little purpose. ■

■ **Borders.** Barak has declared that Israel will not return to its pre-1967 borders; the Palestinians have insisted on a complete Israeli withdrawal from the West Bank and Gaza and have even raised the prospect of Israeli withdrawals from existing Israeli territory.

■ **Water resources.** One of the most contentious issues to be resolved is that of water rights in the occupied territories. Israel draws an estimated 25% to 40% of its water from the aquifer running under the West Bank, and Palestinians complain that they have been deprived of adequate amounts. If Israel withdraws from the Golan Heights, it loses control over most of the headwaters of the Jordan River, which provides it with 40% of its water. Israel would also like to gain access to the waters of the Litani River in southern Lebanon. Water was a major issue in the peace accord with Jordan.

■ **Refugees.** Palestinian negotiators insist that refugees living in Arab countries be granted the right to return to their former homes inside Israel and that those who decide not to return should receive compensation. Israelis fear an influx that could alter the Jewish nature of the state and the Barak government has declared that it will not permit a return of the refugees.

■ **Settlements.** Over 140,000 Jewish settlers live in the occupied territories at present. A minority are hard-line religious nationalists who have often proved hostile to any hint of government compromise. Many Israelis live there, however, because of cheap housing, tax relief and educational benefits, and would probably respond to economic incentives to return. Disbanding settlements will be painful for Israel, but it was done during the evacuation of Sinai in 1982. ■

The Persian Gulf: unfinished business

The Persian Gulf war made a big difference in the domestic politics of the littoral states. Since it ended, all the regional governments (except Iraq) have been dealing with demands for greater political participation, especially by women, more press freedom and respect for human rights. Kuwait held its third election since the war in July 1999 and had an 80% turnout of registered voters, despite the 118°F heat. In Saudi Arabia, Oman and Bahrain, consultative councils have been formed, although they are appointed by the sovereign. Last September, Yemen held its first direct presidential elections.

The oil roller coaster

The prosperity of the Persian Gulf and the mood in the region is closely tied to oil prices. The huge windfall that the oil-producing countries enjoyed from 1973 until 1986 is now over. As oil revenues decline, the population continues to grow at a rapid rate throughout the region—an average of 2.5% in the six Gulf monarchies in 1999. Over one third of the population of the eight Gulf states is under the age of 15. Runaway population growth in Iran after its war with Iraq has now eased, but Iran still has a very young population, with two thirds under the age of 30. This has led to a serious lack of employment and education opportunities and is fueling political discontent.

In 1998, oil prices plunged to their lowest level in two decades. In Saudi Arabia this meant a loss of $20 billion in income, leading to the biggest budget deficit since the end of the Persian Gulf war. Per capita gross domestic product (GDP) dropped to $6,300, from a peak of $16,700 in 1980. Unemployment is now a serious problem in Saudi Arabia, and the state cannot afford the generous benefits (housing, education, health care and numerous subsidies) it instituted when flush with oil wealth. This has prompted a long-overdue reconsideration of the post-oil ethos of entitlement that has arisen in the Persian Gulf states, whereby governments have generously provided for their citizens in return for political quiescence. Crown Prince Abdullah of Saudi Arabia warned in December 1998, "The boom days are over, and they will not come back."

In 1999, however, thanks to more effective discipline on the part of OPEC in reducing production levels, and some recovery of demand in the Far East, prices again rose. This reprieve granted to the oil-producing states has eased immediate financial difficulties, but the loss of income was sobering. "Those who felt rich and arrogant are still rich, but not so arrogant. They have been shaken, and see how vulnerable they are," according to Saad Eddin Ibrahim, a professor at the American University in Cairo. One issue still to be faced is the huge number of expatriate workers; in Saudi Arabia foreigners are estimated to hold 95% of the private-sector jobs, and numbers are similar in the other Gulf states.

Iran: the revolution continues

Almost three years after President Khatami assumed office in Iran, the struggle has intensified over the future of the Islamic revolution that ousted the shah in 1979. Although Khatami still enjoys widespread respect and support for his agenda of law, tolerance and increased freedom, he does not control the real instruments of power, including the army, police and judiciary. The hard-line forces who identify with the country's supreme leader, Ayatollah Ali Khamenei, feeling increasingly beleaguered, have forced some of Khatami's top supporters from office and have occasionally resorted to violence to silence liberal elements. A key complaint against Khatami is his stewardship of Iran's economy, which is in disastrous shape.

Last summer, six days of widespread anti-government rioting and student protests in Tehran, reminiscent of the revolution, shocked the nation. Calls were heard for the downfall of Khamenei—an unheard-of provocation—and one of the most potent symbols of the revolution, the pulpit for the Friday prayers at Tehran University, was burned. Counterdemonstrations orchestrated by the government and a massive show of force restored "order." In the wake of the riots, 1,500 people were arrested and, in secret trials, 45 were given jail terms and fines and 4 were sentenced to death.

During their "days of rage," students felt betrayed when Khatami did not show more support for them and acquiesced to the security crackdown. In fact, the Revolutionary Guards, in effect, threatened to depose Khatami if he did not act. Conservatives, who have amassed a great deal of political and economic power, were shocked at the depth of opposition to government policies. Although Khatami and Khamenei stand for very different types of society, they are both committed to Islamic government and in times of stress have supported each other.

The next milestone in Iranian politics will be elections for the sixth Majlis, or Parliament, scheduled for February 18, 2000. Reformers are hoping to capture enough seats to give the president a solid majority, something he has lacked until now and which could allow him to implement his agenda and promote the creation of a civil society. Many regard Khatami as Iran's last hope, the only one who can save the Islamic form of government by reforming it. The powerful and conservative Council of Guardians, however, which approves candidates, may disqualify reformers, as it has in the past. Regardless of the outcome, though, the struggle for the future of the revolution will undoubtedly continue.

Iraq: a stalled society

Iraq under the rule of Saddam Hussein has sacrificed two decades of development due to the destruction, isolation and impoverishment of the country that resulted from two major wars, one with Iran from 1980 to 1988 and the other with the U.S.-led coalition in 1990–91. Strict UN sanctions against the country, which have been in effect for over nine years, have led to widespread privation and an alarming increase in child mortality. Iraq's middle class, once one of the best-educated and best-paid in the Arab world, has effectively been destroyed. This has serious implications for a post-Saddam Iraq. "Iraq's younger generation of professionals, the political leadership of the future—bitter, angry, isolated and dangerously alienated from the world—is maturing in an environment not dissimilar to that found in Germany under the conditions set by the Versailles Treaty," according to Denis J. Halliday, former UN humanitarian coordinator in Baghdad.

Saddam Hussein still has a firm grip on power, despite frequent reports of antigovernment disturbances. He rules through terror and secrecy, and has encouraged the reversion to a kind of tribalism that pits Iraqis—Sunni, Shia, Arab, Kurd—against each other. Iraq is potentially a rich country, and is second only to Saudi Arabia in its oil reserves. Under a UN resolution that took effect in December 1996 and has been renewed periodically, Iraq is allowed to export $5.3 billion worth of oil every six months to buy food and medicine, with about 40% of the revenues withheld by the UN to pay for war reparations.

APWIDEWORLD PHOTOS

IRANIAN PRESIDENT *Mohammad Khatami, left, meets Saudi Crown Prince Abdullah at the meeting in Tehran of the Organization of the Islamic Conference, December 1997.*

The future of Iraq is entangled to a large degree with policy decisions being made in Washington. With the effective collapse of the coalition that kept Iraq in check during Desert Storm, the U.S. and Britain have taken a hard line in the UN Security Council to continue the sanctions until Iraq fulfills obligations it undertook after the Persian Gulf war to open its arms facilities to international inspection. During the fall of 1999, intensive negotiations were carried out between the five permanent Security Council members on whether to reconstitute an arms-monitoring commission in exchange for a relaxation of sanctions. In the absence of international agreement, the U.S. has been conducting a low-level war in Iraq, bombing targets upon "provocation," as defined by the U.S. This war has been kept largely out of the headlines.

By the fall of 1999, Iraq had begun a "charm offensive" to improve its image. Arab states such as Egypt, the UAE, Qatar and Oman have called for Iraq's rehabilitation, while Saudi Arabia and Kuwait are holding out for a formal apology first. Kuwait also insists that Iraq account for the whereabouts of over 600 people, mostly Kuwaiti, missing since the Gulf war. There is increased resignation to the rule of Saddam, although many blame him for the humanitarian disaster now taking place in Iraq.

So far there is no realistic prospect that the Iraqi opposition can overthrow the government. There is no organized resistance within Iraq, and exile groups are badly fragmented. The largest, the Iraqi National Congress (INC), is an umbrella group created in 1992, committed to the overthrow of Saddam and the creation of a democratic Iraq. The INC has received support from the U.S. Congress and operated in northern Iraq

APWIDEWORLD PHOTOS

A STUDENT *throws a stone at riot police near Tehran University on the sixth day of protests against hard-liners opposing social reforms in July 1999.*

until 1996 when it was routed by Iraqi forces. The only opposition groups currently based in Iraq are two rival Kurdish groups, the Kurdish Democratic party and the Patriotic Union of Kurdistan. One reason the opposition has not been more successful is uncertain U.S. backing: Despite a rhetorical commitment to replace Saddam Hussein, and the approval of $97 million for this purpose by the Congress in October 1998, the Clinton Administration has been reluctant to disburse the funds. ■

U.S. policies for a new millennium

With the end of the cold war and an easing of the security threat to Israel, crisis in the Middle East has become a less worrying prospect for the U.S. Further progress in the peace process would merely reinforce this trend. The main American policy goals in the region for the past 50 years have been achieved—Russian influence has all but collapsed, oil exports are secure (and were not threatened even by two major regional wars) and Israel is effectively at peace with its neighbors. The limits of Washington's ability to influence the outcome of regional conflict has also become more apparent, whether in Iraq, the Balkans or Chechnya.

One dilemma that U.S. policymakers must confront is how strongly to encourage political reform, especially among close allies such as Egypt and Saudi Arabia. Absent reform, popular opposition to corruption and human-rights abuses will grow, leading to instability. Dictatorships may be easier to deal with, but democracy—even with an anti-American tinge—may be a stronger guarantee of long-term security.

In the past, major advances in the peace process, such as occurred at Camp David, Madrid and after Oslo, were achieved with active American intervention. This is likely to be the case again as Israelis and Palestinians begin to confront the final-status issues. Unlike his predecessors, Prime Minister Barak is ready to negotiate peace on all fronts—with the Palestinians, Syria and Lebanon—simultaneously. Such a peace would have widespread positive repercussions throughout the Middle East, including the Persian Gulf.

Peace process

The policies of President Clinton toward Middle East peace are very much in line with those of previous Administrations. The U.S. supports Barak's goal of wrapping up a peace settlement this year on the basis of UN Security Council Resolutions 242 and 338, which call for an exchange of land for peace. It wants to leave the outcome of the final-status issues, however, to the parties themselves. For example, Clinton has avoided taking a position on whether there should be a Palestinian state. The issue of Jerusalem is also sensitive: Despite congressional votes to recognize the city as Israel's capital, U.S. Administrations have refrained so far from doing so, saying it would prejudice the negotiations.

One question that has not been fully addressed is the cost of a permanent settlement to U.S. taxpayers. Massive American aid, probably hundreds of millions of dollars, will be needed to finance an Israeli withdrawal from the West Bank and the Golan Heights, to bolster Israeli military forces, to contribute to the nascent Palestinian state, if there is one, and to compensate Syria. To underwrite a peace agreement, the Congress in November 1999 agreed to provide, over three years, $1.2 billion in military support for Israel, $400 million in economic aid for the West Bank and Gaza, and $200 million for Jordan. Aside from economic aid, the U.S. may be asked to provide monitors to police the Golan Heights following an Israeli withdrawal. (A similar force has operated almost without incident in Sinai since 1981.)

Dealing with Iraq

The Administration's policy on Iraq has prompted considerable debate and criticism. The U.S. seeks to force Iraq to comply with agreements it made at the end of the Persian Gulf war to disclose the extent of its programs to develop weapons of mass destruction and ballistic missiles and to dismantle them. Iraq also has to agree to long-term UN monitoring. (After years of cat-and-mouse games, UN monitors were finally expelled in September 1998.) To achieve its goals, the U.S. supports the continuation of UN sanctions that punish Iraq economically, and it enforces no-fly zones that bar flights by Iraqi aircraft in the north and south of the country, in order to protect Kurdish and Shiite opponents of the government, respectively. The U.S. also seeks to alleviate the humanitarian costs to the Iraqi people of Saddam's policies by allowing the oil-for-food program.

The Clinton Administration, going beyond the aims of the Bush policy, also seeks to change the regime in Iraq. The Administration intends to work with Iraqi opposition forces to achieve this, although so far it has not been willing to provide advance military support for a coup d'état. The President has authority to provide funds to Iraqi opposition groups, but has only given them nonlethal aid so far. The U.S. is also considering filing war-crimes and genocide charges against Saddam Hussein.

The dilemma the U.S. now faces is whether it should work actively to topple Saddam Hussein. Sanctions have been widely criticized as only punishing Iraqi civilians and having no effect in overthrowing Saddam. "American policymakers need to recognize that the only 'box' into which sanctions put Iraqis is coffins," according to Professor F. Gregory Gause III of the University of Vermont.

If sanctions are not working, should the U.S. step up military pressure? The brief "*Wag the Dog*" war waged by the U.S. in December 1998—in which opponents criticized the President for trying to postpone the impeachment crisis—did not settle anything and led to criticism by U.S. allies. But it did end the cycle of constant crises. The unilateral U.S. military policy on Iraq, in sharp contrast to the reliance on UN resolutions and common agreement among the allied coalition on aims during the Persian Gulf war, is also problematic. This policy is costly financially and threatens to alienate allies such as Turkey and some Arab Gulf states that are hurt economically. The intense yet low-level war has not attracted much attention—certainly not like the campaign in the Balkans—but it has no prospect of victory, either.

Iran: slow warming

The rapprochement that was forecast for U.S.-Iranian relations after Khatami's election has proceeded much more slowly than expected. Since the Iranian president's conciliatory statements to the American public in a CNN interview in January 1998, there has been a distinct warming of U.S. rhetoric toward what it previously termed a rogue state. The Administration has made some positive gestures, such as allowing sales of food and medicine and certifying that Iran is making progress in combating drug traffickers. It recently put the Tehran government's bitterest opponents, the Mujahideen, on its terrorist list, devaluing them in the eyes of Congress and depriving them of financial support originating in the U.S.

Executive orders issued by President Clinton in 1995 prohibit practically all trade with Iran, and in 1996 the Congress imposed sanctions on foreign countries that invest more than $20 million in Iran's energy industry. Washington has not enforced them against allies, and many American oil companies that want to operate in the Persian Gulf or Caspian Basin area argue that sanctions put them at a commercial disadvantage and should be lifted. In response to a question put to GREAT DECISIONS readers in 1999, some 80% of respondents favored allowing U.S. companies to do business in Iran.

Iran remains on the State Department list of states that sponsor terrorism, and the U.S. remains concerned about Iran's opposition to the peace process and its presumed effort to develop weapons of mass destruction and ballistic missiles. Until Iranian behavior in respect to these issues changes, the U.S. is not prepared to normalize relations.

In a major policy address to the Asia Society in June 1998, Secretary of State Madeleine K. Albright urged Iran to join the U.S. in drawing up a "road map leading to normal relations." However, in October 1999, Martin Indyk, the assistant secretary of state for Near Eastern Affairs, expressed disappointment at Iran's "hidebound and unimaginative" response to this overture. One new subject of concern is the arrest of 13 Iranian Jews in the spring of 1999 on trumped-up charges of spying for Israel.

AP/WIDEWORLD PHOTOS

ISRAELI PRIME MINISTER *Ehud Barak (seated left) and Palestinian leader Yasser Arafat (seated right) sign a land-for-security agreement September 5, 1999. Standing from left to right are Gilead Sher (Barak's negotiator), Jordan's King Abdullah II, Egyptian President Hosni Mubarak, U.S. Secretary of State Madeleine K. Albright and Saeb Erekat (Arafat's negotiator).*

Part of the problem is that the U.S. government, mindful of the Iran-contra scandal, insists on public talks, whereas the Iranian government prefers private ones. While the two governments publicly avoid each other, people-to-people diplomacy has grown, with the exchange of sports teams, tourists, journalists and writers. Real improvement will have to await the conclusion of the Iranian elections, assuming Khatami's mandate is strengthened and he is willing to deal with the U.S.

The Middle East at the millennium is in a period of transition and transformation, with many uncertainties ahead. In all the states of the region, political disputes are obscuring the real underlying problems that need to be addressed, including the lack of water resources, rapid population growth, unemployment, weak civil society, lack of political participation and the need for economic liberalization.

Among Arabs and Israelis, there has been a transformation of attitudes that has now led to the brink of peace. But to sustain the process, real compromises will have to be made and political leadership of a high caliber is required. Politicians must move beyond the zero-sum mindset that has long characterized the region, and recognize that long-standing conflicts cannot be settled fully to the satisfaction of either side but rather must be managed.

In the Persian Gulf, an unnatural situation has been perpetuated in which the major states, Iran and Iraq, have been excluded from regional affairs and an outside hegemon, the U.S., has stepped in to maintain peace. But while reassuring at present for the Persian Gulf monarchs, a continued large U.S. presence is not a recipe for future harmony either at home or in the region. The littoral states need to confront the serious internal problems they all face. As petroleum analyst Vahan Zanoyan has pointed out, the Gulf states' holiday from more "normal" politics and economics is now over.

Overall, U.S. policies toward the Middle East under Clinton have very much followed the pattern of previous Administrations. There has been an emphasis on military security agreements, assuring oil exports and propping up pro-Western leaders. Especially in light of the nascent civil society in the region, the U.S. might do well to accord a greater role to the underlying problems that may prove equally important to regional security in the long run. These include human rights and democratization, a larger role for women, and the question of real economic reform. These are all issues that will affect the security of the Persian Gulf in the 21st century. ■

Opinion Ballots are on pages 63–64

DISCUSSION QUESTIONS

1. Now that the major U.S. policy goals for the Middle East since World War II (exclusion of Soviet influence, protection of oil exports and security of Israel) have been achieved, what should shape the U.S. agenda on the region in the 21st century?

2. The Persian Gulf has a history of outside intervention, with the U.S. as the predominant external power since the British withdrawal in 1971, and especially since the Gulf War ended in 1991. What should future U.S. priorities be in the Gulf, and under what conditions do you see the prospect of a reduction of troop levels?

3. Should present-day borders in the Middle East be regarded as sacrosanct, or are there reasons to justify changing them? If the Palestinians are granted a state, how about the Kurds? Why are neighboring states committed to maintaining Iraq's territorial integrity?

4. How do you think the information revolution and expansion of Internet use will affect the Middle East in the 21st century? Do you think they will help solve problems or exacerbate them?

5. A major issue in the negotiations between Israelis and Palestinians is that of a Palestinian state. So far the U.S. government has not taken a position in favor of statehood. How do you see the pros and cons of such a state, and what effect would it have on regional politics and security?

6. Americans are sharply divided over U.S. policy toward Iraq, including whether to relax sanctions in light of the humanitarian catastrophe, and how deeply involved the U.S. should be in any attempt to overthrow the regime of Saddam Hussein. Do you think it is time the U.S. modified its policy on Iraq?

7. Twenty years after Iran's revolution, the U.S. and Iranian governments remain estranged, although people-to-people ties are growing. Do you think that it is time to relax sanctions and permit American companies to do business in Iran, or should the U.S. continue to insist on policy changes from the Khatami government first?

READINGS AND RESOURCES

Benvenisti, Meron, **Intimate Enemies: Jews and Arabs in a Shared Land.** Berkeley, University of California Press, 1995. 260 pp. $30.00. Former deputy mayor of Jerusalem addresses the Israeli occupation of the West Bank and Gaza and evaluates the 1993 Israeli-Palestinian accords.

Humphreys, R. Stephen, **Between Memory and Desire: The Middle East in a Troubled Age.** Berkeley, University of California Press, 1999. 297 pp. $29.95. In this discussion of the ideological differences that have shaped conflict in the Middle East, Humphreys focuses on the importance of Islam.

Indyk, Martin S., "U.S. Policy Toward the Middle East." **U.S. Department of State Dispatch,** July 1999, pp. 9–16. The assistant secretary for Near Eastern affairs outlines the Clinton Administration's policy.*

Khalidi, Rashid, **Palestinian Identity: The Construction of a Modern National Consciousness.** New York, Columbia University Press, 1997. 309 pp. $16.50 (paper). A major study of modern Palestinian nationalism.

"The Middle East." **Current History,** January 2000. Entire issue. Experts consider a range of regional issues in an excellent annual review.

Potter, Lawrence G., "The Persian Gulf in Transition." **Headline Series** No. 315. New York, Foreign Policy Association, 1998. 72. pp. $5.95. Explains the historic and strategic importance of the Gulf and provides an assessment of current regional tensions and their effect on future U.S. policymaking.

"Pushing the Limits: Iran's Islamic Revolution at Twenty." **Middle East Report,** Fall 1999. Special issue assesses the current state of affairs in Iran.

You can find links to this document and additional readings on our website at* **www.fpa.org/program.html

Sick, Gary G., and Potter, Lawrence G., eds., **The Persian Gulf at the Millennium: Essays in Politics, Economy, Security and Religion.** New York, St. Martin's Press, 1997. 356 pp. $18.95 (paper). Prominent experts identify issues likely to affect the region in the future.

Tessler, Mark A., **A History of the Israeli-Palestinian Conflict.** Bloomington, Indiana University Press, 1994. 928 pp. $27.50 (paper). An excellent, balanced and comprehensive review.

THE GULF/2000 PROJECT ■ A major research and documentation project on the Persian Gulf based at Columbia University. **http://gulf2000.columbia.edu**

ISRAEL/PALESTINE CENTER FOR RESEARCH AND INFORMATION ■ Founded in Jerusalem in 1989, this is the only joint Israeli-Palestinian think-tank devoted to developing viable solutions for the Israeli-Palestinian conflict. **www.ipcri.org**

MIDDLE EAST INSTITUTE, 1761 N St. NW, Washington, DC 20036; (202) 785-1141; Fax (202) 331-8861. ■ A resource center dedicated to providing impartial information on recent developments in the Middle East. **www.mideasti.org**

MIDDLE EAST RESEARCH AND INFORMATION PROJECT (MERIP), 1500 Massachusetts Ave. NW, Suite 119, Washington, DC 20005; (202) 223-3677; Fax (202) 223-3604. ■ A nonprofit, nongovernmental organization that provides news and perspectives about the Middle East not available from mainstream news sources. Publishes **Middle East Report,** a quarterly magazine. **www.merip.org**

MIDDLE EAST STUDIES ASSOCIATION OF NORTH AMERICA (MESA), University of Arizona, 1643 East Helena St., Tucson, AZ 85721; (520) 621-5850; Fax (520) 626-9095. ■ MESA is a nonprofit, nonpartisan membership organization comprising academics and others interested in the Middle East and North Africa. Publications include the quarterly **International Journal of Middle East Studies. www.mesa.arizona.edu**

U.S. STATE DEPARTMENT, Bureau of Near Eastern Affairs website on "The Middle East Peace Process:" **www.state.gov/www/regions/nea/peace_process.html**

OPINION BALLOTS

Please feel free to xerox opinion ballots, *but be sure to submit only one ballot per person. To have your vote counted, mail ballots by June 30, 2000. Send ballots to:*

FOREIGN POLICY ASSOCIATION, 470 PARK AVENUE SOUTH, NEW YORK, NY 10016-6819

TOPIC 5 Middle East

ISSUE A. In its policy toward Iraq, the U.S. should:

	AGREE	DISAGREE
1. Maintain sanctions until Iraq complies fully with UN resolutions.	❑	❑
2. Relax sanctions to permit humanitarian relief.	❑	❑
3. Support a military overthrow of Saddam Hussein's government.	❑	❑
4. Follow a multilateral, not unilateral, policy.	❑	❑

Other, or comment: ______________________________

____

____

____

Your zip code: ___ ___ ___ ___ ___

Date: / **/2000** *Ballot continues on reverse side...*

TOPIC 5 Middle East

ISSUE A. In its policy toward Iraq, the U.S. should:

	AGREE	DISAGREE
1. Maintain sanctions until Iraq complies fully with UN resolutions.	❑	❑
2. Relax sanctions to permit humanitarian relief.	❑	❑
3. Support a military overthrow of Saddam Hussein's government.	❑	❑
4. Follow a multilateral, not unilateral, policy.	❑	❑

Other, or comment: ______________________________

____

____

____

Your zip code: ___ ___ ___ ___ ___

Date: / **/2000** *Ballot continues on reverse side...*

TOPIC 6 The Euro and the Dollar

ISSUE A. Will the adoption of the euro make it more difficult or less difficult for U.S. companies to do business in Europe?

___ More difficult

___ Less difficult

___ No difference

ISSUE B. Will monetary unification by itself stimulate economic growth in Europe, or will monetary unification not be enough without far-reaching economic reforms?

___ Stimulate growth

___ Not enough without reforms

Your zip code: ___ ___ ___ ___ ___

Date: / **/2000** *Ballot continues on reverse side...*

TOPIC 6 The Euro and the Dollar

ISSUE A. Will the adoption of the euro make it more difficult or less difficult for U.S. companies to do business in Europe?

___ More difficult

___ Less difficult

___ No difference

ISSUE B. Will monetary unification by itself stimulate economic growth in Europe, or will monetary unification not be enough without far-reaching economic reforms?

___ Stimulate growth

___ Not enough without reforms

Your zip code: ___ ___ ___ ___ ___

Date: / **/2000** *Ballot continues on reverse side...*

OPINION BALLOTS

ISSUE B. In the context of a Middle East peace agreement, the U.S. should:

	AGREE	DISAGREE
1. Support the formation of a Palestinian state.	❑	❑
2. Be prepared to send peacekeeping troops to the Golan Heights.	❑	❑
3. Be willing to substantially underwrite the costs of a settlement.	❑	❑

Other, or comment: ______________________________

____

____

ISSUE B. In the context of a Middle East peace agreement, the U.S. should:

	AGREE	DISAGREE
1. Support the formation of a Palestinian state.	❑	❑
2. Be prepared to send peacekeeping troops to the Golan Heights.	❑	❑
3. Be willing to substantially underwrite the costs of a settlement.	❑	❑

Other, or comment: ______________________________

____

____

ISSUE C. In its future policy toward Iran, the U.S. should:

	AGREE	DISAGREE
1. Continue to maintain trade sanctions until all U.S. conditions are met.	❑	❑
2. Permit U.S. companies to do business with Iran.	❑	❑
3. Increase efforts to normalize relations with Iran.	❑	❑

Other, or comment: ______________________________

____

ISSUE C. In its future policy toward Iran, the U.S. should:

	AGREE	DISAGREE
1. Continue to maintain trade sanctions until all U.S. conditions are met.	❑	❑
2. Permit U.S. companies to do business with Iran.	❑	❑
3. Increase efforts to normalize relations with Iran.	❑	❑

Other, or comment: ______________________________

____

ISSUE C. Do you agree or disagree with the following statements?

	AGREE	DISAGREE
1. The U.S. reaps significant benefits from the dollar's international role.	❑	❑
2. The euro will be a serious rival for the dollar at the beginning of the 21st century.	❑	❑
3. The U.S. government and Federal Reserve System should take concerted steps to defend the international preeminence of the dollar against the euro's challenge.	❑	❑
4. Following the adoption of the euro by the European Union, the U.S. should pursue monetary unification in the Western Hemisphere.	❑	❑

Comment: ______________________________

____

____

____

____

ISSUE C. Do you agree or disagree with the following statements?

	AGREE	DISAGREE
1. The U.S. reaps significant benefits from the dollar's international role.	❑	❑
2. The euro will be a serious rival for the dollar at the beginning of the 21st century.	❑	❑
3. The U.S. government and Federal Reserve System should take concerted steps to defend the international preeminence of the dollar against the euro's challenge.	❑	❑
4. Following the adoption of the euro by the European Union, the U.S. should pursue monetary unification in the Western Hemisphere.	❑	❑

Comment: ______________________________

____

____

____

____

The euro's challenge to the dollar

The dollar is used for international trade and financial transactions by people around the world. But will the euro supplant the dollar in international business?

by Barry Eichengreen

APWIDE WORLD PHOTOS

CLOSE TO A THOUSAND *people gathered around a huge replica of the euro symbol in a park in Frankfurt, Germany, on January 1, 1999.*

WITH THE BIRTH of the euro, the dollar has a serious rival in the international sphere for the first time in 50 years. The German deutsche mark, despite its strength and stability, never posed a major challenge, since it was issued by a country only a third the size of the U.S. The Japanese yen long labored under the handicap that Japanese financial markets were tightly regulated, making them unattractive to foreign investors. Free of rivals, the dollar remained far and away the leading currency used in international trade and financial transactions not just by Americans but also by firms, governments and travelers around the world.

BARRY EICHENGREEN *is George C. Pardee and Helen N. Pardee Professor of Economics and Political Science at the University of California, Berkeley, research associate of the National Bureau of Economic Research in Cambridge, Massachusetts, and research fellow of the Centre for Economic Policy Research in London, England. He is the author of* European Monetary Unification *(MIT Press, 1997).*

The euro has the potential to change all this. "Euroland," the popular name for the region comprising the 11 countries that have so far agreed to adopt the new European currency, is a large economy with a population of 300 million. Its economic weight and participation in international trade and investment are comparable to those of the U.S. Its members, which include France, Germany and the Netherlands, have highly developed financial markets. Their newly created European Central Bank has a mandate to pursue price stability and seems every bit as committed as the U.S. Federal Reserve System to be the steward of a strong currency. Together, these facts conjure up visions of the dollar and the euro, like King Kong and Godzilla, engaged in a battle to the death for world financial supremacy.

Is this challenge real, and should Americans care? The answer to neither question is clear. International currency status depends on more than the sheer size and economic weight of the country—or, in Europe's case, countries—issuing it. At the same time, the benefits of being the dominant international currency are probably less than meet the eye. Retaining the benefits may not be worth major sacrifices by the U.S.

Indeed, there is reason to ask if the metaphor of a battle to the death between two supermonsters is useful for understanding the issue. The world economy in the 21st century may not turn out to be one in which only a single currency remains standing. If the world is reorganized into several distinct economic and financial zones ("Dollarland" and "Euroland"), then the two currencies, unlike King Kong and Godzilla, may learn to coexist.

Why the euro?

The advent of the euro is widely hailed as the most important event affecting the international monetary landscape since the breakdown of the Bretton Woods system of pegged-but-adjustable exchange rates in the early 1970s, and possibly since the Bretton Woods Agreement itself, which established the International Monetary Fund and the World Bank in 1944. Between them, the U.S. and Europe account for nearly half of all global production and consumption. Their policy decisions consequently have an outsized impact on the rest of the world. But when the U.S. and Europe have met to discuss monetary issues, there have been upward of a dozen countries at the table, each with its own currency and agenda. Now

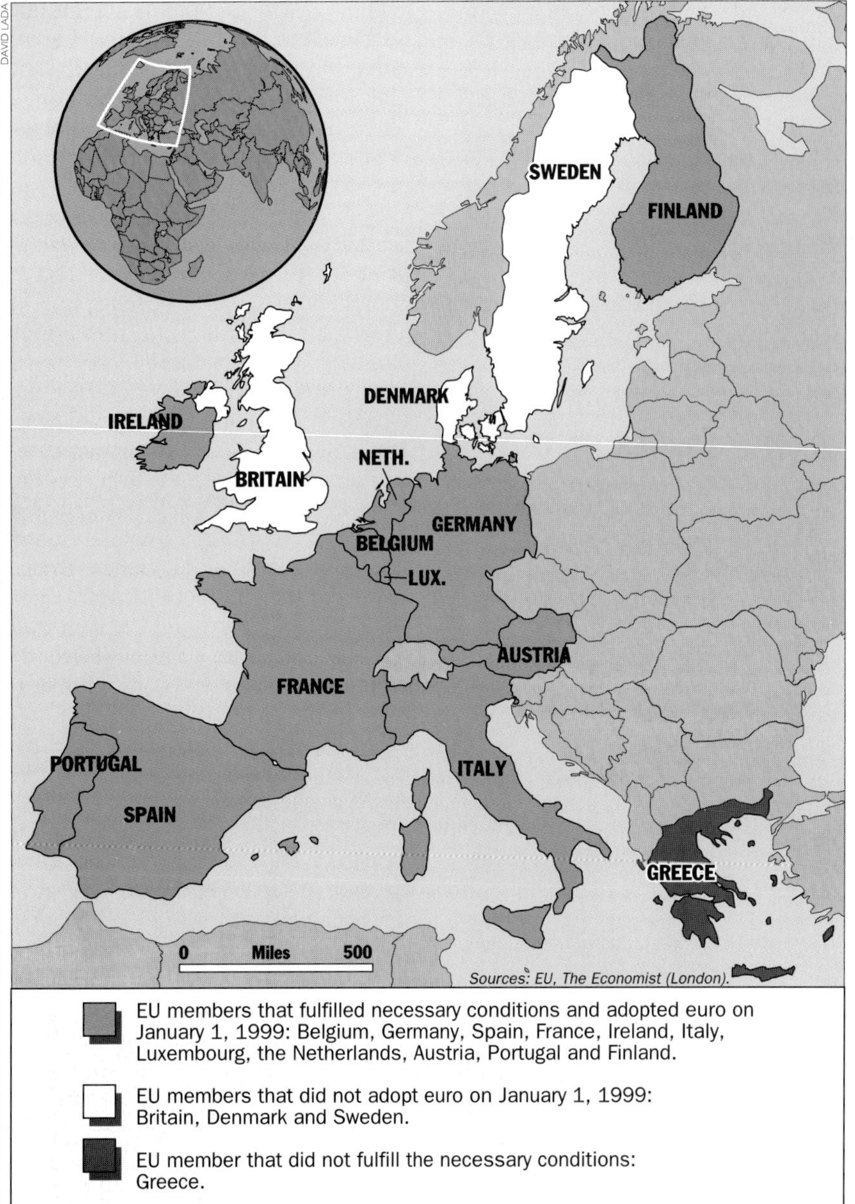
DAVID LADA
SWEDEN
FINLAND
DENMARK
IRELAND
BRITAIN
NETH.
GERMANY
BELGIUM
LUX.
AUSTRIA
FRANCE
PORTUGAL
SPAIN
ITALY
GREECE
0 Miles 500
Sources: EU, The Economist (London).
EU members that fulfilled necessary conditions and adopted euro on January 1, 1999: Belgium, Germany, Spain, France, Ireland, Italy, Luxembourg, the Netherlands, Austria, Portugal and Finland.
EU members that did not adopt euro on January 1, 1999: Britain, Denmark and Sweden.
EU member that did not fulfill the necessary conditions: Greece.

many of the same issues can be addressed on a bilateral basis by the Board of Governors of the Federal Reserve System and the European Central Bank (ECB). The policy problem of which Henry A. Kissinger (secretary of state 1973–77) once warned—that no one knows who to call when the time comes to telephone Europe—no longer prevails in the monetary domain.

The creation of the euro certainly is unprecedented. There is no other instance in history where 11 sovereign states voluntarily abandoned their national monies for an untested transnational currency. It is as if the U.S., Canada and Mexico agreed to abandon their dollars and pesos in favor of a single North American currency, the "nacho." The sacrifice of sovereignty is clear even in the design of the euro banknotes: instead of flags, politicians, or kings and queens, the new notes will feature mythical bridges symbolizing the euro's role in spanning Europe's national economies.

What accounts for this revolutionary step? The standard explanation is that the 15 member states of the European Union (EU)—formerly the European Economic Community (EEC) and then the European Community (EC)—first decided to forge a single market, whose completion required a single currency. Here Europe was merely following America's lead. American producers derive significant advantages from the fact that the 50 U.S. states make up a continental market free of internal tariffs and other barriers to interstate commerce. American firms can sell the same products in all 50 states. They can advertise nationally. They can source materials and inputs from whatever part of the country supplies them at the best price. They can locate their factories in states with the largest pool of workers with the requisite skills. All this enables them to produce higher volumes at lower costs (in the economist's lingo, to exploit "economies of scale"). And in turn this gives them a leg up when competing against imports and exporting to the rest of the world.

The U.S. having emerged from World War II as the leading industrial power with the world's most productive manufacturing sector provided European policymakers with an example to follow. One way in which they sought to do so was by constructing their own continental market. The Treaty of Rome, agreed to in 1957, committed the six founding members of the EEC (France, Germany, Italy, Belgium, Luxembourg and the Netherlands) to create a free-trade area in no more than 10 years, a task they completed ahead of schedule. From the 1970s to the 1990s that area was enlarged to its present 15 members. A landmark on the road was the Single European Act (SEA) in 1986, under which EU member states agreed not just to abolish border controls but to harmonize domestic economic regulations as well. The fact that Europe was then experiencing a crisis of confidence, as unemployment rose to unprecedented heights, provided the motivation for taking this momentous step.

From the beginning, monetary integration was part of the process. Economists and politicians agreed that a true single market required a single currency. Again, U.S. experience illustrates the point. It is impossible to imagine flourishing interstate commerce within the U.S. under the hypothetical scenario of 50 different state currencies issued by 50 state governments. Visualize the difficulty for a U.S. shipper of having to change money every time his truck crossed state lines, or the frustration of a housewife from another state who first had to obtain Wisconsin "cheesos" before purchasing an item from the Land's End catalog! Until Europe solved this problem, it was hard to believe that it could forge a true single market comparable to that of the U.S.

This realization led to a series of increasingly ambitious European monetary initiatives, starting in the early 1970s. The timing is explained by two facts. First, by the early seventies, the Common Market of "the Six" had been completed. Having integrated trade, it seemed natural to turn to the integration of money. Second, with the breakdown of the Bretton Woods system of pegged-but-adjustable exchange rates between 1971 and 1973, currencies began to fluctuate more freely, and their unpredictable movement proved disruptive. In response, the Europeans reached a series of agreements designed to hold their currencies steady: the Snake, the Snake in the Tunnel, and the less colorfully named European Monetary System (EMS). None of these attempts was successful. As private capital markets continued to grow, it became more and more difficult for central banks and governments to keep exchange rates stable when the markets became convinced that they should move. In a sense, the SEA sealed the fate of these agreements. To create a true single market, the SEA mandated the elimination of remaining restrictions on cross-border financial investment within Europe. (Where there had once been controls limiting the ability of Germans to open bank accounts in France, for example, they are now as free to do so as are New Yorkers to open bank accounts in California.) With financial capital free to move, the exchange rate became more difficult to hold still. This tension culminated in the European currency crisis of 1992–93, in which the EMS nearly blew apart.

The irrefutable conclusion was that the only way of eliminating currency instability in Europe was by eliminating European currencies. The Maastricht Treaty adopted by the European Council at the end of 1991 laid out a plan for achieving this. The member states of the EU would adopt their single currency in three steps: a Stage I of closer monetary cooperation, a Stage II of institutional harmonization, and a Stage III in which their exchange rates were irrevocably locked and responsibility for monetary policy was transferred from their national central banks to the newly created ECB. The deadline for the inauguration of Stage III was January 1, 1999, although national currencies would be withdrawn and euro notes and coins issued only at the beginning of 2002.

Who could participate was made to depend on an extensive set of preconditions: to qualify, countries had to reduce their budget deficits, public debts, interest rates and inflation rates and stabilize their exchange rates. In the event, most everyone who aspired to do so qualified. Denmark, Britain and Sweden, which remained reluctant to participate for political reasons, were permitted to opt out, at least initially.

These Danish, British and Swedish reservations are reminders that the creation of the euro has been a political as well as an economic process. Another lesson Europeans drew from World War II, along with the need to keep economic pace with the U.S., was the importance of defusing the political tensions that had made Europe the incubator of two catastrophic 20th century wars. The containment mechanism developed in response was a new set of Europe-wide institutions through which disputes could be hashed out before they festered: the European Parliament, the European Commission and the European Court of Justice. Economic and especially monetary integration was the thin end of this wedge. If Europe was to have a single market, it needed a single currency. If it was to have a single currency, it needed a European Central Bank. If it was to have a European Central Bank, it needed a single political body to hold the monetary technocrats accountable—in other words, a more powerful European Parliament. And what was a more powerful European Parliament but a mechanism for taking political power out of national hands?

Thus, for the postwar generation of French and German leaders, the single currency has been a goal worth pursuing not just for its symbolic value, and not just because it promises to enhance the efficiency of the European economy. Beyond that, it is worth pursuing because it creates additional momentum for political integration. Consequently, those like the Danes, British and Swedish who are reluctant to transfer decisionmaking power from their national capitals to Brussels, the capital of the EU, regard the euro with more than a little trepidation.

Europe's new monetary setup

The ECB, which opened shop at the beginning of 1999, operates out of an office tower in Frankfurt, Germany. Technically, it is part of the European System of Central Banks, together with the participating national central banks

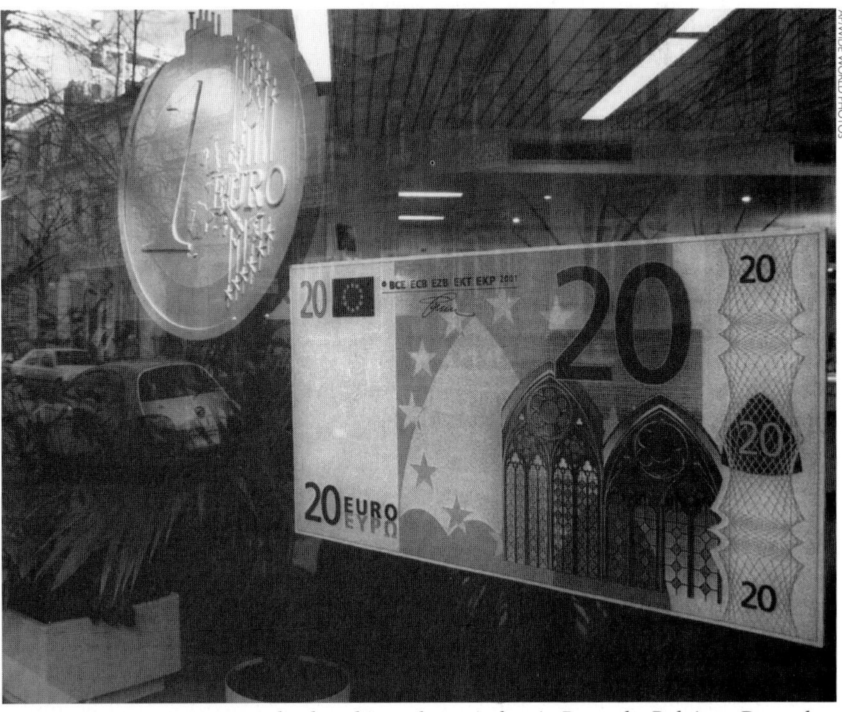

AP/WIDE WORLD PHOTOS

A GIANT EURO BANKNOTE *displayed in a shop window in Brussels, Belgium, December 1998. Adoption of the common currency is viewed as the biggest step toward European unity since the creation of the Common Market.*

(the Bank of France, the German Bundesbank, etc.), just as the Board of Governors of the Federal Reserve Board in Washington, D.C., is part of the Federal Reserve System, together with the 12 regional reserve banks (the Federal Reserve Bank of New York, the Federal Reserve Bank of San Francisco, and so forth). But in the same sense that decisionmaking power in the U.S. system ultimately rests with the Federal Reserve Board in Washington, D.C., final control over Euroland's monetary policy resides with the ECB Board in Frankfurt.

Policy is made by the Executive Board of the ECB, together with the governors of the 11 participating national central banks. The Executive Board is made up of the ECB President (the Dutchman Wim Duisenberg), the vice-president, and four other members appointed by the governments of the participating countries. Together, these 17 individuals define and implement the single monetary policy, take decisions regarding ECB operations in foreign-exchange markets, and manage the international reserves of the participating states (that is, their dollar, Swiss franc, Japanese yen and gold holdings). In other words, they carry out all the normal functions of a national central bank but at the European level. The participating national central banks, such as the Bank of France and German Bundesbank, are reduced to collecting statistics and carrying out the instructions that come down from the ECB.

The ECB is an independent body, by most measures more independent than even the Federal Reserve. Neither the ECB, nor any participating national central bank, nor any member of the Executive Board may seek or take instructions from any external body, including national governments. This independence is a matter of law: it is enshrined in the Maastricht Treaty and carries over to the statute under which the ECB now operates. The governments of the member states are prohibited from attempting to influence the members of the ECB Board in the performance of their tasks. To further secure their independence, the ECB statute provides for long terms in office (five to eight years) for national central bank governors and Executive Board members.

This independence is intended to permit the ECB to pursue its "primary objective" of maintaining price stability. While the ECB, like any central bank, considers economic and financial objectives more broadly, it is permitted to pursue these only insofar as doing so does not conflict with its primary objective of maintaining price stability. This fixation on price stability, like other developments in Europe, reflects the Continent's distinctive history, specifically the two disastrous inflations suffered by Germany in the first half of the 20th century. As a result, German politicians and the German public were willing to turn over the monetary reins to the ECB only after erecting very considerable safeguards against inflation.

None of these restrictions limits the ability of the ECB to hold intra-European exchange rates stable in the interregnum between 1999 and 2002 while the national currencies of the participating countries continue to circulate. Now that the ECB can simply order the Bank of France and German Bundesbank to print as many or few French francs and German marks as it wishes, there are no limits to its capacity to stabilize the franc-mark exchange rate. This fact is evident in how the franc-mark rate moved immediately to its new official parity at the end of 1998 and has not budged since.

What of the currencies of the four EU member states—Britain, Sweden, Denmark and Greece—that are not yet part of Euroland? Their value against the euro continues to fluctuate, less freely in Greece's case than the others, reflecting differences in national preferences and policies. Greece is anxious to become a member of Europe's monetary union, although the incumbent members have insisted that it must first get its domestic economic and financial house in order, while the other three holdouts are adopting a wait-and-see attitude. Countries in Central and Eastern Europe anxious to become members of the EU are similarly anxious to join Euroland. Some of them, like Estonia, have already pegged their currencies to the euro, effectively allowing the ECB to run their monetary policies.

In contrast to its implications for exchange rates within Europe, this structure implies nothing for the exchange rate between the euro and the dollar. ECB officials may desire a stable dollar-euro exchange rate, but if that desire comes into conflict with the pursuit of price stability, their mandate requires them to opt for the latter. Only if European governments unanimously ratified a formal exchange-rate stabilization agreement with the U.S. and other international powers would the ECB be required to adopt an exchange-rate target for the euro. But such an agreement is unlikely. The U.S. is not interested: since it is only moderately dependent on international trade, exchange-rate fluctuations are not American policymakers' primary concern; inflation and unemployment matter more. And with the advent of the euro, Europe has become more like the U.S. in this respect. Instead of a collection of small, trade-dependent economies at risk of disruption by exchange rate movements, Euroland is a single large monetary zone, half of whose trade is with itself and therefore free from internal exchange-rate movements. Only the remaining half of its trade (that is, Europe's trade with other continents) can now be disrupted by fluctuations between the euro and non-European currencies like the dollar. For the new Europe, exchange-rate fluctuations matter less. Fluctuations in the value of the euro against the dollar are more likely to be treated, as central bankers put it, "with benign neglect." ■

The international role of currencies

THE DOLLAR is the main—basically, the only—currency in which people do business in the U.S. In two years, the euro will similarly be the only currency in which people do business in Euroland. But which of these two currencies will Americans and Europeans use when they do business with one another? And which currency will be used for international transactions in other parts of the world? This is the realm in which there could loom a battle between the euro and the dollar.

A currency has three uses: as a unit of account, a store of value, and a means of payment. An international currency is one that is used for these purposes outside the country that issues it. The unit of account is the scale used for describing how much a thing costs; when Americans describe how much an item costs, they give its price in dollars and cents. Dollars are the unit of account for prices in the U.S., like degrees on the Fahrenheit scale are the unit of account for the temperature.

The dollar has an international function as unit of account because people outside American borders use it when quoting prices. Oil prices are quoted in dollars around the world, even though most oil is produced and consumed in countries other than the U.S. Prices on other commodity exchanges are quoted in dollars, regardless of where those exchanges are located, because traders find it convenient to use this single measure. All this is to say that the dollar is widely used as an international unit of account.

Bank notes and financial assets denominated in the domestic currency (for Americans, savings bonds and bank deposits denominated in dollars) are the form in which the residents of most countries store their wealth. An international currency is one that is used for this store-of-value purpose outside the country that issues it. Thus, Russians distrustful of the ruble hold dollar bills. Argentines worried about the stability of their peso hold their savings in dollar-denominated deposits in Buenos Aires banks. That they look to the dollar when seeking a currency in which to store their savings is another way of saying that the dollar plays an international role.

Central banks have wealth in the form of gold and interest-bearing financial assets, including financial claims on other countries. In particular, they find it useful to hold foreign currencies, which they can conveniently buy and sell to influence conditions on international financial markets. More than half the foreign-exchange reserves of central banks worldwide is held in U.S. dollars. This is what economists mean when they say that the dollar is the leading reserve currency.

The means-of-payment function refers to the currency that changes hands when two parties complete a transaction. For transactions within the U.S., that currency is obviously the dollar. Less obviously, the dollar is also the currency that typically changes hands when parties in other countries do business internationally. When a Brazilian firm buys a drill press from a South Korean machine toolmaker, it pays for that purchase in dollars, since the South Korean seller could not easily dispose of Brazilian reals and would not be pleased to receive them. The Brazilian firm therefore buys dollars from its bank, using reals. It pays for the drill press by wiring those dollars to the South Korean company's bank account in Seoul. Finally, the South Korean company changes those dollars into South Korean won at its local bank, since only South Korean won are widely accepted at home. Meanwhile, the dollar has served as the international means of payment.

International currencies have existed for as long as there have been international transactions. In the 17th and 18th centuries the Dutch guilder was a prominent international currency, reflecting Holland's importance in long-distance trade and its precocious financial development. By the 19th century the guilder had been overtaken by the pound sterling, reflecting Britain's

APWIDE WORLD PHOTOS

ON DECEMBER 31, 1998, *Commission President Jacques Santer (left), European Central Bank President Wim Duisenberg (center left), Luxembourg Prime Minister and Finance Minister Jean-Claude Juncker (center right) and French Finance Minister Dominique Strauss-Kahn toast the introduction of the euro.*

emergence as the first industrial nation and the world's leading commercial and financial power. And by the middle of the 20th century, sterling was in decline, having been dethroned by the dollar.

The dominance of the dollar

A look at the international role of the dollar shows that 57% of the foreign-exchange reserves of central banks around the world are in dollars, compared to less than a quarter of the total for all Euroland currencies and a meager 5% for the Japanese yen. Nearly 40% of the minor currencies that are pegged to one of their major counterparts are pegged to the U.S. dollar. (That the French franc is next in line reflects France's continued close ties to its one-time colonies in West and Central Africa.) Strikingly, no country pegs to the yen, notwithstanding Japan's international financial aspirations.

But this preference of governments for the dollar is nothing compared to the preference of producers, consumers and investors. At last report (in the spring of 1998), the dollar was bought or sold in fully 87% of all trades in foreign-exchange markets. The dollar is the invoicing currency (the unit of account) in nearly half of all trade-related transactions. The dollar is used to denominate more than half of all private financial transactions. Less is known about whose cash is held outside the home country, since much of it is used for illicit purposes like drug smuggling, tax evasion and money laundering. But the best guess of the Federal Reserve and the German Bundesbank is that perhaps 80% of the total is greenbacks.

This has been the pattern since World War II, from which only the U.S. economy emerged intact. In the immediate postwar years, in other words, there was no viable international alternative to the dollar. But as the other industrial nations rebuilt their economies, their currencies began to reacquire some of their international functions. Since the early 1970s, the share of global foreign reserves accounted for by dollars has fallen from 80% to its present 57%. The fact that 87% of foreign exchange trades worldwide involves the dollar is impressive, but 10 years ago that number was above 90%. That the dollar, while still the dominant international currency in *absolute* terms, is in *relative* decline had raised hopes and fears that the greenback was poised for a fall even before the euro appeared on the scene.

The euro as a rival to the dollar

It is argued that the euro will quickly come to rival the dollar in the international sphere. In one fell swoop, its champions trumpet, the birth of the euro has erased any remaining international advantage of the dollar. Twenty-two million more people live in Euroland, and hence will use the euro on an everyday basis, than live in the U.S. The residents of Euroland are even more active in international trade than the residents of the U.S.: exports and imports amount to 25% of the output and income of Euroland, but only 20% in the U.S.

HACHFELD, CARTOONISTS & WRITERS SYNDICATE/cartoonweb.com

This means that there is no longer any reason to expect South Korean or Brazilian companies striking a deal to pick the dollar as the currency with which to do it. Firms doing business with Europe will find it attractive to use euros, since they can use the same unit of account, store of value, and means of payment whether they are doing business in France, Germany or any one of their nine other Euroland partners. And since they will be already using the euro in their business with Europe, they will find it natural to also use the euro when doing business in other parts of the world.

These arguments are strong, but they will become stronger still as Euroland expands. Euroland will expand geographically until it reaches the borders of the EU, once member states like Greece meet the requirements for admission and holdouts like Britain, Denmark and Sweden, which would be welcomed by the incumbents, decide to climb aboard. It will expand further as the EU itself is enlarged to the East. There is agreement in principle on EU membership for the more advanced, democratic nations of Eastern Europe. (Among the larger East European countries, the Czech Republic, Hungary and Poland are typically regarded as prime candidates.) Looking further down the road, one can imagine the EU expanding still further to include other East European countries, perhaps also Malta, perhaps Turkey. On joining, such new members will have to accept the EU's existing agreements (the "*acquis communitaire*"), including the commitment to adopt the single currency.

In addition to expanding geographically, Europe will expand economically. Euro enthusiasts suggest that the European economy will grow even faster than the U.S. economy. In this view, the euro will work like a monetary turbocharger, allowing the European hotrod to speed ahead of the American jalopy. This hope rests on three foundations. First, the Single Market, for which the euro is the cement, will allow European producers to exploit economies of scale. It will allow them to build bigger factories and plan longer production runs because they can sell to a larger market. The flaw in this argument is that as the cost of airfare, telephony and corporate intranet communications comes down, nothing prevents Pirelli, the Italian tire company, from operating a plant in southern California as easily as in northern Italy. The Single Market may be rendered irrelevant, in other words, by the global market.

Second, euro enthusiasts argue that the Single Market and the single currency will force European governments to deregulate their overregulated economies. Starting a new company is more difficult in Europe than in the U.S. because European entrepreneurs face more bureaucratic red tape. The hope is that by intensifying competition among the member states, the advent of the euro will force European governments to remake their economies along more market friendly lines. Just as the 50 U.S. states compete with one another to attract new employment by offering the most hospitable business environment, the members of Euroland will have no choice but to do the same or see companies flee to neighboring countries. The fly in this ointment is that at the same time market forces are pressing for deregulation, politicians may be pressing for reregulation. Special interests seeking regulatory protection through the polity may now be able to obtain it from the European Parliament, in other words, as well as from their national capitals.

Finally, the optimists insist that the euro will force Europe to become more flexible by removing the easy ways out. If European wages are too high, it will no longer be possible to raise prices to maintain profits, because the ECB has a mandate to prevent inflation. If Italian goods are too expensive for German consumers, it will no longer be possible to boost Italian exports by devaluing the lira because there will be no lira to devalue. Easy escape routes having been foreclosed, Europe will have no choice but to take the hard steps needed to become more efficient. Wages will have to become more flexible, as in the U.S. Barriers to hiring and laying off workers will have to be reduced. Taxes will have to be cut. In order to avoid being painted into a corner, Europe will have to take a leap. The other scenario, of course, is the one in which he who paints himself into a corner ends up painted into a corner. In other words, the necessary reforms may not be forthcoming. Europe could end up with a rigid, high-unemployment economy.

Only time will tell whether the euro boosts European economic growth, since there are plausible arguments on both sides of the debate. But for the time being, the hypothetical in which the dollar is toppled by a turbo-powered Europe that leaves the U.S. in its dust is merely that: hypothetical.

History is on the dollar's side

Champions of the dollar argue that it is not simply the size of its home market that makes an international currency. In practice, they insist, the history and management of that market matter for international-currency status.

History matters because reliance on an international currency is habit forming and because habits are shared. An international currency is one that people use because everyone else uses it. It pays for Brazilian importers to use dollars because they know that South Korean exporters use dollars. By settling on dollars, they minimize confusion and costs. Neither has a reason to start using euros unless he believes that the other is about to start using euros. And if millions of importers and exporters around the world are currently invoicing and settling their transactions in dollars, the natural expectation for each is to assume that most of the others will continue using dollars, and therefore to continue doing so. No single trader then has an incentive to shift to another currency. This means that an incumbent international currency, like an incumbent politician, has a built-in advantage when competing to retain its status.

The advantages of incumbency are evident in history. The Dutch guilder remained an important international currency long after Holland had been overtaken as a commercial and financial power by Britain, simply because so many participants in international markets had long used the guilder and had little reason to change. The pound sterling remained the leading international currency well into the 20th century, long after the country was overtaken economically by the U.S. and Germany.

Incumbent politicians can still lose elections despite their advantages in raising funds and accessing the media. Incumbent international currencies can lose ground as well. If a currency is seriously mismanaged, like the British pound was in the middle decades of the 20th century, foreigners will drop it like a hot potato. But few people now think that the Fed will disastrously mismanage the dollar anytime soon. In its battle with the euro, history is on the dollar's side. ■

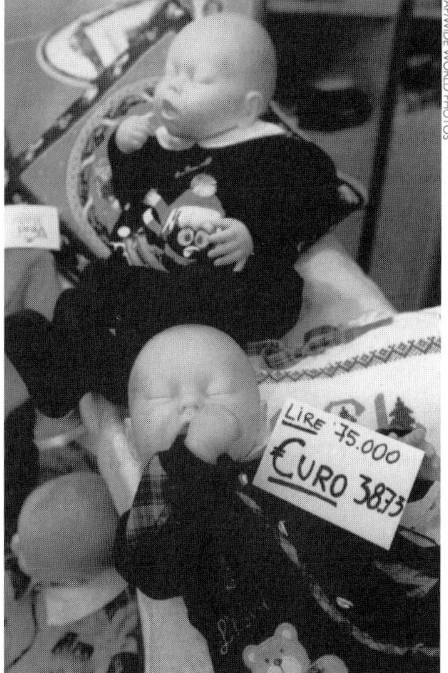

APWIDE WORLD PHOTOS

A BABY JUMPER *in a Milan, Italy, clothing store is priced both in Italian lire and in the euro. Though coins and banknotes will not be issued until 2002, people can designate the new currency for their bank accounts and credit cards.*

The importance of the markets

A CURRENCY TENDS to acquire an international role once the country issuing it has developed a large financial market. The deeper and more liquid that market, the easier it is to get in and out without disturbing the level of prices, something that is attractive to investors. Central banks similarly like to hold their foreign-exchange reserves in a currency that is traded in deep and liquid markets, where they can get in and out without drawing attention. Hence, the larger and more liquid a country's financial markets, the more likely is its currency to acquire an international role.

The advent of the euro will create an immensely large European financial market, larger even than that of the U.S. The market value of the bonds, equities and bank assets issued in EU countries at the end of 1995 amounted to roughly $27 trillion, whereas the comparable figure for the U.S. was "only" $23 trillion. This is another argument for why the euro could overtake the dollar.

But the attractions of a financial market depend on more than just its size. In addition, its allure hinges on how it is regulated and managed. The dollar is attractive to foreigners because so many U.S. treasury bonds and so much corporate paper (debt securities issued by U.S.

companies) are traded every day. Prices adjust smoothly, and business is rarely disrupted by sharp market moves. Credit for this goes partly to vigorous regulation by public agencies like the U.S. Securities and Exchange Commission, which discourages market cornering, insider trading and other anticompetitive practices that would make U.S. markets less attractive. In addition, an important role is played by the Fed, which provides liquidity to the markets when they threaten to seize up. For example, the Fed injected massive amounts of liquidity into U.S. financial markets in October 1987, following the Wall Street crash. It reduced interest rates in the second half of 1998 when the stability of U.S. financial markets was again threatened, this time by the all-but-failure of the Connecticut-based investment fund Long-Term Capital Management.

That the Fed stands ready to maintain orderly conditions is critical for making the U.S. market attractive to foreign participants. This too is evident in history. The U.S. acquired its role as a major player in international financial markets only after the Federal Reserve System was established in 1913. Before then, the U.S. commercial paper market was shallow and volatile. Financial crises were a chronic problem. Only after the Fed was created and began to carry out its backstopping functions did the market deepen and settle down. Only then did the dollar become attractive to foreigners. Only then did it acquire an international role.

Whether the euro dethrones the dollar may therefore depend on responsibilities assumed by the ECB. It is anticipated, in line with traditional Bundesbank practice, that the ECB will engage in relatively limited day-to-day liquidity management. Emulating the Bundesbank, it will provide refinancing to the private sector perhaps once a week. While such occasional transactions are appropriate for bank-based financial systems like that on which Europe has traditionally relied, they are less suited to securitized financial markets like that which Europe is currently trying to build. Limiting the volatility of such markets requires continuous liquidity management by the central bank, not just periodic intervention. If the ECB does not intervene regularly to damp down sharp swings in liquidity, interest rates on European instruments will not exhibit the attractive stability of their American counterparts. The activities of the ECB will then contribute little to the creation of a deep and stable European financial market. And the euro will not be attractive to traders and investors deciding what currency to utilize in their international transactions.

The point is not that financial markets in Europe will stagnate. Those markets will develop in response to the same advances in information- and risk-management technologies that have stimulated their growth in the U.S. Still, it is unlikely that European stock and bond markets will quickly come to rival U.S. markets in the absence of a central bank ready to support the market. And in turn this will make the euro less attractive than the dollar for international purposes.

International role of the dollar

How much should Americans and the government officials who represent them care about the dollar's international role? The answer is "probably a little," but not enough to justify serious compromises in the pursuit of other objectives.

The dollar's international-currency status confers several modest advantages on the U.S. Above all there is the advantage of convenience. The fact that the dollar is used in international as well as domestic transactions is of special benefit to Americans. Foreign firms have to use dollars and their domestic currency, depending on whether they are doing business at home or abroad, but American firms can use dollars regardless of with whom they deal. Both German and U.S. college students traveling in Asia carry dollars in their wallets, which is especially convenient for the Americans, who do not even have to go to the foreign-exchange counter at the bank in order to obtain them.

While U.S. banks have more customers because the dollar is so widely used in international transactions, this advantage will lose importance as financial markets are deregulated and banks offer new products. In the past, South Korean exporters and Brazilian importers who used dollars in their international business kept them in accounts in U.S. banks. Now that global banking is being deregulated, nothing prevents foreign banks from also allowing their customers to make dollar-denominated deposits. Foreign firms thus no longer have to come to New York to open dollar bank accounts.

Finally, there is what economists call seigniorage. Seigniorage is the additional income the U.S. gets when dollars are held abroad. It costs the U.S. Bureau of Engraving and Printing three cents to print a dollar bill. But foreigners have to give us a dollar's worth of goods and services in order to obtain one of those green pieces of paper. They are effectively giving the U.S. an interest-free loan when they hold dollar bills, since they could take their dollars if they wished and use them to purchase

HENG, CARTOONISTS & WRITERS SYNDICATE/cartoonweb.com

U.S. merchandise, which then would no longer be available to American consumers.

How much is this interest-free loan worth? The Fed estimates that $265 billion of U.S. currency is held abroad. At an interest rate of 5%, this makes the loan the U.S. receives worth $13 billion. A billion here, a billion there, and pretty soon you're talking about real money. Still, for a trillion-dollar economy like that of U.S., $13 billion is small potatoes.

On balance, the dollar's international-currency status confers several modest benefits on the U.S. But those benefits are less important to the prosperity and welfare of its citizens than a robust economy. The implication is that the Fed should not raise interest rates simply to make the dollar more attractive to foreign investors if doing so would place the economic growth and stability at risk. International-currency status is worth keeping, but not at the cost of significant sacrifices of other objectives.

Battle to the death or peaceful coexistence?

The image of King Kong and Godzilla suggests a knockdown, drag-out battle between the euro and the dollar. The world, in this view, is big enough for only one international currency.

In fact, this may no longer be true. With advances in electronic trading, it costs less for manufacturing firms and financial institutions to buy and sell different currencies. It becomes easier to develop an internationally active market in the euro alongside the internationally active market in the dollar. There is less reason to believe that the growth of the market in one currency will automatically drive the market in the other out of existence.

Moreover, with the regionalization of the world economy, both the dollar and the euro may be developing their own natural constituencies. The euro has a natural constituency in Eastern Europe. East European countries trade mainly with West European countries due to geographic proximity. Eastern Europe will naturally find it convenient to use the euro when conducting those transactions. Furthermore, the overriding foreign policy objective of East European countries is membership in the EU, and the EU is willing to have them.

A BANK CUSTOMER *counts U.S. dollars withdrawn from an ATM in Buenos Aires, Argentina, that dispenses both dollars and pesos. U.S. currency circulates freely in the economy.*

It has therefore given them tariff breaks and other concessions to encourage them to trade even more with Western Europe. In turn, this makes them more likely to prefer the euro.

Similar points can be made for countries on the southern and eastern rims of the Mediterranean basin. Such countries may have dimmer prospects for EU accession, but they share proximity to the European market. Neighbors tend to trade with neighbors. For the countries of North Africa and the Middle East, this means trading with Europe. It implies the development of a zone from Morocco in the west to Turkey in the east dominated by the euro.

The same logic points to the dominance of the dollar in the Western Hemisphere. Latin America, the Caribbean and, of course, Canada trade mainly with the U.S. A Free Trade Area of the Americas, if negotiated, would reinforce this pattern. Since they sell mainly into the U.S. market, the countries of the Western Hemisphere will continue to use dollars in their international transactions. Those wishing to peg their currencies in order to minimize disruptions to their exports will peg to the dollar. This conjures up a picture of a dollar zone stretching from Tierra del Fuego in the south to the Yukon Territory in the north.

But even if the forces at work are the same in the Old World and the New, the process will surely play itself out differently. In Europe, the growing importance of the euro will make it attractive for additional countries to become members of Euroland. As they do so, they will acquire seats on the board of the ECB and gain some say over the conduct of their monetary policy. In the Western Hemisphere, no one seriously contemplates giving Canada and Mexico, much less all the countries of the Caribbean and Latin America, seats on the Federal Reserve Board. The idea would be rejected by the U.S. Congress as soon as it was raised. The difference is that the creation of the euro is part of Europe's drive for political integration. In our hemisphere, there is no comparable sentiment to make Canada and Mexico the 51st and 52nd states.

Thus, even if other countries in the Western Hemisphere tie their currencies to the dollar, they still will not have a seat on the Federal Reserve Board. Even if they abandon their national currency altogether and allow the dollar to circulate internally in its place, as Panama has done, they will still not have a vote when the Open Market Committee of the Fed decides whether to change interest rates. They will just have to accept whatever level of interest rates the Fed deems appropriate for the U.S.

Some observers warn that Europe's attempt to place 11 national economies in a single monetary straitjacket will be a source of political tension. This may be true, but the rather different arrangement likely to develop in our hemisphere could become a serious source of tension as well. ■

Opinion Ballots are on pages 63–64

DISCUSSION QUESTIONS

1. How did the dollar become the world's leading international currency?

2. Is the advent of the euro, Europe's single currency, a bane, a blessing or a matter of indifference for the U.S.?

3. Will monetary unification inaugurate a period of fast growth and prosperity in Europe, enhancing the appeal of the euro as an international currency?

4. Should the U.S. care about the international role of the dollar? What can the U.S. government do to maintain the currency's international role? Should it alter other policies to ensure the maintenance of the dollar's dominant international role?

5. The three Nafta countries (the U.S., Canada and Mexico) have three different currencies. Does Europe's experience suggest that the U.S. should pursue monetary integration with its neighbors to the north and south?

6. Economists have wildly differing opinions about whether monetary unification will accelerate European economic growth. Where do you come down on this issue?

READINGS AND RESOURCES

Alogoskoufis, George, Portes, Richard, and Rey, Hélène, "The Emergence of the Euro as an International Currency," **Center for Economic Policy Research,** Discussion Paper No. 1741. London, 1997. $8.00 (paper). A strong statement by three Europe-based economists on why the euro will pose an immediate challenge to the dollar.

Bergsten, C. Fred, "The Impact of the Euro on Exchange Rates and International Policy Cooperation," in **EMU and the International Monetary System.** Washington, DC, International Monetary Fund, 1997, pp. 17–48, $35.00 (paper). Describes why the euro should quickly come to rival the dollar in the international sphere, and why its impact will be profound.

Economic Report of the President, 1999. Washington, DC, U.S. Government Printing Office. 454 pp. $19.00 (paper).

Eichengreen, Barry, and Frankel, Jeffrey, "The SDR, Reserve Currencies, and the Future of the International Monetary System," in **The Future of the SDR in Light of Changes in the International Financial System.** Washington, DC, International Monetary Fund, 1996, pp. 337–77, $27.50 (paper). An introduction to the effects of international currencies.

Hartmann, Philipp, **Currency Competition and Foreign Exchange Markets: The Dollar, the Yen and the Euro.** New York, Cambridge University Press, 1999. 214 pp. $39.95. Hartmann, one of the leading economists in Europe, presents a major new study of the future role of the euro.

McCauley, Robert N., "The Euro and the Dollar," **Essays in International Finance,** No. 205. Princeton, NJ, Princeton University, International Finance Section, 1997. 88 pp. $10.50 (paper).

Noyer, Christian, **The International Implications of the Introduction of the Euro.** Tokyo/Osaka, Feb. 25/26, 1999. A speech by a member of the ECB Board.*

You can find links to this document and additional readings on our website at* **www.fpa.org/program.html

CENTER FOR EUROPEAN POLICY STUDIES (CEPS), Place Du Congres 1, B-1000 Brussels, Belgium; (32.2) 229.39.11; Fax (32.2) 219.41.51 ■ A European organization that offers information about the EU's monetary policy and its implications for the global market. Links to its publications are available on the CEPS web site: **www.ceps.be**

EUROPA ■ The European Union's server contains press releases from EU institutions, a calendar of upcoming events, official euro rates and the latest statistics. Source of information on EU and its institutions. Supplies direct access to the home pages of many EU institutions. **www.europa.eu.int**

EUROPEAN CENTRAL BANK (ECB), Postfach 16 03 19, D-60066 Frankfurt am Main, Germany; 49 69 1344 0; Fax: 49 69 1344 6000. ■ The ECB publishes a "Working Paper" series, a set of articles intended to present the results of economic research conducted within the ECB. Hard copies of the papers are available free of charge from the ECB. **www.ecb.int**

EUROPEAN UNION, DELEGATION OF THE EUROPEAN COMMISSION TO THE U.S., 2300 M St. NW, Washington, DC 20037; (202) 862-9500; Fax (202) 429-1766. ■ The EU delegation offers a wide variety of resources, including a list of publications related to the EU-U.S. partnership. **www.eurunion.org**

EUROPEAN VOICE ONLINE ■ Website of European Voice, a Brussels-based weekly newspaper published by The Economist Group. Offers coverage of all aspects of the politics and business of EU. **www.european-voice.com**

INSTITUTE FOR INTERNATIONAL ECONOMICS (IEE), 11 Dupont Circle NW, Washington, DC 20036; (202) 328-9000; Fax (202) 328-5432. ■ A private, nonprofit, research institution that aims to educate the public with its research on international economic policy. **www.iie.com**

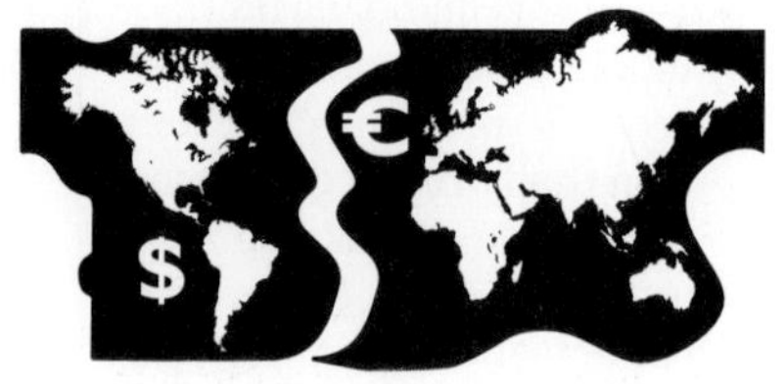

Africa: prospects for the future

The renaissance in Africa presents its leaders with many challenges. What are U.S. interests in Africa? What role should the U.S. play?

by Peter J. Schraeder

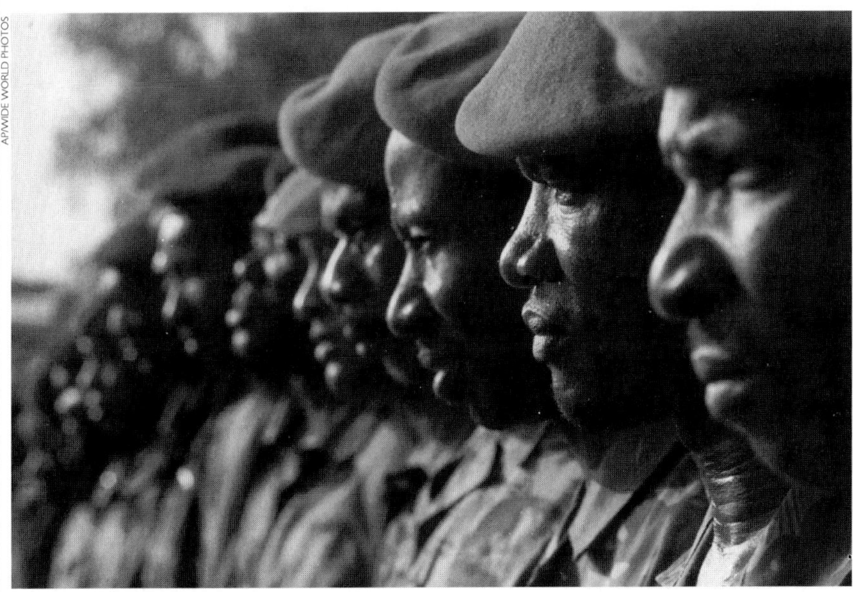
AP/WIDE WORLD PHOTOS

U.S.-TRAINED MALIAN TROOPS *listen to U.S. Secretary of State Madeleine K. Albright as she tells them of the importance of peacekeeping, October 1999. The troops, part of the African Crisis Response Initiative, will be deployed in Sierra Leone.*

An "African renaissance" of historic proportions is under way. The 1994 inauguration of Nelson Mandela as South Africa's first democratically elected president symbolized the efforts of thousands of pro-democracy groups to instill democratic practices throughout the African continent. Mandela's willingness to embrace his former captors embodied the vision of a new generation of leaders committed to multiracial and multiethnic societies based on tolerance, universal human rights and the rule of law. Policymakers, technocrats and private entrepreneurs are also at the forefront of restructuring once moribund economies to unleash the African entrepreneurial spirit. This renaissance is perhaps best captured by the flourishing of the media and literature as they enjoy the progressive decline of state censorship. A new generation of journalists, writers and scholars remains firmly committed to strengthening the democratic achievements of the last decade of the 20th century.

PETER J. SCHRAEDER *is associate professor in the Department of Political Science at Loyola University Chicago, and author, most recently, of* African Politics and Society: A Mosaic in Transformation *(Boston/New York: College Division of Bedford/St. Martin's, 2000).*

As Americans begin debating U.S. foreign policy as part of the 2000 presidential election, the time is ripe for a reassessment of U.S.-Africa relations. Though the African mosaic is diverse, with 53 independent countries and a number of complex issues, one question stands out: Should the next U.S. President draw upon America's traditional role as aid-giver and play an activist role in the African renaissance, or will budgetary constraints and competing interests in other regions reinforce what is viewed by some as a policy of neglect, at best?

Democratization

Dozens of countries in Africa, Asia, Latin America, and Eastern and Southern Europe made transitions from authoritarian to more democratic forms of governance during the last quarter of the 20th century. This trend has prompted visions of a "third wave of democratization" (the first began in the 1820s and the second in the 1940s). In the case of Africa, this third wave coincided with the fall of the Berlin Wall in 1989. The collapse of single-party regimes throughout Eastern Europe and the former Soviet Union set powerful precedents for African pro-democracy activists who already had begun organizing against human-rights abuses and political repression against the backdrop of severe economic stagnation in their respective countries. The most notable outcome, often referred to as "Africa's second independence" or "Africa's second liberation," was the discrediting of more than 30 years of experimentation with single-party political systems in favor of more democratic forms of governance based on multiparty politics and the protection of human rights.

In the early 1980s, truly competitive elections were held in only five African countries: Botswana, Gambia, Mauritius, Senegal and Zimbabwe. But between 1990 and 1994, more than 38 countries held competitive elections. Most important, 29 of the multiparty contests of this period constituted "founding elections" in which the office of the head of government is openly contested following a period during which multiparty political competition was impossible.

Optimism or pessimism?

The prospect of a new wave of democratization has fostered both optimism

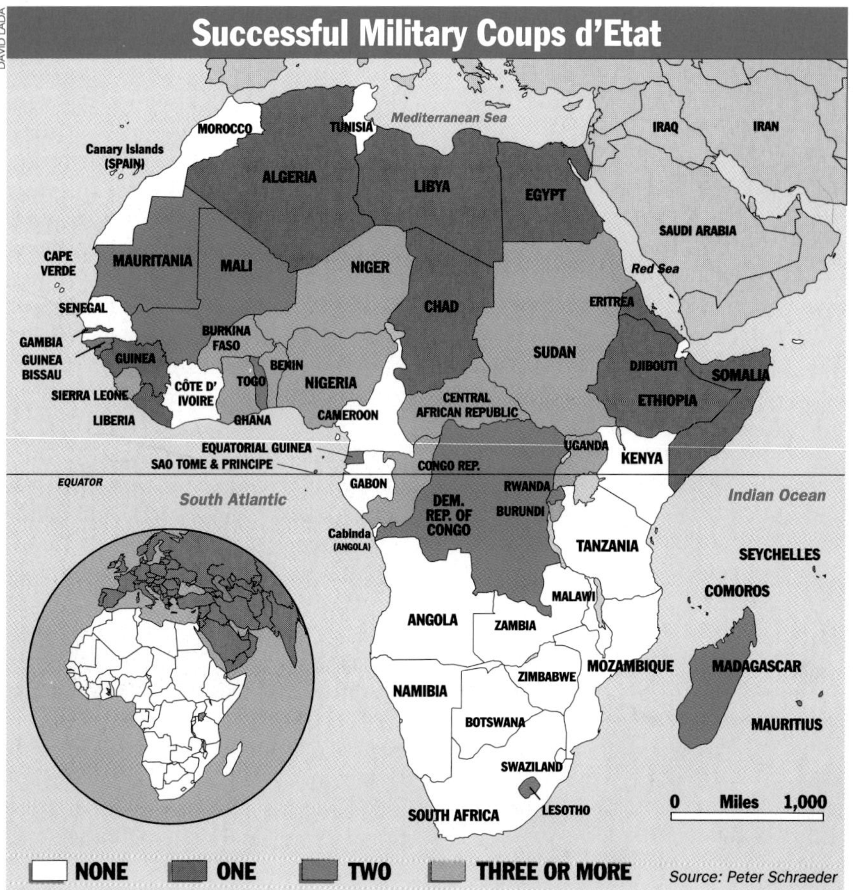

Successful Military Coups d'Etat

and pessimism: optimism generated by a host of democratic successes that culminated in what numerous observers have referred to as the South African "miracle," and pessimism based on the simple reality that several transitions resulted in "democratic decay," often ending in military coups d'état and a return to authoritarianism. Colonel Ibrahim Maïnassara Baré of Niger achieved the dubious honor of leading the first successful coup d'état against a democratically elected government in francophone West Africa since the beginning of the third wave of democratization. In a throwback to an earlier reign, Colonel Baré announced that there would be multiparty elections in 1996, presented himself as the "civilian" candidate of the ruling party and won what international observers agreed was a grossly flawed electoral contest.

Even when a successful transition to more democratic governance is made, newly elected leaders are confronted with the long-term challenge of ensuring the consolidation of democratic practices in still-fragile political systems. "The frequency of democratic breakdowns in this century—and the difficulties of consolidating new democracies—must give serious pause to those who would argue . . . for the inevitability of global democracy," explains Larry Diamond, a senior research fellow at the Hoover Institution. "As a result, those concerned about how countries can move 'beyond authoritarianism and totalitarianism' must also ponder the conditions that permit such movement to endure . . . . To rid a country of an authoritarian regime or dictator is not necessarily to move it fundamentally beyond authoritarianism."

The authoritarian-democratic paradox

In 1991 Zambia made a successful transition from a single-party system headed by President Kenneth Kaunda to a multiparty system under the leadership of President Frederick Chiluba of the Movement for Multiparty Democracy. Eighteen months after achieving victory, Chiluba reinstated a "state of emergency" that had existed throughout Kaunda's rule, and arrested and detained without charges 14 members of the official opposition, the United National Independence party. Critics drew parallels between Kaunda's use of states of emergency during the 1970s and the 1980s to silence political opponents and Chiluba's use of them to curb rising criticism of his regime's inability to resolve economic problems.

Chiluba's predicament illustrates Africa's new authoritarian-democratic paradox. As with the first generation of African leaders, who took office beginning in the 1950s, Chiluba and the other newly elected leaders of the 1990s are confronted with popular expectations that higher wages and better living conditions will be widely and quickly shared following multiparty elections. When the weak Zambian state was saddled with even the minimal checks and balances of a democratic system, economic progress was stymied, and weariness and disenchantment grew.

Although largely trained within an authoritarian tradition, Chiluba is now expected to abide by the "rules of the game" of Zambia's multiparty political system. When strict adherence to those rules threatened to seal his political fate in the 1996 presidential elections, however, he put them aside, especially after Kaunda accepted opposition backing and entered the race. To fend off his opponents, Chiluba oversaw the ratification of two constitutional amendments that harked back to the authoritarian excesses of his predecessor and undermined the very democratic political system he had sought to create. The first requires that the parents of any presidential candidate be Zambians by birth. The second limits presidential candidates to two terms of office. Since Kaunda's parents were born in neighboring Malawi, and he had ruled Zambia for 27 years (1964–91), he was forced to withdraw from the race. Chiluba's political maneuvering removed the only serious challenge to his rule and ensured his reelection.

Some proponents of democratization argue that the true test of Africa's newly established systems is their ability to foster an "alternation of power" between rival political parties. Benin stands out as the best example of a newly established, multiparty democracy that has successfully weathered an alternation of power via the ballot box. Following a 1990 national conference, founding elections were held in 1991 in which a technocrat, Nicéphore Soglo, was elected president. Mathieu Kérékou, the former Marxist dictator, graciously accepted defeat and retired from politics only to return as the leading opposition candidate in the 1996 presidential elections. With Soglo's reelection campaign severely hampered by the poor performance of the economy and public perceptions of his disregard for the average citizen, Kérékou overcame the odds, emerged victorious and now serves as a powerful example of the consolidation of democratic practices on the African continent.

Whether democratic consolidation will overcome democratic decay largely depends on how the newly elected elites respond to the authoritarian-democratic paradox. Will they graciously accept defeat and join the ranks of the "loyal opposition," as was the case in Soglo's defeat in 1996, or will they increasingly turn to a variety of authoritarian tactics to keep themselves in power at any cost, as did Chiluba?

Civilian militaries

African militaries emerged from the shadows during the 1950s to become some of the most important institutions in politics and society. The main way they achieved power was the coup d'état: the sudden and illegal overthrow of an existing government by a portion of the state's armed forces. By the end of the 1960s, more than two dozen successful coups had ushered in a period that soon left more than 50% of all African countries governed by military regimes. Even in cases where they led their troops back to the barracks after turning over power to elected civilian regimes, military leaders maintained—and often enhanced—their newfound levels of political influence. Once they enjoyed the fruits of power, these so-called leaders in khaki were prone to return to presidential mansions in subsequent coups, leading foreign observers to characterize African militaries as the primary forces for change throughout the continent.

Most African countries have experienced at least one attempted or successful military coup, and several have experienced two or more. The record for the greatest number (six) is jointly held by Benin, Burkina Faso and Nigeria. Only six African countries—Botswana, Djibouti, Cape Verde, Eritrea, Namibia and South Africa—have never faced armed challenges from their military, police or other security personnel. Nonetheless, the common assumption in Africa is that civilian-dominated systems constitute the norm. Even military leaders intent on staying in power are forced to offer, at minimum, rhetorical support for an eventual "return" to civilian rule, usually accompanied by some sort of timetable. The notion of "demilitarization," sometimes referred to as promoting the "civilianization" of military regimes, became increasingly important in the post-1989 era as policymakers and citizen movements sought firmer transitions to democracy.

In contrast to the 1960s, when military coups reached their peak, the second half of the 1980s and the 1990s have witnessed a sharp decline in military intervention. This trend may suggest a growing strength among democratic transitions in the post-cold-war era. At the same time, it is important to note that the transition to civilian governments during the 1950s ultimately stalled, only to be followed by an explosion of coups that made the 1960s the "decade of the military." Today's civilian leaders thus view the potential reemergence of African militaries—the so-called khaki contagion—as a threat to the democratization process throughout Africa. ■

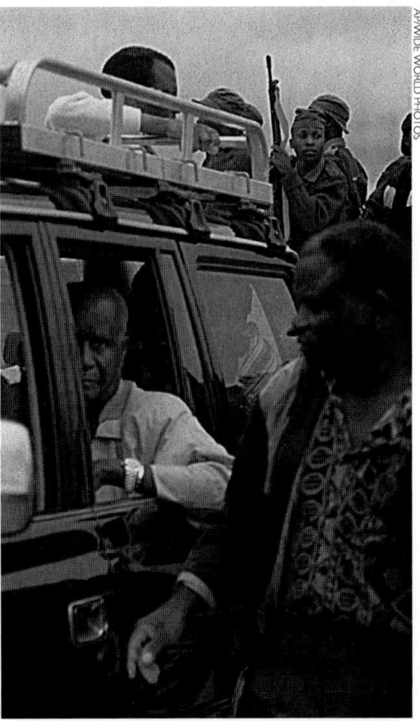

APWIDE WORLD PHOTOS

FORMER ZAMBIAN PRESIDENT *Kenneth Kaunda peers out of a police vehicle, December 1997, after he was arrested and ordered detained for 28 days. Opposition groups accused President Frederick Chiluba of using the emergency declaration to crack down on political enemies.*

The crisis of the African state

THE 1950–70 period was marked by the creation of highly authoritarian and centralized states seeking to co-opt or silence the very elements of civil society that had contributed to the independence struggle, most notably political parties, labor unions and student groups. These states were significantly challenged during the 1970s and the 1980s by a series of economic, political and military developments often referred to as the crisis of the African state. African leaders found their hold on power simultaneously threatened by the demands of faltering national economies, the resurgence of civil society, and in some cases civil unrest and conflict. Hobbled by decades of corruption and economic mismanagement, the "predatory states" of the earlier independence era increasingly proved incapable of maintaining control over their respective territories, and became known as lame Leviathans and shadow states.

The most noteworthy outcome was the inability of African leaders to contain domestic violence and conflict. As explained by Christopher Clapham, a noted British Africanist, an especially threatening trend was the rise of guerrilla insurgencies. First and foremost, liberation insurgencies were directed against colonial empires unwilling to cede power peacefully, as well as against white minority regimes in Southern Africa. Other guerrilla groups sought greater rights for specific regions of already independent nation-states. In the

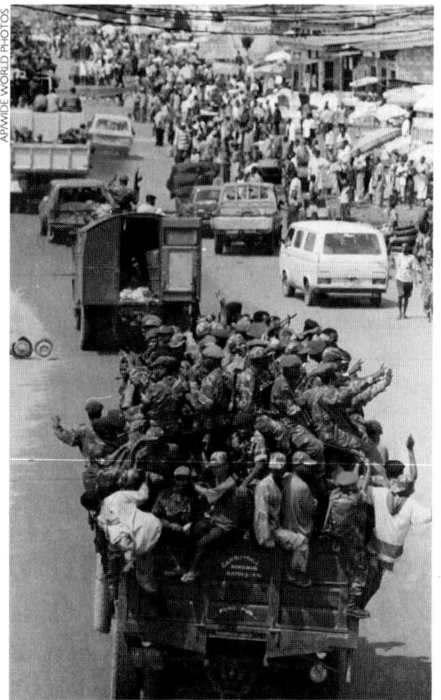

REBEL SOLDIERS *in Kinshasa await pronouncement by Laurent Kabila about a new government. Kabila proclaimed himself president and changed the name of the country from Zaire to the Democratic Republic of the Congo.*

extreme, such separatist insurgencies sought secession and recognition of their territories as independent nation-states. Although another group of reform insurgencies sought to maintain the territorial integrity of existing nation-states, their leaders were nonetheless committed to overthrowing existing regimes. A fourth group, warlord insurgencies, lacked a coherent vision beyond the immediate goal of overthrowing the regime in power. Such insurgencies usually were unable to reestablish centralized states after achieving victory, often leading to the continuation of conflict among competing warlords and their respective armies.

The crisis of the African state clearly demonstrated that highly authoritarian governments were ineffective managers. It also highlighted the rising importance of African civil societies. Just prior to their marginalization in the post-independence era, civil societies had played important roles, and during the 1990s they expected to wield equal if not greater levels of influence in their newly restructured societies. The international dimension had also changed with the cold war's end. African leaders could no longer count on the diplomatic, financial or even military support of foreign powers to compensate for an increased inability to manage internal affairs.

Experiments in restructuring state-society relations

Can a new generation of leaders succeed in fostering an economic and political renaissance? Skeptics point to Laurent-Désiré Kabila, the former guerrilla leader whose forces overthrew the dictator Mobutu Sese Seko in the Democratic Republic of the Congo (Congo-Kinshasa; formerly Zaire), in 1997. Rather than establish democratic practices and a timetable for national elections, Kabila created a new dictatorship. In a series of moves that harked back to the rise of authoritarianism under Mobutu, he banned opposition parties, arrested several leading opposition figures, outlawed human rights organizations and arrested journalists who criticized the new regime. In an ironic but unsurprising twist of fate, the Kabila regime in 1999 found itself confronted with a guerrilla insurgency in the eastern provinces funded by Kabila's former military benefactors, Uganda and Rwanda.

There are, however, other more hopeful situations. One group of victorious guerrilla leaders, often referred to as the "new bloc," led disciplined and battle-tested guerrilla armies to victory over discredited states. Bloc members include Issaias Afwerki of Eritrea, Meles Zenawi of Ethiopia, Yoweri Museveni of Uganda and Paul Kagame of Rwanda. All share a commitment to a free-market economy, the reduction of corruption at all levels of government, the rule of law and the creation of responsible police and mili-

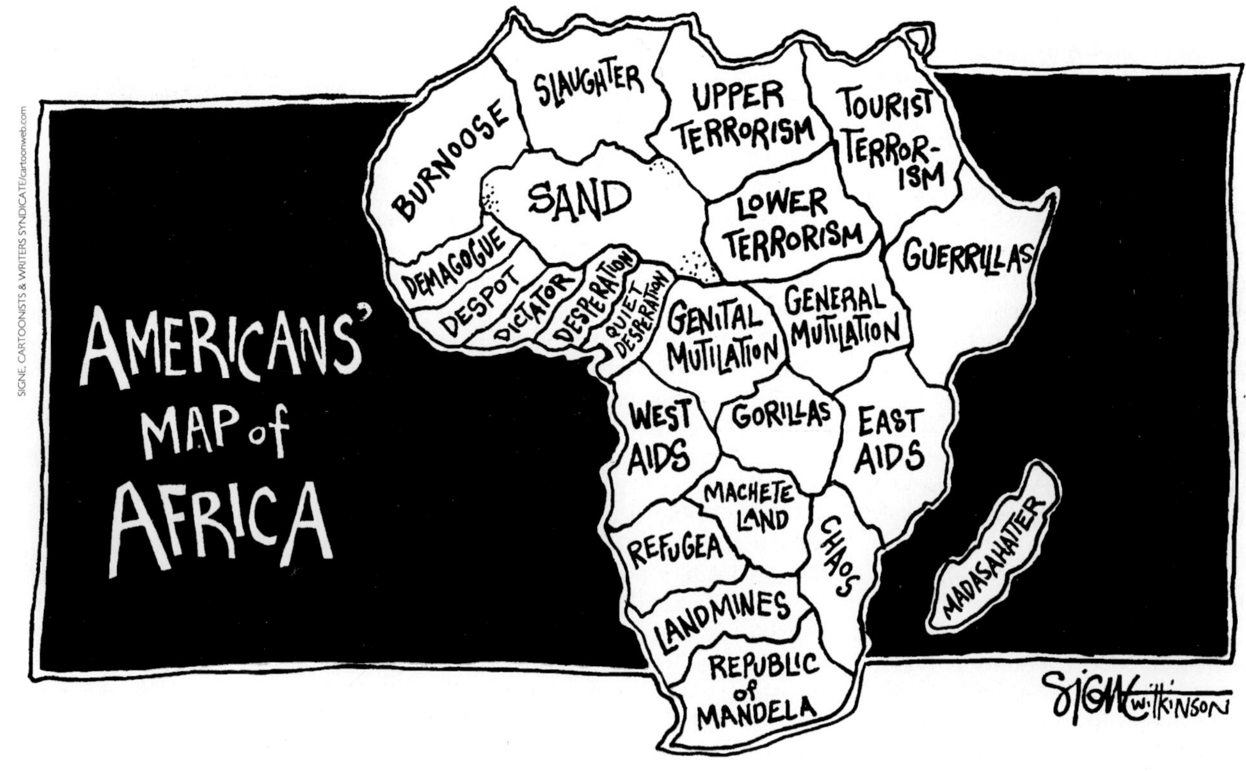

ETHIOPIAN CIVILIANS WALKING *to a military camp at Adigrat to enroll in the militia, June 1998. Since Eritrean planes bombed civilian targets in Adigrat, enrollment in the militia has increased.*

tary forces. However, this new bloc also tends to view multiparty democracy as a luxury that must take a backseat to the promotion of politico-military stability and socioeconomic development. In the case of Uganda, for example, Museveni's regime has instituted a "no-party" system that does not allow candidates to campaign under the banner of opposition parties. As a result, this bloc increasingly finds itself criticized by citizens as well as international observers who question the long-term wisdom of stifling political dissent.

A second restructuring that attracted tremendous debate revolves around Ethiopia's ethnically based federal system. In 1991, after nearly 30 years of civil war, the Ethiopian People's Revolutionary Democratic Front (EPRDF) overthrew a highly authoritarian and centralized state that had been ruled by the U.S.-supported monarchy of Emperor Haile Selassie (1930–74) and then the Soviet-supported Marxist regime of Mengistu Haile Mariam (1977–91). EPRDF leaders firmly believed that both the Selassie and Mengistu regimes intensified ethnic hatreds and polarized the nation. They fielded a guerrilla army and led it to victory, one outcome of which was the determination of Eritrean guerrilla forces to demand independence for their province.

In a 1993 referendum, 99.8% of voters favored independence.

The EPRDF leadership believed that the only way to "save" the remaining portions of the multiethnic Ethiopian state was to create a federal system comprising 12 ethnically based states and two autonomous cities. Although critics have argued that such an arrangement will further polarize politics as ethnic leaders compete for federal resources, proponents have countered that the move quelled separatist tendencies. Meanwhile, Ethiopia's experiment in federalism has been marred by the authoritarian practices of the Tigrean People's Liberation Front, the politico-military core of the EPRDF, which controls both the presidency and the vast majority of the seats in the Council of People's Representatives, the national legislature.

The most comprehensive example of state-society restructuring revolves around the ongoing transformation of South Africa's former apartheid system into a multiracial and multiethnic democracy. Prior to 1994, South Africa had been ruled by a white minority regime that instituted racial and social segregation. As part of democratization, South Africans were challenged to confront their collective past and to create a culture of forgiveness through public hearings of the Truth and Reconciliation Commission. Subsequent negotiations among the major political parties resulted in the adoption of a constitutional framework in 1997 that separated powers between the executive, legislative and judicial branches; created a three-tiered structure of municipal, provincial and federal governments; and established a bill of rights for individuals and civil society. Although the constitution recognizes the importance of protecting the "cultural rights" of individual racial and ethnic groups, the unified federal system is not based on race or ethnicity.

South Africa's carefully crafted state-society balance is threatened by a dramatic rise in crime and the continued poverty of a large portion of the population. Constitutional guarantees of political freedoms may mean little to working parents who cannot safely walk about their townships or earn enough money to move their families out of poverty. Indeed, the suggestion that the new constitution will eventually evolve into a living testament to the multiracial and multiethnic ideals of the African National Congress (ANC) misses the crucial elements in this political transition: the vast majority expects and demands immediate rewards to make up for the past injustices of apartheid.

"However it evolves, it seems safe to conclude that the [South African] constitution provides a solid basis for representative, transparent and accountable governance, with meaningful protection and promotion of fundamental rights," concluded a special report by the Carnegie Foundation. "As such, it does hold promise as an inspiration for other countries in transition, particularly those that are attempting to build viable state-society coalitions under conditions of diverse cultures, deep economic disparities and limited political authority and financial resources."

OAU and conflict resolution

The Organization of African Unity (OAU) has the potential to play an important role in the resolution of conflicts emerging from such restructuring experiments. However, the OAU's two bedrock principles—support for the territorial integrity of member states and noninterference in internal affairs—historically have impeded its ability to mediate both internal conflicts and those among member states. The 1967–70 Nigerian civil war, for example, which yielded automatic support for the territorial integrity of Nigeria, seriously called into doubt (at least from the view of the secessionist Igbos) the OAU's ability to serve as an impartial negotiator. It is for this reason that the OAU Commission of Mediation, Conciliation and Arbitration was stillborn, and the majority of African-initiated arbitration efforts have been carried out on an ad hoc basis by African presidents. For example, former President Hassan Gouled Aptidon of Djibouti used his country's stature as the headquarters for the Intergovernmental Authority on Drought and Development to mediate the conflict between Ethiopia and Somalia. According to I. William Zartman, a specialist in conflict resolution, such efforts historically have had a 33% success rate, and then only temporarily as warring parties returned to the battlefield.

The ability to dispatch peacemaking or peacekeeping forces is critical to conflict resolution. The OAU founding fathers attempted to prepare for this by planning the creation of an African High Command: a multinational military force comprising military contingents from OAU member states. The African High Command never made it beyond the planning stage, however, leading once again to a variety of ad hoc measures. In 1981 the OAU sponsored the creation of a short-term all-African military force designed to resolve an expanding civil war in Chad. With approximately 4,800 troops from Congo-Kinshasa, Nigeria and Senegal, the OAU force failed to achieve any concrete solution due to financial, logistical and political difficulties, and within a few months was forced to withdraw.

Search for an interventionist solution

The OAU's shortcomings have fostered intervention by four sets of actors: the United Nations, as demonstrated by the Security Council's 1991 decision to sponsor a series of U.S.-led military operations in Somalia, usually referred to as Operation Restore Hope; African regional organizations, such as the Economic Community of West African States, which sponsored a series of Nigerian-led military operations in Liberia; foreign powers, most notably the former Soviet Union, the U.S. and France; and African powers, as demonstrated by Nigeria's 1997 dispatch of troops to neighboring Sierra Leone to restore a civilian government to power. From the perspective of pan-Africanists, such interventions are ultimately undesirable: rather than representing the consensus of OAU member states, they appear driven by the self-interests of the intervenors.

In the wake of the cold war, African leaders agreed in 1997 to create an African Defense Force made up of military units of OAU member states equipped by foreign powers, most notably the U.S., France and Britain. The African Defense Force would remain under the command of the OAU. Unresolved issues revolve around which countries should be eligible to contribute forces (e.g., should involvement be limited only to democratic countries?) and what type of decisionmaking body should authorize interventions (e.g., should intervention be the consensus of all OAU member states, or a smaller representative body?). ■

Response of the Clinton Administration

PRESIDENT Bill Clinton's 11-day visit to Africa in 1998 was intended to signal a significant change in U.S. policy and a firm commitment to strengthening the African renaissance. "In coming to Africa," Clinton explained in an address to the Great Hall of Parliament in Capetown, South Africa, "my motive in part was to help the American people see the new Africa with new eyes, and to focus our own efforts on new policies suited to the new reality."

Clinton Administration pronouncements are not unlike those of their Democratic party predecessors, who also sought to underscore their "fresh thinking" when it came to Africa. In rhetoric that would resonate just as strongly with Africanists during the late 1950s and early 1960s as it did during the late 1990s, then Senator John F. Kennedy derided Washington's inability to come to grips with the rising tide of African nationalism, and he underscored the need to embark on a "bold and imaginative new program for the development of Africa." President Jimmy Carter entered office on a pledge to transcend his predecessors' cold-war preoccupations in favor of such positive goals as promoting human rights and basic human needs.

The Kennedy and Carter Administrations nonetheless came under fire from Africanists who criticized the chasm between rhetoric and action. Despite his sharp attacks on European colonialism, Kennedy kept close military ties to Portugal in order to protect access to Portuguese-controlled military bases in the Azores. And Carter's human-rights rhetoric notwithstanding, the U.S. continued to align itself with authoritarian dictators, including Zaire's Mobutu.

Reassessing military force

In October 1993, dozens of U.S. soldiers were killed or wounded in a fierce battle in Mogadishu, Somalia, during a humanitarian military mission launched by the previous president, George Bush. Media images of victorious Somali forces holding a U.S. helicopter pilot hostage and dragging the corpse of a U.S. soldier through the streets unleashed a firestorm of criticism and debate. What became known as America's "debacle" in Somalia served as a crucial turning point in Clinton Administration foreign policy toward Africa.

The White House renounced a campaign to significantly expand multilateral peacekeeping through the creation of a UN rapid deployment force. A formal Presidential Decision Directive, PDD-25, outlined fairly restrictive conditions that had to be met before the U.S.

would agree to any further UN-sponsored military operations, regardless of whether American troops took part. Among the most important conditions was the consent of all warring parties prior to the deployment of military forces. The simple message was that the U.S. "cannot resolve the conflicts of the world but does not believe that the UN is capable of making and keeping peace, particularly when hostilities among parties still exist."

The most important outcome of the new directive, which in essence denied U.S. support for UN-sponsored military operations designed to impose peace, was an extremely cautious approach to other conflicts in Africa. In the case of Rwanda, for example, the Clinton Administration was clearly wary of being drawn into a civil conflict that, according to a UN report issued in 1994, had resulted in the execution of between 500,000 and 1 million unarmed civilians. Fearful of being drawn into "another Somalia," the Clinton Administration not only initially blocked the dispatch of 5,500 troops requested by UN Secretary General Boutros Boutros-Ghali, but instructed Administration spokespersons to avoid labeling the unfolding ethnic conflict as "genocide," lest such a label further inflame American public sympathy and a demand for intervention, as had been the case in Somalia.

This unwillingness to support UN-sponsored peacekeeping missions has led to de facto support for African military solutions under the guise of "African solutions for African problems." It is precisely for this reason, argue critics of U.S. foreign policy toward Africa, that the Administration originally proposed creation of an African Crisis Response Force, subsequently reformulated as the African Crisis Response Initiative. Africans, not Americans, were to take the lead in resolving conflicts—a regional dynamic that stands in sharp contrast to extensive White House attempts at resolving the Arab-Israeli conflict in the Middle East or the series of crises in the Balkans.

One controversial implication is tacit support for military solutions imposed by African regional powers. For example, the Administration quietly supported Rwanda's military efforts to install a pro-U.S. government in Congo-Kinshasa under Kabila, and at this writing the U.S. is also supporting efforts by Rwanda, Eritrea and Ethiopia to undermine what is perceived as a radical Islamic fundamentalist regime in the Sudan. The Administration has embraced the so-called new bloc—Afwerki of Eritrea, Zenawi of Ethiopia, Museveni of Uganda and Kagame of Rwanda—who control battle-hardened guerrilla armies. Apart from the fact that they hold the reins, these regimes are believed able to maintain stability and create "responsible and accountable" governments. Paradoxically, a stress on stability may in fact run counter to the long-term goal of promoting democracy.

PRESIDENT CLINTON GREETS *OAU Secretary General Salim Salim during the opening session of the Conference on U.S.-Africa Partnership for the 21st century, while Secretary of State Madeleine Albright (center left) and Assistant Secretary of State for African Affairs, Susan Rice, look on.*

U.S. involvement, for and against

Entering office at a time when civil conflicts were multiplying across Africa, the Administration was expected to formulate a comprehensive policy of conflict resolution. The new Administration was initially split. One school felt African issues would unnecessarily distract the President and potentially plunge the White House into political controversies at home. A second, more activist point of view, also inspired by the U.S. experience in Somalia, asserted that disaster could have been avoided by preventive action. "The choice is not between intervening or not intervening," explained one White House policymaker. "It is between getting involved early and doing it at a cheaper cost, or being forced to intervene in a massive, more costly way later."

With White House attention focused elsewhere, the African affairs bureaus of the national security bureaucracies, such as the State Department, the Pentagon and the Central Intelligence Agency (CIA), grew in importance, along with economic policy units, most notably within the Department of Commerce. The net result has been fragmented foreign policy. In the case of Somalia, lack of high-level coordination led to what many Somali specialists considered an ill-conceived military operation from the start (i.e., famine was merely the symptom of an underlying political problem that could not be resolved through military intervention). As separate bureaucracies pursued different, often contradictory goals, the emphasis on political reconstruction was at best contradicted by the military's approach in the field, and at worst mere rhetoric.

The first high-level analysis of growing contradictions in policy toward Somalia nonetheless occurred only after the deaths of U.S. soldiers—some eight months after Clinton assumed office. To his credit, Clinton recognized the shortcomings of policy as it had evolved and quickly announced the impracticality of a military solution imposed from abroad. However, the structural problem inherent in the foreign policy apparatus—the lack of high-level attention and coordination of U.S. policies toward Africa—is as much a problem today as ever.

Uneven approach to democratization

Africanists have been understandably disappointed. "Democracy" was one of the common threads in Clinton's campaign speeches, during which he stated that "we should encourage and nurture the stirring for democratic reform that is surfacing all across Africa from the birth of an independent Namibia to the pressure for democratic reforms in Kenya." Though U.S. support for South Africa's transition to a democracy indicates rhetoric can be transformed into viable policies, in Congo-Kinshasa the cornerstone of Administration policy is a permutation of the same "Mobutu or chaos" thesis that dominated State Department, Pentagon and CIA thinking from the 1960s through the 1980s. Under this bureaucratically inspired view, regional instability and, ultimately, Communist expansion into the heart of Africa was the only alternative to Mobutu's continued hold over power. "Regardless of the fact that we are no longer faced with a Communist threat," explained one member of the State Department's Africa bureau, "the destabilization of Zaire [Congo-Kinshasa]—which borders nine other African countries—could have a tremendously negative impact on regional stability." With the experiences of Somalia and Rwanda still etched in their minds, the Africa specialists of the national security bureaucracies have successfully argued for the need to tread softly as, according to another member of the State Department's Africa bureau, the situation in Congo-Kinshasa "could easily turn into a Somalia and a Rwanda rolled into one, although this time in one of Africa's largest and most populous nations."

It is particularly striking to hear members of the State Department's Africa bureau argue that, like his predecessor, Kabila is both "part of the problem and part of the solution" to resolving the crisis in the region. As is the case with U.S. support for other members of the new bloc of African leaders, a responsive and accountable government capable of restoring order, ensuring territorial integrity and ending transborder threats will be viewed as a success—even if it is at the expense of democracy.

The Administration's ambivalence can be nicely summed up by comparing Clinton's trip to Africa with one made by Secretary of State Madeleine K. Albright in December 1997. Clinton's itinerary was purposely whittled down to emphasize his commitment to democratization: four of the six countries visited—Botswana, Ghana, Senegal and South Africa—are among Africa's leading democracies. Albright, however, visited seven countries, six of which—Ethiopia, Uganda, Rwanda, Congo-Kinshasa, Angola and Zimbabwe—are ruled by leaders who seized power with the barrel of the gun rather than by democratic elections. The message sent by the Albright visit was that the Administration's true priority is the cultivation of strategically located, pro-U.S. regimes capable of maintaining stability where civil wars and ethnic conflicts once raged.

A final component of the Administration's approach has been to deemphasize foreign aid in favor of trade and investment. Foreign aid to Africa has steadily decreased from a peak of $1.8 billion in 1985 to approximately $800 million in 1999; meanwhile, a 1996 initiative, built around the proposed Africa Growth and Opportunity Act, would stimulate U.S. investments and sales throughout Africa. Africans have sharply criticized the gradual decline in U.S. aid, and some, most notably Mandcla, havc denounced the political and economic conditionalities associated with the Africa Growth and Opportunity Act. Indeed, although a version of the Africa Growth and Opportunity Act has passed both the House and the Senate, powerful domestic criticism, most notably within the Congressional Black Caucus and the textile industry, threatens the viability of any trial bill.

The Administration's aggressive trade policy has intensified economic competition between the U.S. and other industrialized democracies with an eye on Africa. This has strained U.S.-French relations because stakes are so high in the lucrative petroleum, telecommunications and transport industries in francophone Africa. In the eyes of French policymakers, the penetration of American and other Western companies constitutes at best an intrusion and at worst an aggression against France's former colonies. The seriousness with which this issue is taken became clear when France's minister of cooperation, Michel Roussin, said a series of meetings had been held at the beginning of the 1990s on how best to defend French economic and political interests against those of the U.S.

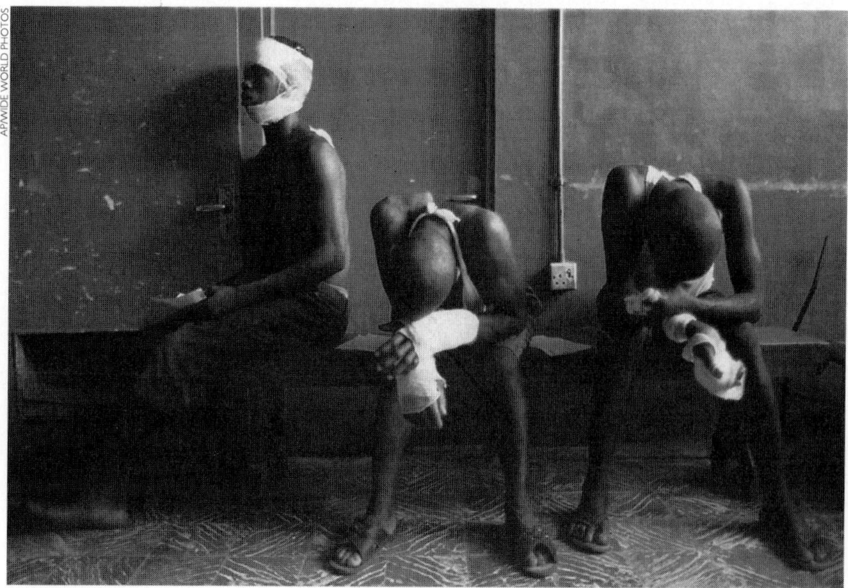

AP/WIDE WORLD PHOTOS

YOUNG SIERRA LEONE *men, who have had their ears, hands or fingers chopped off by rebels roaming the countryside after being ousted from power, wait outside a hospital operating room in Freetown, Sierra Leone, May 1998.*

Options for the new millennium

Grappling with ways to strengthen the African renaissance at the beginning of the new millennium, African leaders are confronted with the simple reality that even the best of intentions are often not enough, while American leaders are confronted by the knowledge that enlarging the renaissance will require enormous political will and greater understanding of an extremely diverse continent that has never been a U.S. priority. Even the best of American intentions can be deemed contradictory or as even constituting an "Uncle Scrooge" approach devoid of either true interest or sincerity. But Clinton's visit and other steps in the right direction mean the time is ripe to build on the successes thus far and to promote debate about the future. Three policy options stand out:

❑ **1. The U.S. should speak out publicly and put pressure on all African governments—including those that have been freely elected—that do not respect the political rights and civil liberties of their citizens, especially when civilian democracies have been overthrown by military coups d'état.**

Pro: Making democracy the sine qua non of enhanced U.S.-African ties is consistent with U.S. values and an appropriate and constructive way to treat all foreign countries. In the absence of strong, national institutions, this is the most effective way to foster democratic norms. It also clearly conveys U.S. commitment to democratic practice.

Con: U.S. policymakers should of course condemn military coups, but they have no business interfering in the internal affairs of other countries, especially those with democratic elections. Democracies come in many varieties, and the U.S. should be careful not to impose its own model on other countries. Acting in such a way might jeopardize other, more important issues on the U.S. agenda for foreign policy toward Africa.

❑ **2. The U.S. should make the African Crisis Response Initiative (ACRI) the thrust of its approach to conflict resolution in Africa.**

Pro: The guiding principles of the OAU—support for the territorial integrity of member states and noninterference in internal affairs—historically have impeded its ability to mediate internal conflicts and those between two or more member states. Ad hoc arrangements, such as Nigeria's unilateral intervention in Sierra Leone, raised questions as to the desirability of regional, often undemocratic countries (Nigeria was under military rule at the time) taking matters into their own hands. African countries need external help in the creation and maintenance of a continent-wide force capable of responding to internal crises and state collapse. U.S. training of national armies, such as Senegal's, has helped improve peacekeeping and should be strengthened.

Con: Ever wary of the consequences of direct U.S. military intervention, Washington supports ACRI as a way to wash its hands of its military responsibilities on the African continent. The slogan "African solutions for African problems" in essence signals the lack of political will to put American soldiers in harm's way. ACRI itself remains flawed, because of such unresolved issues as which countries should be eligible to contribute forces and what type of decisionmaking body should be capable of authorizing when and where to intervene. In the extreme, U.S. support of local military forces will ultimately intensify regional military conflicts, as witnessed by Rwanda's ongoing military intervention in Eastern Congo-Kinshasa.

❑ **3. The U.S. should actively implement the Africa Growth and Opportunity Act and make it the centerpiece of U.S.-African economic relations.**

Pro: In an era of declining foreign aid, the promotion of trade and investment serves as a solid indicator of U.S. interest in Africa. Trade and investment—the cornerstone of economic growth and development—are key to strengthening fledgling African democracies and preventing the return of military rule. Trade will ultimately benefit African and American producers and economies alike.

Con: Trade and investment are not reliable substitutes for foreign aid because they gravitate to countries that are already economic leaders, to the potential detriment of the most impoverished African countries. Several prominent African leaders, including Nelson Mandela, have sharply criticized the Africa Growth and Opportunity Act and the political and economic conditions that would accompany its extension to individual African countries. Congressional critics say increased trade and investment in Africa would hurt certain U.S. economic sectors, most notably the textile industry in the U.S. South. ■

REUTERS/ARCHIVE PHOTOS

PRISONERS WITHIN GITARAMA PRISON, *which holds some 6,500 inmates, look out from behind the bars of a dormitory window in April 1996. Some 68,000 prisoners reside in the overcrowded and grossly inadequate Rwandan jails.*

Opinion Ballots are on pages 85–86

DISCUSSION QUESTIONS

1. What are the problems and prospects associated with the "third wave of democratization" in Africa?

2. What are the essential components for ensuring the successful "demilitarization" or "civilianization" of African military regimes?

3. How should state-society relations be restructured so as to provide a firm basis for African economic growth and political development?

4. What are the primary beliefs of the so-called new bloc of African leaders concerning the process of democratization? Do these beliefs ultimately facilitate or hinder the consolidation of African democracy in the long-term?

5. What actors and/or international organizations ultimately should be responsible for resolving African conflicts, in every way including the ultimate interventionist tool of direct military intervention?

6. How prominent should the African continent be in the global hierarchy of U.S. foreign policy in comparison to other regions, most notably Asia (including Japan and China), Latin America (including Central America and the Caribbean), the Middle East, Russia and Eastern Europe (the former Communist states), and Western Europe?

7. How involved should U.S. policymakers be in attempting to facilitate and strengthen the "African renaissance"?

8. What are some of the challenges and pitfalls associated with U.S. foreign policy efforts to promote democratization and conflict resolution in Africa?

9. What should be the relative importance of the following U.S. foreign policy goals in Africa: democratization, conflict resolution, and trade and investment?

READINGS AND RESOURCES

Bratton, Michael, and Van de Walle, Nicolas, **Democratic Experiments in Africa: Regime Transitions in Comparative Perspective.** New York, Cambridge University Press, 1997. 352 pp. $19.95 (paper). Comprehensive analysis of all democratic transitions that took place in Africa 1989–94.

Clough, Michael, **Free at Last? : U.S. Policy Toward Africa and the End of the Cold War.** New York, Council on Foreign Relations, 1992. 145 pp. $14.95 (paper). A noted observer of U.S. foreign policy toward Africa examines the political, economic and military trends.

Ottaway, Marina, **Africa's New Leaders: Democracy or State Reconstruction?** Washington, DC, Carnegie Endowment for International Peace, 1999. 120 pp. $10.95. A critical analysis of the new bloc of African leaders and the implications of their rule for the future of democracy in Africa.

Reno, William, **Warlord Politics and African States.** Boulder, CO, Lynne Rienner Publishers, 1999. 260 pp. $19.95 (paper). An analysis of the implications of the enfeeblement and breakdown of African states during the 1990s.

Rice, Susan E., **United States Policy in Africa: Moving Forward as Partners.** An address before World Vision's Washington Forum, "Africa on the Eve of the New Millennium." Washington, DC, April 30, 1999.*

Rothchild, Donald, **Managing Ethnic Conflict in Africa: Pressures and Incentives for Cooperation.** Washington, DC, Brookings Institution, 1997. 350 pp. $15.96 (paper). An extremely detailed examination of U.S. responses to ethnic conflict in Africa by a leading authority.

Schraeder, Peter J., **United States Foreign Policy Toward Africa: Incrementalism, Crisis and Change.** New York, Cambridge University Press, 1994. 373 pp. $29.95 (paper). A theoretical analysis of U.S. foreign policy toward Africa during the cold-war era that focuses on the evolution of U.S. foreign policy toward the Democratic Republic of Congo, Ethiopia, Somalia and South Africa.

Smock, David R., and Crocker, Chester A., eds., **African Conflict Resolution: The U.S. Role in Peacemaking.** Washington, DC, United States Institute of Peace, 1995. 176 pp. $14.95 (paper). An overview of the challenges and pitfalls of U.S. involvement in peacemaking operations in Africa.

Villalón, Leonardo A., and Huxtable, Phillip A., eds., **The African State at a Critical Juncture: Between Disintegration and Reconfiguration.** Boulder, CO, Lynne Rienner Publishers, 1997. 334 pp. $22.00 (paper). An extremely useful collection of case studies by noted Africanists on the nature and evolution of the "crisis of the African state."

THE AFRICA FUND, 50 Broad St., Suite 711, New York, NY 10004; (212) 785-1024; Fax (212) 785-1078. ■ Since 1966, the Africa Fund has worked for an informed U.S. policy toward southern Africa, mobilizing community leaders throughout America and providing guidance, information and contacts. **www.prairienet.org/acas/afund.html**

AFRICANEWS ONLINE, P.O. Box 3851, Durham, NC 27702; (919) 286-0747; Fax (919) 286-2614. ■ Contains up-to-date news stories and features about a wide spectrum of issues concerning Africa. **www.africanews.org**

AFRICA POLICY INFORMATION CENTER (APIC), 110 Maryland Ave., NE, #509, Washington, DC 20002; (202) 546-7961; Fax (202) 546-1545. ■ A nonprofit organization dedicated to disseminating information on African issues. The APIC offers maps, news, documents, publications and reports. **www.africapolicy.org**

AFRICAN STUDIES ASSOCIATION (ASA), Rutgers University, Douglas Campus, 132 George St., New Brunswick, NJ 08901-1400; (732) 932-8173; Fax (732) 932-3394. ■ A nonprofit organization with a mission to bring together people with a scholarly and professional interest in Africa. **www.sas.upenn.edu/African_Studies/ASA/ASA_Groups.html**

You can find links to this document and additional readings on our website at* **www.fpa.org/program.html

OPINION BALLOTS

Please feel free to xerox opinion ballots, *but be sure to submit only one ballot per person. To have your vote counted, mail ballots by June 30, 2000. Send ballots to:*

FOREIGN POLICY ASSOCIATION, 470 PARK AVENUE SOUTH, NEW YORK, NY 10016-6819

TOPIC 7 Africa's Prospects

ISSUE A. What should serve as the guiding principle of U.S. foreign policy toward Africa? (choose one)

___ **1.** Promoting democratization

___ **2.** Prevention of genocide

___ **3.** Encouraging trade and foreign investment.

ISSUE B. How important should the African continent be in the global hierarchy of U.S. foreign policy in comparison to other regions of the world? (choose one)

___ **1.** The single most important region.

___ **2.** More important than most other regions.

___ **3.** Less important than most other regions.

___ **4.** Not important at all.

Your zip code: _____ _____ _____ _____ _____

Date: / /2000 *Ballot continues on reverse side...*

TOPIC 7 Africa's Prospects

ISSUE A. What should serve as the guiding principle of U.S. foreign policy toward Africa? (choose one)

___ **1.** Promoting democratization

___ **2.** Prevention of genocide

___ **3.** Encouraging trade and foreign investment.

ISSUE B. How important should the African continent be in the global hierarchy of U.S. foreign policy in comparison to other regions of the world? (choose one)

___ **1.** The single most important region.

___ **2.** More important than most other regions.

___ **3.** Less important than most other regions.

___ **4.** Not important at all.

Your zip code: _____ _____ _____ _____ _____

Date: / /2000 *Ballot continues on reverse side...*

TOPIC 8 Humanitarianism

ISSUE A. Do you agree or disagree with the following statements?

	AGREE	DISAGREE
1. The interventions in Kosovo and East Timor have set a precedent for dealing with humanitarian disasters elsewhere in the world.	❑	❑
2. International humanitarian assistance needs to be regulated by a global body.	❑	❑

ISSUE B. Who should take the lead in spelling out criteria for humanitarian interventions?

___ **1.** The UN

___ **2.** The U.S.

___ **3.** NATO

___ **4.** The Red Cross

Your zip code: _____ _____ _____ _____ _____

Date: / /2000 *Ballot continues on reverse side...*

TOPIC 8 Humanitarianism

ISSUE A. Do you agree or disagree with the following statements?

	AGREE	DISAGREE
1. The interventions in Kosovo and East Timor have set a precedent for dealing with humanitarian disasters elsewhere in the world.	❑	❑
2. International humanitarian assistance needs to be regulated by a global body.	❑	❑

ISSUE B. Who should take the lead in spelling out criteria for humanitarian interventions?

___ **1.** The UN

___ **2.** The U.S.

___ **3.** NATO

___ **4.** The Red Cross

Your zip code: _____ _____ _____ _____ _____

Date: / /2000 *Ballot continues on reverse side...*

OPINION BALLOTS

ISSUE C. As for dealing with African conflicts, which of the following U.S. foreign policy tools are appropriate and which ones are not?

	APPROPRIATE	NOT APPROPRIATE
1. Noninvolvement	❏	❏
2. Diplomacy	❏	❏
3. Economic and military aid	❏	❏
4. Covert intervention	❏	❏
5. Direct military intervention	❏	❏

ISSUE D. Who should be ultimately responsible for resolving African conflicts?

	RESPONSIBLE	NOT RESPONSIBLE
1. African countries	❏	❏
2. African regional organizations, most notably the Organization of African Unity (OAU)	❏	❏
3. Foreign powers, most notably the U.S.	❏	❏
4. International organizations, most notably the UN	❏	❏

ISSUE C. As for dealing with African conflicts, which of the following U.S. foreign policy tools are appropriate and which ones are not?

	APPROPRIATE	NOT APPROPRIATE
1. Noninvolvement	❏	❏
2. Diplomacy	❏	❏
3. Economic and military aid	❏	❏
4. Covert intervention	❏	❏
5. Direct military intervention	❏	❏

ISSUE D. Who should be ultimately responsible for resolving African conflicts?

	RESPONSIBLE	NOT RESPONSIBLE
1. African countries	❏	❏
2. African regional organizations, most notably the Organization of African Unity (OAU)	❏	❏
3. Foreign powers, most notably the U.S.	❏	❏
4. International organizations, most notably the UN	❏	❏

ISSUE C. Do the principles of neutrality and impartiality still provide a useful guide to humanitarian action, or are these principles now obsolete?

___ **1.** Still useful

___ **2.** Now obsolete

Comment: ______________________________

____

____

ISSUE D. Should humanitarian assistance be limited to delivery of such supplies as food or medical aid, or should it do more in addressing the root causes of the crises?

___ **1.** Deliver supplies

___ **2.** Address root causes

Comment: ______________________________

____

____

ISSUE C. Do the principles of neutrality and impartiality still provide a useful guide to humanitarian action, or are these principles now obsolete?

___ **1.** Still useful

___ **2.** Now obsolete

Comment: ______________________________

____

____

ISSUE D. Should humanitarian assistance be limited to delivery of such supplies as food or medical aid, or should it do more in addressing the root causes of the crises?

___ **1.** Deliver supplies

___ **2.** Address root causes

Comment: ______________________________

____

____

Humanitarianism: facing new challenges

In the increasingly complex world of humanitarian assistance, how big a role should international politics play?

by Joanna Macrae

APWIDE WORLD PHOTOS

A MEMBER OF THE RED CROSS *is flanked by two columns of Rwandan Hutu refugees heading to Gisenyi, after crossing the border with Zaire in 1996. Up to 10,000 refugees crossed the border in one day, fleeing the rebel-held city of Goma.*

HUMANITARIANISM used to seem so simple: picture an African child standing on a parched plain, a sack of food aid behind him offering the promise of life and hope. Now, the new image is more complex and fragmented: children as perpetrators, as well as victims, of violence; soldiers as relief workers; well-educated, urban Europeans as well as African farmers lined up for relief assistance; and mounting allegations that, far from helping, relief aid is actually making things worse.

So, what's changed? As the world reels from the unexpected and as yet uncertain successes in its first "humanitarian" war, in Kosovo, it is worth reflecting on why the apparently banal world of trucks of food has become a matter of high international political interest and debate.

Disastrous wars

While wars are inevitably associated with death and destruction, they are not necessarily associated with humanitarian crises. For example, between 1980 and 1988 the Iran-Iraq War claimed the lives of an estimated half a million people, 90% of whom were soldiers. Despite the war, and in part because of it, both governments involved were strengthened, consolidating their positions internally. While individual families mourned the death and injury of their loved ones, this war was not associated with famine, disease and large-scale displacement.

The international character of the Iran-Iraq War, and the means by which it was fought, stand in stark contrast to the majority of conflicts that have taken place since 1945, most of which have been fought within the borders of states. It would be wrong to characterize the origins of these conflicts as purely internal, since in many cases opposing sides depended on external support in order to prosecute them. During the cold war (1945–91), many internal conflicts were structured along ideological lines and became regionalized and internationalized with the respective superpowers and their allies providing political and military support to the warring parties.

However, the fact that the majority of conflicts are fought within the borders of sovereign states makes them particularly deadly. In these conflicts, the goal of warfare is not simply the occupation and control of territory but the definition of a nation's identity. In this context, war is no longer about military victory, it is about destroying the identity and dignity of the opposition. In this case, the "opposition" comprises not only soldiers, but the civilians in whose name they claim to be fighting.

It is for this reason that since 1945 civilians have accounted for 90% of war deaths worldwide. It is for this reason too that war-affected populations are among the most vulnerable people on earth. Worldwide some 40 million people are displaced from their homes by conflict. Africa's 15 million displaced people outnumber the population of all but six of the countries on the continent. The particular vulnerability of this group has been well documented. In Africa, infant and child mortality is at least 10 times higher among displaced populations than elsewhere on the continent, accounting for one fifth of its total child deaths.

JOANNA MACRAE *is a research fellow in the Humanitarian Policy Group at the Overseas Development Institute in London and coeditor of* Disasters: The Journal of Disaster Studies, Policy and Management. *Her areas of interest include the role of aid in conflict management and the changing institutional relationship between aid and foreign policy.*

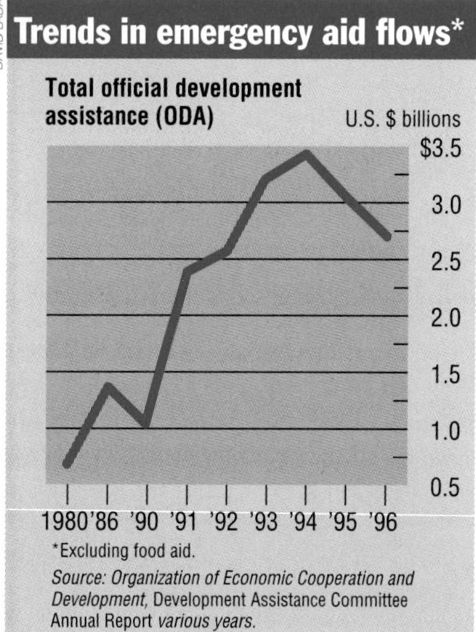

Trends in emergency aid flows*

*Excluding food aid.

Source: Organization of Economic Cooperation and Development, Development Assistance Committee Annual Report *various years.*

An important characteristic of contemporary conflicts is that they have been fought in extremely poor countries. Even without the particular effects of conflict, populations in these countries are already at the margins of survival, often living on less than one dollar a day and subject to the vagaries of the weather and international commodity prices in order to secure their livelihoods. These are the world's most deprived populations in terms of access to basic services such as water, health and education. This is the case not only in Africa and parts of Asia, but, for example, in parts of the former Eastern bloc, where survival rates have diminished for many sections of the population since the early 1980s.

This structural vulnerability to disaster has deep roots. Many Third World countries saw a significant downturn in their fortunes during the 1970s, as the effects of recession in the West rippled around the globe. By 1982, the Third World's share of global trade had dropped by 2%, while in Africa, terms of trade of low-income African countries fell by nearly 14% between 1979 and 1982. While trade revenues were falling, monetarist policies, reinforced by the major international development agencies such as the World Bank, reduced international financial liquidity, increasing interest rates significantly. Throughout the 1980s the debt burden continued to expand. Public debt in Africa alone increased from U.S.$5.2 billion in 1970 to U.S.$151 billion in 1991. At the same time, the high price of oil forced these countries to devote an increasingly large share of declining national income to the purchase of oil and oil-related products, including fertilizers.

Against this background, a mounting crisis in the world food supply occurred during the 1970s and 1980s, and in particular, a growing dependence of the Third World on the West to meet the gaps in food supply. Between 1949 and 1951, 12 million metric tons of grain were imported by developing countries. In 1972, 36 million metric tons were imported. This food gap continued to grow throughout the 1980s. In 25 of the 36 developing countries for which data are available, food production declined significantly in the period from 1980 to 1992. During this time, food-aid imports increased from 1.6 million to 4.2 million metric tons annually.

This economic crisis was reflected in the political domain. As the ability of Third World states to sustain themselves declined and they were unable to provide access to basic goods and services or social and economic security, so reliance on coercive methods of government increased. In 1960, 26 of the developing states that were then independent were under some form of military control. By 1982 this number had reached 52, and by 1992 it was up to 61. In this context, it is unsurprising that persistent and violent challenges to the state emerged throughout the Third World.

Thus, Third World conflict can be understood not only as a *cause* of poverty and suffering among civilian populations, but also as *symptomatic* of the vulnerability of these political economies. This vulnerability is to a degree economic, but it is primarily political, reflecting a crisis of governance and public institutions. It is for this reason that conflict-related emergencies are differentiated from natural disasters by calling them "complex *political* emergencies," denoting the primarily political character of these disasters.

The tactics of modern warfare can push populations from a position of chronic poverty to disaster. The deliberate destruction of livelihoods—the burning of crops and discriminatory employment practices—means that populations lack the ability to produce and to buy food and other necessities. Prices of basic goods, including food, usually escalate rapidly as supplies are reduced and as military, commercial and political forces manipulate markets, deliberately restricting the flow of goods, particularly into besieged towns. Although such tactics disempower and demoralize the enemy, they also allow some to profit from the parallel market.

In this context, people's options narrow quickly. Unable to produce or procure adequate food through their usual means, many people are forced to sell their remaining assets and/or to move in search of security and other means of securing a livelihood. As the successive conflicts in the former Yugoslavia have shown, forcible displacement of civilian populations through the use of direct violence and by making their lives and livelihoods untenable because of discrimination is part of a process of political and social engineering. It is about one section of the population redrawing political maps, and about seizing the assets (such as land and housing) of another. Thus, the humanitarian crises associated with wars from Afghanistan to Zaire have not just been unfortunate but unintended by-products of conflict—they have been its goal.

Survivors of the famine in Biafra will testify that there is little that is new in these strategies. (Biafra was the part of Nigeria that declared its independence in 1967. Starvation and disease resulted when Nigerian forces surrounded it and cut off supplies. Biafra ceased to exist in 1970.) What has changed significantly over the last three decades has been the international response to these war-induced humanitarian crises.

Relief during the cold war

Given that the tactics of internal warfare are designed to kill civilians or to force them to abandon their livelihoods and their homes, it is unsurprising that those who try to prevent or mitigate the effects of these strategies are undertaking a very difficult and highly political role. One commentator aptly described the intercession of relief agencies in war as "...akin to spectators in a stadium running down onto the field while a football game is in progress so as to reduce the incidence and severity of the tackling."

During the cold war, the ability and willingness of international actors to watch and intervene in the deadly "game" of war was limited. Efforts to provide its victims with humanitarian relief were confined by the boundaries of sovereignty. In the context of the superpower stand-off there was absolute respect for the principle of negative sovereignty, in other words, an agreement by states not to intervene in the internal affairs of others. Governments' abuses of the human rights of their citizens were seen to fall within the domain of internal affairs, and, with few exceptions, were not seen to constitute a major threat to international peace and security that would justify intervention.

Within this framework of respect for sovereignty, the scope for humanitarian action was limited and heavily weighted in favor of the sovereign power. The provision of relief assistance was confined largely to the periphery of conflict—to relatively secure government-held territory, particularly towns, and most significantly to the assistance of refugees who had fled their countries of origin and crossed an international border into a second country.

Within war zones, and particularly in rebel-held territory, international assistance was heavily circumscribed not only by high levels of violence but also by the dependence of aid agencies on securing the consent of governments to their engagement. Furthermore, at least until the 1980s, the majority of relief assistance was provided through national governments. For example, it is notable that in 1976 the then European Community channeled over 90% of its relief budget through national governments in affected countries.

The important exception to this general rule was the work of the International Committee of the Red Cross (ICRC). Since the late 19th century, the ICRC has sought to alleviate the worst effects of war. Initially, it focused on developing a body of law to regulate the conduct of conflict and prevent its worst excesses, and to mitigate the suffering of soldiers wounded and captured in battle. As the concept of total war took hold, first in the Boer War (1890–1902) and then in the lead-up to World Wars I and II, the ICRC took on an increasing role in providing relief to civilians.

The work of the Red Cross Movement rested upon two key principles—neutrality and impartiality. Neutrality means not taking a political position in relation to the conflict in terms of its origins and outcomes. Impartiality means the provision of relief on the basis of need and regardless of political affiliation, race, nationality or creed. These principles derive from both an ethical belief in the essential humanity of people and their equal right to assistance, and also from an essentially pragmatic stance. Because the ability of the ICRC to secure access to all was contingent upon its acknowledging that humanitarian intervention would not provide military advantage to either side, it maintained close contacts with military and political leaders at high levels in conflicts and would intervene only with the consent of both sides. Where such consent was withheld, as in the case of Biafra, the ICRC would not intervene.

Biafra was a formative moment in the history of humanitarian action in another way. As one commentator has noted, after this war the ICRC would "...never be alone in the field and never free of the competition that has come to mark modern humanitarian work." Quietly and very slowly the international humanitarian system began to expand. One of the first indications of this expansion was the formation by a group of French doctors in 1971 of Médecins Sans Frontières (MSF), or Doctors Without Borders, recently awarded the Nobel Peace Prize. This group of "revolutionary humanitarians" included some who had been disillusioned by the response of the Red Cross in Biafra, and in particular its failure to speak out publicly regarding the scale of horror and suffering in that war. This group interpreted ICRC's discretion, which it argued was vital to its neutrality, as complicity in massive abuse of human rights. Since that time, MSF has grown enormously, now boasting an international network of agencies which seek not only to provide assistance, but also to bear witness to unfolding conflicts and effects and advocate publicly for an end to abuses of human rights.

Humanitarian space

As the cold war thawed, so the scope for humanitarian action began to expand. The effective military disengagement of the West (and indeed of the Eastern bloc) from Africa in the mid-1980s provided one of the first indications of the demise of absolute respect for sovereign borders, which in turn offered new opportunities for humanitarian action. Some of these first tentative

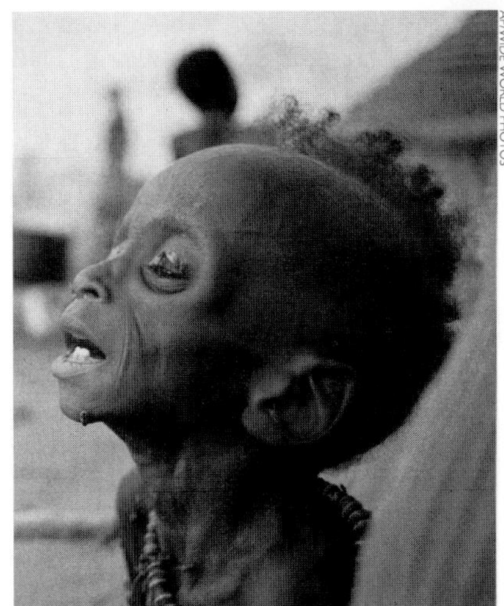
AP/WIDE WORLD PHOTOS

AT AJIEP, IN SUDAN, *a starving boy cries inside a compound run by Doctors Without Borders. The group provides medical aid in countries devastated by natural disasters, such as drought and earthquakes, or unnatural ones, such as war.*

steps toward humanitarian interventionism were taken in the Horn of Africa. The cross-border operations into rebel-held areas of Ethiopia and what is now Eritrea were organized by indigenous organizations affiliated with the liberation fronts. The aid convoys that crossed into Ethiopian territory from Sudan were "illegal" and were undertaken without the consent of the Ethiopian authorities. Initially the relief effort relied only on private funds from international nongovernmental organizations (NGOs) and from the diaspora of people from these regions. From the late 1980s, however, these agencies received the majority of their funds from the U.S. Agency for International Development (AID) and the European Commission, albeit channeled discreetly through intermediary private voluntary organizations (PVOs).

What this represented was an extension of emerging development-assistance policy into the humanitarian sphere. In the development sphere, there was a radical rethinking of the role of the state in economic and political development, with an increasing emphasis on the role of the private sector, including PVOs, in the financing and provision of basic services. In countries experiencing emergencies brought on by conflict, some political analysis suggested that, far from being part of the solution, the state had become part of the problem. Rather than engage with the state in order to bring about its re-

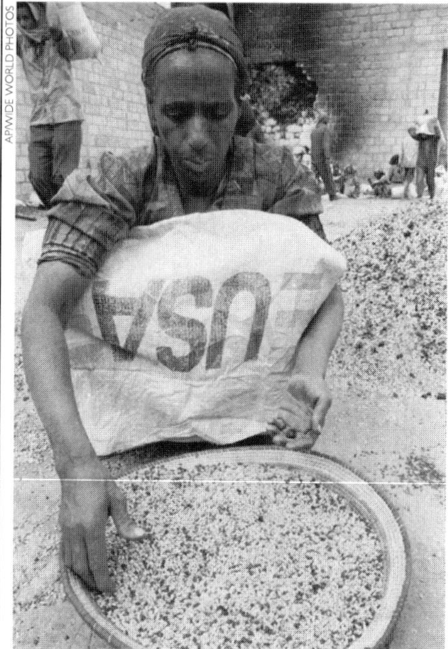

AN ETHIOPIAN WOMAN *cleans wheat grain salvaged from a storehouse after it was bombed by Eritrean forces. The wheat was part of 2,000 tons of grain destined for distribution to 13,884 displaced persons in Adigrat, Ethiopia.*

form, to varying degrees international assistance agencies sought to work outside it. Relief aid represented the culmination of this approach.

In countries such as Ethiopia after 1974, Cambodia in 1982 and Sudan after 1989, for example, development assistance was virtually suspended by Western nations in protest against the policies of the respective regimes. Only relief, channeled through international—usually private—organizations, remained in place. Relief therefore came to symbolize not simply the existence of massive humanitarian need, but an effective questioning of sovereignty. While development assistance implied legitimacy of regimes, relief did not. Despite its antistate rhetoric, development assistance still conferred legitimacy upon, and required the authority of, state institutions for its implementation.

It was against this backdrop that the humanitarian system familiar in the late 1990s began to emerge. It constitutes a complex network of agencies, private and public. Fueled with funds by both donor governments and the general public in Western countries, the assistance community comprises three major pillars: the Red Cross Movement (ICRC and the national Red Cross societies); specialist agencies and funds of the United Nations (UN Office of High Commissioner for Refugees or UNHCR, UN Children's Fund or UNICEF and the World Food Program or WFP are the most important operational agencies); and PVOs. All of these different bodies have the advantage of enabling donor governments to provide assistance in conflict-affected countries without channeling resources through the recipient government.

Thus the rise of relief, and the evolution of its strategies, was a response to the crisis of governance and of welfare in many developing countries. It was also a political message from powerful donor countries to Third World states regarding expected norms of behavior and the changing rules of international relations.

Nowhere was this new order more evident than in the international response, led by the U.S., to the humanitarian consequences of the conflicts in northern Iraq and Somalia. In the case of Iraq, military force was deployed in order to allow Kurdish refugees in Turkey to return to their homes. In the aftermath of this crisis, the UN General Assembly adopted Resolution 46/182. This sought to improve the UN's coordination of relief operations and to sustain the momentum for humanitarian intervention initiated by the formation of safe-havens in Iraqi Kurdistan. Importantly, it stated:

> The sovereign, territorial integrity and national unity of states must be fully respected in accordance with the Charter of the UN. In this context, humanitarian assistance *should* be provided with the consent of the affected countries, and *in principle* on the basis of an appeal by the affected country (emphases added).

As a review of the initiative notes, the inclusion of terms "should" and "in principle" set a precedent for violation of sovereignty if the international community justified intervention on humanitarian grounds. This resolution thus paved the way for a doctrine of humanitarian intervention.

The optimism that force could be used for a humanitarian purpose has wavered over the past decade. The experience in Somalia had dented, seemingly irrevocably, the idea that international troops, particularly U.S. troops, could and should intervene on humanitarian grounds in other people's wars. U.S. PVOs and the global news network CNN were pivotal in generating support for the deployment of these troops in 1992, whose mandate was to protect the delivery of food aid to hundreds of thousands of Somalis. Such a deployment was seen to be necessary because of the high rates of violent looting and manipulation of food aid by the different warlords. The mission ended in disaster. A military stand-off between U.S. troops and Somalis resulted in deaths on both sides and culminated in a revenge attack on U.S. troops. Captured by the world's media, the pictures of the mutilated bodies of U.S. soldiers dragged through the streets of Mogadishu, Somalia's capital, will probably be among the seminal images of the century. The withdrawal of the U.S. contingent was inevitable.

When arguing for a concerted international response to the famine in Somalia, then UN Secretary General Boutros Boutros-Ghali contrasted the sluggish response to African suffering with that of the humanitarian effects of the war in Bosnia-Herzegovina. Here, UN forces had been deployed to protect relief convoys at an early stage of the war. The volume of relief allocated to populations in Bosnia-Herzegovina dwarfed that provided to any other emergency at that time. The budget for former Yugoslavia of the UNHCR, the lead agency in the country, exceeded that for the whole of Africa. This generosity in terms of relief did not stop the killing, however, underscoring once again the need to protect the people for whom the aid was destined.

The legacy of Somalia was felt in spring 1994, when ethnic conflict in one of the smallest and poorest countries in the world led, in just three months, to the slaughter of an estimated 500,000 to 800,000 Rwandans. In the aftermath of the conflict and the genocide, 2 million people fled to neighboring countries. These terrible events were to expose the fact that, in the aftermath of Somalia, the international community had yet to develop an alternative strategy to deal with violence within states' borders.

In the UN Security Council, the U.S., among other permanent members, resisted the use of the term "genocide" for the unfolding events in Rwanda, precluding its obligation to intervene under the Genocide Convention. The UN Security Council also failed to provide a response when strong evidence emerged that the massive refugee camps in Zaire (now Congo) were being controlled by the political and military forces responsible for the genocide. The mandate of the UNHCR, which was running the camps, stipulates that those responsible for war crimes and crimes against humanity are not entitled to refugee status or assistance. The UNHCR and the hundreds of PVOs working alongside it, however, lacked the mandate or the tools to separate those who were armed and responsible for the genocide from the innocent victims. Aid agencies could not act as policemen, advocates, judges and jailers. Instead, they stood accused of feeding the killers and of enabling them to regroup in order to mount an attack on the newly formed government in Rwanda. In the end, the Rwandan government seized the initiative and dismantled the camps, forcing their inhabitants either to return to Rwanda or to flee deeper into Zaire. In the course of this turmoil, large civilian populations disappeared from the international radar screen, among whom were an estimated 50,000 children.

By the late 1990s, the experiences of Somalia, Bosnia-Herzegovina and Rwanda, together with those of the quieter, but nevertheless tragic emergencies in countries such as Afghanistan, Angola, Liberia, Sierra Leone, Sri Lanka and Sudan, were raising profound questions for all those who called themselves humanitarians and claimed humanitarian concerns. More money than ever before was being spent on emergency aid (see chart on p. 88). Despite this, and some have argued because of it, suffering continued seemingly unabated. ■

A new humanitarianism?

THE MOUNTING and diverse critiques of humanitarian action are spawning the formation of what has been dubbed a new humanitarianism. As yet, it would be wrong to see this as a single, coherent doctrine. Rather, the different actors who constitute the humanitarian system and who interact with it in the political and military domains are each proposing different modifications to the existing framework of humanitarian action.

Kosovo: precedent or exception?

A first strand of the new humanitarian discourse is the need to shift emphasis from the protection of humanitarian supplies to the protection of people threatened by violence. A major evaluation of the international response to the conflict and genocide in Rwanda concluded that aid had been used as a substitute for political action—a Band-Aid applied much too late to prevent much of the suffering and death in that region. Similarly bleak conclusions might be drawn from any number of conflicts in recent decades. However, it was the specter of Bosnia-Herzegovina that was particularly haunting for European and U.S. policymakers.

The North Atlantic Treaty Organization (NATO) military action against Serbia in 1999 is presented by many as being a response to this criticism. Military action followed months of diplomatic efforts within the European Union, the Organization for Security and Cooperation in Europe and the UN. The deployment of human-rights monitors had failed to yield improvements in security, and the situation for the Kosovar population was becoming steadily more dangerous and difficult. The bombing of Serbia, which began on March 24, 1999, was not authorized by the UN Security Council. The NATO allies did not seek a Security Council resolution, confident that both China and Russia would veto it. Rather, the allies argued that their intervention in the internal affairs of a sovereign state was legitimate because it was designed to alleviate extreme abuses of human rights and thus prevent a major humanitarian crisis from emerging. An additional, although less frequently asserted, justification was that the action was a response to a threat to international peace and security, since a large outpouring of Kosovar refugees could have destabilized the region.

Both the legality and the legitimacy of the intervention, as well as the effectiveness of the NATO strategy, have been widely debated. Despite emphasizing the severity of the threat to civilian Kosovars, the allies relied on aerial bombardment without deploying ground troops, leaving the estimated half a million displaced Kosovars unprotected. The NATO bombardment also precipitated an intensification of Serbia's strategy of ethnic cleansing, leading to massive and rapid displacement of over a million people. Questions have been raised, too, about the sustainability of the political framework put in place by the UN after the Serb

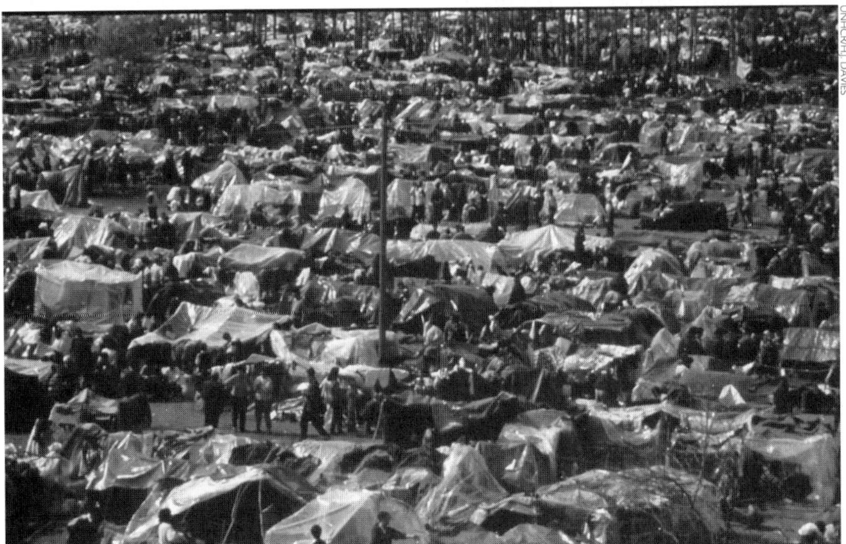

UNHCR/H.J. DAVIES

THOUSANDS OF KOSOVARS *were contained in an open field at a border crossing called Brace in Macedonia, with virtually no medical assistance, little food and limited access for aid agencies. The Macedonian government feared the massive influx of ethnic Albanians could destabilize its own fragile ethnic mix.*

withdrawal. Whatever the political and legal rights and wrongs, for humanitarian actors a distinct set of issues have emerged from the Kosovo case.

First, while welcoming a political intervention to address the root causes of humanitarian crises, the legitimacy and legality of such a deployment of force is important to clarify. Appealing to humanitarian objectives to legitimize such an intervention means appealing to universal values regarding the essential humanity of all people. If military intervention to secure humanitarian objectives is selective, then its legitimacy is potentially compromised, particularly in the eyes of non-Western populations and their governments. The fact that no similar actions are planned to respond to the equally alarming humanitarian crises in Africa, still less in Chechnya, the separatist Russian republic, makes it easier for such actions to be portrayed as part of a new world order where the West is imposing its values on others. Both Russia and China have failed to adhere to international legal standards in their treatment of minority groups, and, in the case of Russia, to conform to international humanitarian law during the course of the conflict in Chechnya. The fact remains, however, that they are permanent members of the Security Council.

The lack of a global consensus regarding humanitarian principles and values, and the use of force in securing them, could mark a new source of tension between the West and other powers. The lack of a rule book also opens the possibility that others may claim illegitimately the right to intervene militarily in second countries on "humanitarian" grounds. In other words, any softening of sovereignty implies a reanalysis of the rules governing intervention by states in each other's affairs. Some people argue that a way out of this problem is to codify the conditions under which the international community is obligated to intervene militarily to prevent or mitigate humanitarian suffering. This is something that has been resisted because it would imply an obligation to act universally, with the political and financial costs this would entail.

The problems regarding the selectivity of response have significant implications for those involved in the delivery of humanitarian assistance. If the enterprise of delivering humanitarian assistance becomes closely associated with a wider process of political and military experimentation regarding the post-cold-war order, then the pillar of neutrality on which the humanitarian enterprise has rested is removed.

Historically, humanitarian aid agencies have sought to maintain their independence from the political arena. This neutrality, and the appearance of neutrality, are more difficult to sustain in situations where they become associated with a particular political position.

NINAN, CARTOONISTS & WRITERS SYNDICATE/cartoonweb.com

In the case of Kosovo, this association was determined not only by the nationality of many humanitarian organizations based in and largely funded by NATO countries. It is also potentially compromised by the close association of civilian, humanitarian organizations with military and political actors at field level. If soldiers are working alongside civilian groups in building camps, and donor-government representatives are becoming involved in routine decisions regarding the allocation of scarce humanitarian resources, the distinctions between them become quickly blurred.

Political humanitarianism?

Some commentators, particularly in the U.S., argue that the blurring of the lines between humanitarian assistance and international politics is an inevitable part of the coming of age of the humanitarian enterprise. It is naive, they argue, to think that humanitarian assistance is anything other than political. Inevitably, the provision of resources in these environments will have a political impact; the trick is to use the leverage provided by such assistance positively to build on local capacities and to provide a basis for peace. Under this approach, the whole concept of neutrality is outmoded and needs to be replaced by a much more active, political form of humanitarianism, integrated with foreign policy objectives of peace and security. This approach is comfortable for many U.S. PVOs, which are often linked to constituencies in recipient countries, for example, through church groups. These links make a pure interpretation of neutrality inherently difficult to sustain.

Others argue, however, that such an integration is problematic ethically and operationally. At an ethical level, they argue, it is far from clear that the foreign policy objectives of the major powers always coincide with the interests of conflict-affected populations. For example, action came only very late in East Timor (decades after the Indonesian campaign against pro-independence militia began), and not at all in Chechnya. The concept of neutrality, they argue, does not mean being politically blind to the potential for warring parties to manipulate relief supplies for their own ends. Rather, it is an active concept, requiring humanitarian actors to undertake extensive political analysis in order to protect the integrity of their work. They distinguish, however, between a politically *informed* approach to humanitarian action and one which is politically *driven* by the foreign policy interests of donor countries.

Defenders of the principle of neutrality also point to the fact that its importance is not only moral, but also practical. Negotiating access to the victims of conflict has frequently been contingent upon aid agencies proving to the warring parties that such assistance would not give military advantage to the opposing side. If humanitarian assistance becomes associated with a particular side in a conflict, then it may also be seen by the opposing side as a legitimate target, so reducing access to victims on that side of the conflict.

Regulating the humanitarian system

A further feature of the humanitarian assistance landscape is increasing concern about how to ensure the legitimacy and accountability of aid interventions in conflict-affected countries. However flawed in practice, the accountability of international aid has traditionally rested on the idea that the recipient state would sanction and monitor flows within a particular country. Indeed this remains the norm for development aid relations. How then to ensure the accountability of assistance in those countries that political scientist Robert Jackson has called quasi-states, in other words, those countries where a central government does not exist (for example, Somalia), is not recognized as the legitimate authority by the community of states (for example Cambodia from 1982 to 1991), or where the state's involvement in human-rights abuses at home and behavior toward third countries renders it an international pariah (for example, Sudan, Serbia, Iraq)?

The lack of a clear framework of governance has important implications for the way in which aid functions. If recipient-country governments are not regulating the quality, distribution and volume of aid flows, who is? For example, in these situations, who should decide where scarce resources should go and how they should be distributed to ensure equitable and efficient coverage? This issue is particularly problematic given the number and diversity of aid agencies working in emergencies, each of which works according to its own mandates and procedures and funding arrangements.

One solution is to try to maximize the participation of national professional and civil groups in decisionmaking, in other words, to legitimize decisionmaking nationally. In authoritarian societies, however, those with power frequently lack legitimacy, while those with legitimacy may lack power. Thus, a key role for humanitarian assistance becomes the empowerment of civil groups, enabling them to play a more effective role in decisions regarding resource allocation and management. So, for example, training might be given to civil wings of rebel movements to enhance the workings of emerging judicial and public-administration structures. This sort of work has been undertaken by the UN in southern Sudan, with funding from the U.S. government. This approach responds to a criticism that the provision of large volumes of humanitarian assistance has allowed warring parties to abrogate their responsibilities to civilian populations under their control, blocking the formation of strong and effective state-society relations. By developing the capacity of political groups to provide the administrative and judicial framework for public life, the relations between them and society become more firmly embedded and legitimate. Such a process might result not only in improved respect for civilians during the course of a conflict, but also provide the basis for future governance.

Others counter, however, that the majority of warring parties consistently behave badly with respect to civilians under their control and that investments in the capacity-building approach are slow to mature and uncertain in their yield. It is often difficult to identify a "good guy" in today's wars. To engage with rebel groups responsible for massive abuses of human rights is to condone such abuses and to strengthen those very institutions that are responsible for violence. In the meantime, children are dying and there is a need to save them now. Furthermore, the boundaries between civil, political and military society are usually blurred in conflict-affected societies. Some church authorities were heavily implicated in the genocide in Rwanda, for example.

The UN has sought to respond to the problem of decisionmaking in situations of contested and uncertain statehood by adopting what it has called a Strategic Framework approach. This seeks to provide a unified mechanism through which all the different actors—UN, PVOs, NGOs, bilateral donors—can analyze needs and allocate assistance. However, the extent to which it can act as a legitimate authority to decide on the allocation of international aid resources is defined by the willingness of UN agencies, PVOs, NGOs and donor governments to allow the UN coordinating body—say, for Afghanistan—to determine how their money should be spent. Unsurprisingly, most have proved unwilling to relinquish their control over programming decisions, rendering the Strategic Framework process little different from information-exchange forums, common in humanitarian programming.

The Strategic Framework is an example of an attempt to fill the hole of governance in defining complex political emergencies. The lack of an effective and legitimate organization to regulate humanitarian action means that the numerous UN, international organizations and PVOs are working within the limits of their own mandates and resources. Until recently, there were no rules or standards against which their performance could be measured.

The need to define rules to guide humanitarian action in wartime was highlighted during the early 1990s when a growing body of evidence suggested that aid was being manipulated by warring parties. Recognizing this, and the threat that this posed to the credibility of humanitarian assistance, a number of PVOs got together with the Red Cross Movement to develop the Code of Conduct for Disaster Relief. This builds on the fundamental principles of the Red Cross to guide the provision of relief assistance and identifies 10 core principles (see box above).

In particular conflicts, aid agencies have also worked together to establish more country-specific strategies to guide their work. Thus, for example, in Liberia and Sudan, the UN and PVOs have formulated principles to guide their work and to hold aid agencies and rebel

Codes of Conduct for the International Red Cross and Red Crescent Movement and NGOs in Disaster Relief: Principle Commitments

1. The humanitarian imperative comes first;

2. Aid is given regardless of the race, creed or nationality of the recipients and without adverse distinction of any kind. Aid priorities are calculated on the basis of need alone;

3. Aid will not be used to further a particular political or religious standpoint;

4. We shall endeavor not to be used as an instrument of government foreign policy;

5. We shall respect culture and custom;

6. We shall attempt to build disaster response on local capacities;

7. Ways shall be found to involve program beneficiaries in the management of relief aid;

8. Relief aid must strive to reduce vulnerabilities to future disaster as well as meeting basic needs;

9. We hold ourselves accountable to both those we seek to assist and those from whom we accept resources;

10. In our information, publicity and advertising activities, we shall recognize disaster victims as dignified human beings, not hopeless objects.

movements accountable for violations of these codes. These are important initiatives and testify to the recognition by aid agencies of the complex political environment within which they work and the need to develop explicit strategies for navigating it. However, experience suggests that warring parties' adherence to the tenets of international humanitarian law and human-rights law is contingent upon their own strategic interests, and does not primarily reflect a response to pressure from humanitarian actors. This implies that the impact of humanitarian principles in terms of reducing manipulation of aid and in facilitating access while not insignificant is not likely to be defining. Rather, there is a need for a parallel political process which exerts pressure on warring parties to conform to the rules of war.

Furthermore, while many aid agencies have subscribed to principles to guide their interventions, there is no global body that monitors their adherence to them or that can apply sanctions if and when they do not conform to these principles. Thus, if an agency delivers aid which then attracts an attack from rebels, or if poorly trained medical professionals mistreat patients, at present there is no mechanism to hold either the agency or the individual accountable.

Some have argued that there is a need to define and establish a global body to regulate the conduct of humanitarian operations and to hold accountable those agencies which do not meet basic standards of care and attention. Others, such as MSF, have argued that attempts to define and implement such codes represent a threat to the independence of humanitarian action. They fear that donor governments will use these standards inappropriately to select the agencies to which they provide support and so exert unwarranted political influence on the organization of relief. In the U.S., the concern is rather that the heavy hand of regulation will increase the costs and reduce the flexibility and innovation of humanitarian action. Here the emphasis remains on self-regulation. ■

Humanitarian community at crossroads

A REVIEW OF CURRENT TRENDS and debates suggests that the humanitarian community finds itself at a historical crossroads.

The unparalleled flow of resources into the humanitarian sector can be seen as a reflection of a new generation of international relations whereby borders and sovereignty no longer define the boundaries of humanitarian action. Now more assistance is reaching more people in more and more difficult circumstances, sometimes by use of force. Behind this headline, however, something more complex is taking shape. The expansion in humanitarian space can be seen as an expression of the increased willingness of the international community to invest in accessing conflict-affected populations.

Paradoxically, it can also be seen as symptomatic of a process of wider political disengagement. In the majority of countries, the provision of humanitarian assistance is not accompanied by high profile political or military intervention. Rather, international actors are increasingly delegating responsibility for essentially political tasks to the humanitarian sphere. More often than not it still remains the case that humanitarian action is a substitute for political action. Not only do humanitarian actors continue to work in extremely violent conflicts unsupported and unprotected by international political and military engagement, they are also under pressure to play an enhanced role in conflict management. Thus, they are at the forefront of political processes of negotiating access and observing the conduct of conflict. They are also often at the front line between warring parties and the international community. For example, in Afghanistan, there was strong pressure on the UN and PVOs from governments, including the U.S., to withhold humanitarian assistance until the ruling Islamic-fundamentalist Taliban reversed its policy of discrimination against women. Even in the high profile cases such as Bosnia-Herzegovina, it has been argued that the outpouring of humanitarian assistance was motivated not purely by altruism, but by a concern to contain the conflict, and in particular to avert large-scale population movements into Western Europe.

The humanitarian sphere is characterized by new uncertainties and increasing diversity in terms of the definition of its objectives. Some critics argue that humanitarian aid is doing little to address the root causes of the crises in which it works, simply handing out food aid year in, year out. They argue that the time has come for humanitarians to get off the fence and to become part of a coherent political strategy for the resolution of conflict. Others suggest, however, that the palliative function of humanitarian assistance is an end in itself. While the ability of the international community to formulate consistent and coherent conflict-resolution strategies remains patchy, humanitarian actors should stick to their original function of trying to make the conduct of war more humane and to allow people to survive it with dignity.

These debates are not new. The trade-offs between neutrality and complicity in mass human-rights abuses were familiar to the International Committee of the Red Cross in dealing with concentration camps in Germany during World War II, for example. However, in the post-cold-war world, articulating a response to these dilemmas has become particularly pressing.

This urgency derives from changes in the political environment within conflict-affected countries and from changes in international political relations more broadly. The nature of conflict appears to be changing significantly. Intertwined with political objectives regarding the organization and control of state power are also complex patterns of conflict to control access to key resources, particularly primary commodities such as timber (Cambodia, East Timor), diamonds (Sierra Leone, Liberia and Angola), opium (Myanmar, Afghanistan) and oil (Sudan, Angola). These resource conflicts reflect the breakdown of the political and economic structures conventionally associated with statehood. The flow of these resources is increasingly unregulated and untaxed by the state, depriving it of essential revenues to conduct basic functions of government—from maintaining a functioning judiciary to the provision of health and education services. The level of violence associated with attempts to control these valuable assets is high, and in highly fragmented and sometimes factionalized armed movements the means of regulating it through conventional command and control structures is limited.

This pattern of conflict is stretching conventional strategies of delivering humanitarian assistance. Instead of two opposing sides, there may now be four or five. The framework of respect for humanitarian assistance seems to be breaking down as more and more aid workers are taken hostage and killed. Conflict resolution is also becoming a more difficult task, as the number of actors and their different interests grow. Even if peace agreements are secured, translating improved military security into social and economic security and thus reducing the need for international assistance becomes highly problematic, since the institutional and political framework for secure livelihoods and the provision of basic services is typically lacking.

Civilians stand in the midst of such conflicts, lacking protection from violence and thus the ability to develop and maintain sustainable livelihoods. It has become painfully clear that the primary need of populations living in such environments is not only or even primarily food aid, but security. The questions are how to achieve this and can it be sustained? This is the major challenge facing the international community, one which has stimulated a new wave of political experimentation, starting in Iraqi Kurdistan and seen most recently in Kosovo and East Timor.

While the world awaits the results of these experiments and their codification into international norms, humanitarian assistance remains one of the only forms of international engagement in the majority of internal wars. Yet support for this most fundamental gesture of human solidarity—the provision of food, health care and shelter to those in the midst of war—appears to be on the wane. With the exception of the Kosovos, it is now becoming routine that donors provide

IN A DISTANT CORNER of the WORLD, A SPARROW FALLS to EARTH....

less than half the funds requested by the UN in its emergency appeals. Despite the increase in the total volume of assistance in the past decade, it is not enough to meet the increased need.

Humanitarian assistance remains on the front line of internal conflicts and of international debates regarding whether and how to pick up the pieces of other people's wars. How these debates are resolved will be revealing in terms of the nature of the post-cold-war political order. On the one hand is the promise of a political humanitarianism and on the other the prospect of a humanitarian politics. The former looks to achieve an integration of political and humanitarian action, seeing assistance as part of a strategy of conflict prevention and resolution. Taken to its logical conclusion, it implies taking sides, providing assistance (humanitarian and otherwise) to one side rather than the other, and taking a clear and loud advocacy position. The latter is a more minimalist position. It implies limiting the objectives of humanitarian assistance to the provision of palliative relief and maintaining a fire wall between such assistance and wider political processes of diplomacy and military action. It implies a more structured division of international labor between the different spheres.

It is difficult to know how to interpret the mounting dissent within the humanitarian community and to assess its implications. It is not clear whether and how warring parties will be able to distinguish between the different schools of humanitarian thought and will therefore realign their position in relation to international efforts to provide assistance. There has been no consensus, either, on the accountability of humanitarian actors.

U.S. policy options

Although most humanitarian crises result in international action, U.S. decisions about how and whether to respond have wide repercussions.

■ Does it make sense for the U.S. to fund different types of humanitarian actors, which adopt very different interpretations of their roles and functions in conflict situations? Or should the U.S. strive for greater consistency and coherence in its approach?

■ Should the U.S. respond to complex political emergencies whether or not it has a geostrategic interest? Should it send troops or just equipment and advisers?

■ Should the U.S. give more support to multilateral initiatives, for example, by increasing payments to the UN for peacekeeping? Can the U.S. successfully opt out of multilateral actions?

+++

Whichever course comes to predominate, the humanitarian sphere will fail unless there is a clear international political strategy for dealing with the ravages of internal war. Of itself, humanitarian assistance can provide invaluable succor to those who have lost much, but without a process of political action, it cannot resolve humanitarian suffering. The question now is how and whether these two spheres should be linked? The jury remains out. ■

Opinion Ballots are on pages 85–86

DISCUSSION QUESTIONS

1. Should the U.S. and its allies develop a set of criteria that would trigger international military intervention when populations are subject to mass violations of human rights?

2. Should international assistance be regulated by a global body to ensure its quality and that it is not doing more harm than good? If so, which organization should play such a role? If not, what other mechanisms might be used to make the humanitarian system more accountable?

3. Do you think recent humanitarian interventions in Kosovo and East Timor set a precedent for future responses to conflict-related emergencies? To what extent are similar interventions likely or desirable in other, on-going wars in Africa and elsewhere?

4. In the absence of such a political intervention and thus the persistence of widespread insecurity and widespread abuses of human rights, should the UN and other international agencies provide relief aid to the victims of conflict?

5. To what extent do the principles of neutrality and impartiality still provide a useful guide for humanitarian action? What might be the implications of giving up these principles?

6. In the absence of effective and legitimate state structures in conflict-affected countries to guide decisions regarding the allocation of aid resources, should there be a global mechanism in place to coordinate needs assessment and to channel resources accordingly?

7. Should humanitarian assistance be subject to conditions in the same way that development assistance is? For example, if warring parties do not respect international humanitarian law, should aid be withheld? Who should decide?

8. Should humanitarian assistance focus on the delivery of basic, material supplies such as food and medical aid, or should it be used for economic development?

READINGS AND RESOURCES

International Federation of Red Cross and Red Crescent Societies, **World Disasters Report, 1998.** New York, Oxford University Press, 1998. $29.95 (paper). An annual publication that details trends and events in the humanitarian sphere.*

Miller, Judith, "Sovereignty Isn't So Sacred Anymore." **The New York Times,** April 18, 1999, Section 4, p. 4. Highlights the new doctrine for the role of human rights in international relations.

Minear, Larry, and Weiss, Thomas G., "Humanitarian Politics." **Headline Series** No. 304. New York, Foreign Policy Association, 1995. 72 pp. $5.95. Discusses the change in the early post-cold-war era in the political and military conditions that generate the need for humanitarian action.

Moorehead, Caroline, **Dunant's Dream: War, Switzerland and the History of the Red Cross.** Emeryville, CA, Publishers' Group West, 1999. 816 pp. $26.60. An authoritative history of the Red Cross Movement that traces the origins of the concept of humanitarian action in wartime and recounts the Red Cross's moral dilemmas from World War I to Chechnya and Bosnia.

O'Hanlon, Michael, **Saving Lives With Force: Military Criteria for Humanitarian Intervention.** Washington, DC, Brookings Institution Press, 1997, 100 pp. $12.95 (paper). O'Hanlon contends that modern Western militaries are capable of successfully intervening to stop an ongoing cycle of warfare in a country whose government has collapsed.

You can find links to this document and additional readings on our website at* **www.fpa.org/program.html

Rieff, David, "The Precarious Triumph of Human Rights." **The New York Times Magazine,** Aug. 8, 1999, pp. 36–41. Charting the new course of human rights and how it drives foreign policy.

Scheffer, David J., "Realizing the Vision of the Universal Declaration of Human Rights." **U.S. Department of State Dispatch,** Oct. 1998, pp. 17–23. Scheffer addresses the U.S. response to human-rights violations in Iraq, Kosovo and Afghanistan.

AMNESTY INTERNATIONAL U.S.A., 322 Eighth Ave., New York, NY 10001; (212) 807-8400; Fax (212) 627-1451. ■ An impartial and independent organization that campaigns for the preservation of human rights. The on-line resources contain the latest news and links to Amnesty affiliates worldwide as well as human-rights-related websites. **www.amnesty.org**

HUMAN RIGHTS WATCH, 350 Fifth Ave., 34th fl., New York, NY 10118-3299; (212) 290-4700; Fax (212) 736-1300. ■ An independent, nongovernmental organization dedicated to monitoring and preserving human rights around the world. Publications include the annual **World Report. www.hrw.org**

HUMANITARIANISM AND WAR PROJECT, Brown University, 2 Stimson Ave., Box 1970, Providence, RI 02912; (401) 863-2728; Fax (401) 863-3808. ■ An independent policy research initiative based at Brown University's Watson Institute. In addition to country-specific case studies from Armenia to Cambodia to Sudan, this project also produces thematic, comparative studies. Its publications are available on the Internet. **www.brown.edu/Departments/Watson_Institute/H_W**

RELIEFWEB ■ The major electronic resource on humanitarian issues. A project of the UN Office for the Coordination of Humanitarian Affairs (OCHA). **wwwnotes.reliefweb.int**

INDEX TO GREAT DECISIONS TOPICS (1989–99)

AFRICA

'98—Africa Today: Worst of Times, Best of Times
'96—Africa: Should the U.S. Care?
'94—South Africa: Forging a Democratic Union
'94—Islam and Politics: Egypt, Algeria and Tunisia
'92—Africa South of the Sahara: Fresh Winds of Democracy?
'89—Horn of Africa: Empty Cornucopia?

ASIA

'99—The Asian Financial Crisis: The IMF and Its Critics
'99—Japan: The Shadow of the Miracle
'98—China and the U.S.: What Priorities in a Changing Relationship?
'98—Turkey: Emerging Regional Power or State in Crisis?
'97—Northeast Asia: Strategic Crossroads
'96—Economic Cooperation in the Asia-Pacific: Openings for the U.S.?
'95—China, Taiwan, Hong Kong: U.S. Challenges
'93—China: New Reforms, Old Politics?
'93—India & Pakistan: Collision or Compromise?
'91—Japanese-U.S. Trade: Harmony or Discord?
'90—Vietnam, Cambodia and the U.S.: Return Engagement?
'89—China: Redefining the Revolution

LATIN AMERICA

'99—Latin America: A Broad Overview
'98—Cuba: Time to Rethink U.S. Strategy?
'96—Mexico: Embattled Neighbor
'94—Argentina, Brazil, Chile: Democracy & Market Economics
'92—Latin America's New Course: Bridge to Closer U.S. Ties?
'91—Cuba: What Future for Castro and Communism?
'90—Nicaragua and El Salvador: War or Peace in Central America?
'89—Latin American Debt: Living on Borrowed Time?

MIDDLE EAST

'99—Iran and the Caspian Basin: Tradition and Transformation
'97—Middle East: Peace and the Changing Order
'95—Middle East: Lasting Steps to Peace?
'92—Middle East After Desert Storm: As the Dust Settles
'91—The Middle East: New Frictions, New Alignments
'90—Palestinian Question: Is There a Solution?
'89—The Persian Gulf: Reassessing the U.S. Role

RUSSIA, FORMER U.S.S.R. AND EASTERN EUROPE

'97—Russia and the U.S.: Growing Cooperation?
'95—Russia and Its Neighbors: U.S. Policy Choices
'94—Conflict in Former Yugoslavia: Quest for Solutions
'93—Russia & the Central Asian Republics: After Independence, New Directions?
'92—Breakup of the Soviet Union: U.S. Dilemmas
'91—Nationalism's Revival: Soviet Republics & Eastern Europe
'90—U.S.S.R. and Eastern Europe: End of an Era?

WESTERN EUROPE

'99—Implementing NATO Enlargement: Difficult Choices Ahead
'98—Turkey: Emerging Regional Power or State in Crisis?
'97—European Integration: What Future for Europe and the U.S.?
'93—Germany's Role: in Europe? in the Atlantic Alliance?
'91—The New Europe: What Role for the U.S.?

DEFENSE AND SECURITY

'99—Implementing NATO Enlargement: Difficult Choices Ahead
'99—Weapons of Mass Destruction: Reemerging Threat?
'96—What Future Role for NATO?
'96—Failing Nations: What U.S. Response?
'96—The Intelligence Community: Time for Reform?
'95—Nuclear Proliferation: Can It Be Capped?
'94—Defense: Redefining U.S. Needs and Priorities
'90—Third World Arms Bazaar: Disaster for Sale?
'89—Arms Agreements: Too Little Too Late, or Too Much Too Soon?

ECONOMIC ISSUES

'99—The Asian Financial Crisis: The IMF and Its Critics
'98—Financing Development: Time for a New Look?
'97—Globalization: Workplace Winners and Losers
'95—Global Finance: America's Role and Stakes
'94—Trade with the Pacific Rim: Pressure or Cooperation?
'93—Trade & the Global Economy: Projecting U.S. Interests
'90—The U.S., Europe & Japan: Global Economy in Transition?
'89—Farmers, Food & the Global Supermarket

ENVIRONMENT

'97—Environmental Threats to Stability: The Role of Population Growth
'96—Water: A Dangerous Endangered Resource?
'94—Environmental Crisis in Former Soviet Bloc: Whose Problem? Who Pays?
'92—Planet Earth: Dying Species, Disappearing Habitats
'91—Women, Population & the Environment
'90—Global Warming & the Environment: Forecast Disaster?

U.S. FOREIGN POLICY

'99—The Information Age: New Dimensions for U.S. Foreign Policy
'98—Special Interests: Is U.S. Foreign Policy for Sale?
'98—Human Rights: What Role in U.S. Policy?
'96—Foreign Policy and the U.S. Political System
'95—Promoting Democracy: America's Mission?
'94—New World Disorder? U.S. in Search of a Role
'93—U.S. in a New World: What Goals? What Priorities?
'92—U.S. Agenda for the '90s: Domestic Needs, Global Priorities
'91—Rethinking Foreign Aid: What Kind? How Much?
'89—Ethics in International Relations: Power & Morality

OTHER CRITICAL ISSUES

'99—U.S. Role in the UN: A Changing Dynamic?
'98—Religion's Role in World Affairs: Challenges for the U.S.
'97—Today's Media: What Voice in Foreign Policy?
'97—Terrorism and Crime: A More Dangerous World
'95—United Nations at Fifty: Reaching Out or Overreaching?
'95—Immigration: An End to Open Doors?
'93—UN: What Role in the New World?
'93—Children at Risk: Abroad and at Home
'92—The Refugee Crisis: How Should the U.S. Respond?
'92—The AIDS Pandemic: Global Scourge, U.S. Challenge
'91—Media's Role in Shaping Foreign Policy
'89—International Drug Traffic: An Unwinnable War?

OPINION BALLOT 1999 HIGHLIGHTS

TOPIC 1: INFORMATION AGE

ISSUE A. Do you think society is better served by governments having access to all kinds of information, or is personal privacy more important?*

Government access	25%
Personal privacy	65%

ISSUE B. Do you agree or disagree with the following statements?

	AGREE	DISAGREE
The U.S. government should take an active role in regulating the Internet.	46%	43%
The U.S. should exploit its advanced technology and develop a new information strategy for the State Department.	82%	8%
The information revolution will lead to the triumph of democracy around the world.	40%	44%
The new global economy facilitated by the information revolution is good for the U.S.	81%	8%
The new media are trivializing international issues.	54%	34%

TOPIC 2: IMF

ISSUE A. Do you agree or disagree with the following statements?

	AGREE	DISAGREE
IMF assistance creates "moral hazard" problems.	69%	23%
IMF assistance delays meaningful reform in countries in crisis.	44%	48%
The strict conditions attached to IMF loans aggravate the economic problems of countries in crisis.	53%	38%
The IMF is "the only thing between us and financial chaos."	37%	55%
The liberalization of international capital movement has gone too far.	39%	50%
The IMF should push for more flexible exchange rates.	72%	15%
The IMF should urge countries to embrace greater capital convertibility.	70%	14%
The U.S. should increase its funding of the IMF.	39%	50%

TOPIC 3: JAPAN

POLITICAL ISSUES

ISSUE A. Is Japan destined to suffer from political gridlock for the foreseeable future? (choose one)

No	11%
Yes, for a year or two	48%
Yes, for the foreseeable future	34%

ISSUE B. What effect can pressure from the U.S. and other countries have on the Japanese government's ability to be decisive? (choose one)

None	29%
A positive effect	45%
A negative backlash	17%

**Note: These percentages and others reported may not add up to 100 because some repondents did not mark particular ballots or volunteered other information.*

ECONOMIC ISSUES

ISSUE A. What should be the main goal of U.S. economic policy toward Japan at this time? (choose one)

Reducing the trade deficit.	20%
Increasing imports from the U.S.	11%
Increasing imports from Asian countries.	3%
Stimulating domestic economic growth.	20%
Fixing the banking problem.	35%

ISSUE B. If the Japanese economy does not meet U.S. expectations, how should the U.S. respond? (choose one)

Threaten trade sanctions.	5%
Threaten decreased security cooperation.	1%
Persuade the G-7, IMF and other international organizations to raise public pressure on Japan.	45%
Wait for Japan's leaders to sort out their own problems.	39%

ISSUE C. Do the U.S. and other countries have a right to interfere in Japan's domestic economic policies when those policies have serious effects outside Japan?

Yes	44%
No	46%

ISSUE D. Do other countries have the right to interfere in domestic U.S. economic policies when those policies have serious effects outside the U.S.?

Yes	40%
No	49%

TOPIC 4: WEAPONS OF MASS DESTRUCTION

ISSUE A. To try to control the spread of nuclear weapons, the U.S. should:

	YES	NO
Ratify the Comprehensive Test Ban Treaty.	85%	6%
Reduce its deployment and stockpiles of nuclear weapons in accordance with the Start accords.	83%	9%
Abandon the ABM Treaty and deploy unlimited defensive interceptor missiles on U.S. soil.	21%	67%
Increase assistance to Russia to assure that dismantled weapons are held secure.	82%	10%
Encourage the establishment of nuclear-weapons-free zones.	79%	10%
Expand future Start agreements to include China.	86%	6%

ISSUE B. For each of the following statements, indicate whether you agree or disagree.

	AGREE	DISAGREE
Chemical and biological weapons are so reprehensible that no country will dare use them.	8%	82%
Biological weapons are attractive to developing countries because they can be developed with relatively small investments of capital and technology.	84%	6%
Because of dual use of many chemical and biological agents, total compliance with treaty specifications is almost impossible to verify.	80%	9%
With chemical and biological weapons, terrorists pose a greater threat than "rogue states."	77%	11%

Results of 27,525 ballots received as of June 30, 1999, and tabulated by Calculogic Corporation of Englewood, New Jersey.

TOPIC 5: IRAN AND THE CASPIAN BASIN

ISSUE A. In dealing with Iran in the future, the U.S. should:

	AGREE	DISAGREE
Continue to maintain trade sanctions on Iran.	20%	72%
Oppose pipelines being built across Iran.	30%	59%
Allow U.S. companies to do business there.	80%	12%
Make concrete concessions to strengthen Khatami's government and permit a renewal of relations.	80%	11%
Support a "nuclear deal" as in the case of North Korea.	52%	32%

ISSUE B. With regard to pipelines to export Caspian oil and gas, the U.S. should:

	AGREE	DISAGREE
Offer incentives to companies to build the Baku-Ceyhan route.	36%	42%
Let economic criteria determine the route even if this rules out Baku-Ceyhan.	59%	21%
Not oppose pipeline projects crossing Iran.	58%	23%

ISSUE C. What is most important for U.S. interests in the Caspian basin countries?

Repairing environmental damage.	16%
Access to energy deposits.	28%
Degree of political participation.	9%
Respect for human rights.	17%
Support for U.S. foreign policy goals.	19%

TOPIC 6: NATO ENLARGEMENT

ISSUE A. Should NATO continue the process of enlargement or should it stop with the current three invitees?

Continue enlargement.	54%
Stop enlargement.	39%

ISSUE B. Should Russia be invited to join NATO?

Yes	38%
No	53%

ISSUE C. In the future, NATO should:

Confine its activities to the territory of NATO members.	34%
Engage in "out of area" missions within Europe.	30%
Act to protect and promote its members' interests anywhere in the world.	25%

ISSUE D. What should NATO's policy be toward membership for the Baltic republics (Estonia, Latvia, Lithuania)?

Offer them membership as soon as they meet NATO standards.	29%
Postpone offering membership until the countries become members of the European Union.	19%
Postpone offering membership until NATO's relations with Russia improve.	29%
Never offer membership.	9%

ISSUE E. How important are the following criteria in determining whether a country should be offered membership in NATO?

Democracy	43%
Economics	10%
Military capabilities	4%
Geographic/strategic importance	24%
Political support in Allied capitals	8%
Russian reaction	4%

TOPIC 7: LATIN AMERICA

ISSUE A. What is most important for relations between the U.S. and the nations of Latin America?

Democracy	25%
Drugs and crime	8%
Economic responsibility	28%
Environment	3%
Human rights	12%
Immigration	3%
Trade	19%

ISSUE B. Regarding Cuba, the U.S. should (choose one):

Retain the full embargo and the Helms-Burton legislation.	5%
Repeal Helms-Burton legislation, but retain the embargo.	7%
Lift the embargo and open relations with Cuba.	79%

ISSUE C. On Nafta, the U.S. should enlarge the North American Free Trade Agreement to include Chile.

Yes	78%
No	10%

TOPIC 8: U.S. ROLE IN THE UN

ISSUE A. What should be the primary concern of UN activities in the world?

Peacekeeping	59%
Humanitarian relief	24%

ISSUE B. Concerning institutional reform of the UN, what is most urgent?

Transform the Trusteeship Council.	17%
Use regional and nongovernmental organizations to a greater extent.	45%
Reduce overlapping activities.	37%

ISSUE C. Regarding payment of its financial obligations to the UN, the U.S. should:

Pay its dues and arrears immediately.	72%
Pay its dues and arrears only when the conditions of the Helms-Biden bill are met.	20%

ISSUE D. For each of the following statements, indicate whether you agree or disagree:

	AGREE	DISAGREE
The UN is due for a drastic overhaul, given all the changes in the world over the past 50 years.	66%	21%
The UN should confine its activities to countries that invite it to act as mediator or observer.	28%	59%
The U.S. Congress should have the power to veto participation in UN peacekeeping operations.	31%	56%

ISSUE E. For each of the following activities, check whether the UN, private/nongovernmental organizations or unilateral/regional actors perform them best:

	UN	Private/ NGO	Unilateral/ regional
Disaster relief	19%	49%	14%
Health/medical assistance	31%	42%	10%
Development assistance	35%	25%	21%
International trade arrangements	44%	8%	31%
Human-rights watch	52%	23%	8%
Arms limitations	64%	2%	17%
Conflict resolution	60%	4%	19%

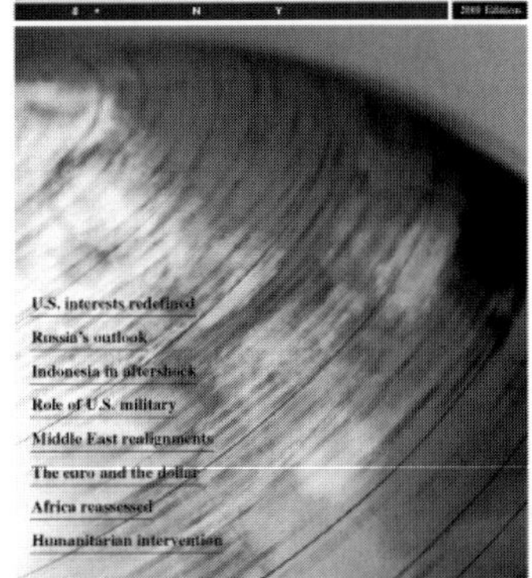

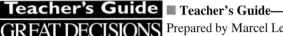

■ **Teacher's Guide—**

Prepared by Marcel Lewinski, master teacher and curriculum developer, this valuable resource contains glossaries for each article, teaching strategies and activities, and reproducible handouts. $19.00 + $3.00 shipping and handling. Product Order No. 31484.

■ **Television Series—**

Hosted by Peter F. Krogh, a leading foreign policy spokesperson and Dean Emeritus of the Georgetown University School of Foreign Service, this is the longest-running television program devoted solely to international affairs and foreign policy. Expanded to 13 half-hour programs, the 2000 series will begin airing on PBS affiliates across the country in the second week of January. You can also order 8 programs on VHS tape for your discussion group: $35.00 + $5.00 shipping and handling. Product Order No. 31485.

■ **FPA Citizen's Guide to U.S. Foreign Policy Issues: Election 2000—**

by the Editors of the Foreign Policy Association

Nonpartisan briefs on key issues facing the nation. Published quadrennially by FPA. Traditionally endorsed by the chairmen of the Democratic National Committee and the Republican National Committee, as well as the president of the League of Women Voters of the United States. To be published June 2000. $ 9.95 + $3.00 shipping and handling. Product Order No. 31491.

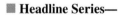

■ **Headline Series—**

These lively and provocative pocket-size publications on current world topics are published four times a year. Written by recognized foreign policy scholars and other experts, they are short (64-80 pp.), concise and readable. Single issues are $5.95; double issues $11.25. A one-year subscription costs $20.00.

"The Japanese Economy at the Millennium: Correspondents' Insightful Views" (HS 319, Product Order No. 31492)

"...And Justice for All: The Universal Declaration of Human Rights at 50" (HS 318, Product Order No. 31479)

"Turkey Today: Troubled Ally's Search for Identity" (HS 317, Product Order No. 31475)

"Right Makes Might: Freedom and Power in the Information Age" (HS 316, Product Order No. 31466)

"The Persian Gulf in Transition" (HS 315, Product Order No. 31461)

"The U.S. Role in the Twenty-first Century World?" (HS 314, Product Order No. 31452)

"Does Russia Have a Democratic Future?" (HS 313, Product Order No. 31451)

"Taiwan Faces the Twenty-first Century: Continuing the 'Miracle' " (HS 312, Product Order No. 31445)

★ ★ ★ ★ ★ ★ ★ ★ ★ ★ ★

OPINION BALLOTS ■ Vote for the foreign policy option of your choice! You can make your opinions count by filling in a ballot after you read and discuss each topic. If you prefer to wait until you have finished discussing all eight topics, you can use the ballot envelope that is bound into this book to mail your ballots to the Foreign Policy Association. Either way, please send your ballots no later than the June 30th cutoff date in order to have your opinions included in the final *National Opinion Ballot Report*. The *Ballot Report* will be prepared by the FPA, with the advice of a public opinion analyst, and will be presented to the White House, the Departments of State and Defense, and members of Congress, as well as the nation's media.

UPDATES ■ Concise, informative supplements to the briefing book articles on developments since the book went to press. They are available free in February and August.

PROGRAM MATERIALS ■ **Great Decisions Program Handbook** and **Tips for Discussion Group Leaders**—Upon request, FPA will provide this material, free of charge, to help you create a better program.

ON TAPE ■ **Great Decisions on Audiotape**—
In a special agreement with FPA, Oregon Great Decisions has produced a series of audiotape cassettes for all eight **Great Decisions** topics. Available as a four-tape set or sold individually. When ordering individually, keep in mind, topics are recorded sequentially, i.e. Topics 1 & 2, Topics 3 & 4, etc.

The Great Decisions 2000 on Tape Set, $19.95 + $2.50 postage and handling, individual tapes, $7.95 + $2.50 postage and handling.

For more information, call Oregon Great Decisions at (541) 688-8754. Send orders, along with payment to: Oregon Great Decisions, 27777 Snyder Road, Junction City, OR 97448.

EARN CREDIT ■ **American Military University (AMU),** a private, accredited, national distance learning institution, offers you the opportunity to earn graduate, undergraduate or continuing education (CEU) credits in conjunction with **Great Decisions.** A Certificate of Completion is also available. Please write to AMU at 9104-P Manassas Drive, Manassas Park, VA 20111, or call (703) 330-5398 for more information.

DISCUSSIONS ONLINE ■ At FPA online, you can:

- Take part in a discussion on foreign policy with other FPA members
- Get the latest updates to the **Great Decisions** articles
- Download the **Tips for Discussion Group Leaders** booklet
- Read the results of our latest *National Opinion Ballot Report*
- Use our Readings and Resources page to link directly to the **Great Decisions** suggested readings
- Check out our Reference Maps, designed especially for the Web
- Get the latest information on Foreign Policy Association events and speakers.

Visit FPA Online today!
http://www.fpa.org

To order FPA materials or to request a free catalogue, contact:

Foreign Policy Association
470 Park Avenue South
New York, NY 10016-6819
(800) 477-5836
Fax: (212) 481-9275

FPA Invites You To...

Become a National Associate. Your participation as a National Associate will enable FPA, an independent, nonpartisan educational organization, to carry out its mission to develop awareness and understanding of global issues and informed opinion on U.S. foreign policy.

To become a National Associate, please use the envelope bound into this book. National Associates receive a membership card; FPA's most recent *Headline Series, "The Japanese Economy at the Millennium: Correspondents' Insightful Views,"* by Nicholas Kristof and Sheryl WuDunn; the 1999 National Opinion Ballot Report; a complimentary issue of *Foreign Policy Forum*; and the latest catalog of FPA publications.

Become an FPA Civic Volunteer. Lead your community in a dialogue on "great decisions" that affect our daily lives. FPA's volunteer corps of civic leaders organizes and leads **Great Decisions** discussion groups, supplemented by lecture series, town meetings, media programs, and other forums that encourage thoughtful deliberation and civic action. Through their efforts, citizens across the country join together to share viewpoints and strengthen the democratic process.

Participate in the Foreign Policy Process

Join a **Great Decisions** foreign policy discussion group in your community.

Participate in the opinion ballot process (ballots are included in this book).

Lead a new **Great Decisions** group in your area.

Coordinate several groups by becoming a **Great Decisions** Regional Organizer, acting as the liaison between the Foreign Policy Association and **Great Decisions** groups in your area, as well as introducing the program to new audiences.

"Never doubt that a small group of thoughtful, committed citizens can change the world. Indeed, it's the only thing that ever has."

—Margaret Mead

Do you have any questions about starting, joining, leading or participating in a **Great Decisions** group? Please call **(800) 628-5754.**

FPA wishes to thank the following Great Decisions participants who generously supported the program.

National Associates

Mr. Benjamin F. Adams
Ms. Anne M. Allan
Mr. Bhaskar K. Arumugam
Mrs. Mary J. Auerbacher
Mr. Eric Axelbank
Mr. Harry Balfe
Dr. R. G. Elliott
Ms. Marinda Ferrell
Ms. M. Helen Gillis
Mr. Bernard M. Granum
Mr. Mark Hanington
Mr. Manfred F. Harpole
Mr. E. James Hickey
Mr. James R. Hinkle
Mr. Albert H. Huntington, Jr.
Ms. Patricia A. Jobe
Ms. Katharine H. Kappas
Ms. Cynthia Kassouf
Mr. Edib Kirdar
Mr. Robert O. Lehrman
Mr. William J. Mares
Mr. Brian McCotter
Mr. Stanley Muroff
Mrs. Irene B. Negus
Mr. Ralph H. Nestmann
Ms. A. Carolyn Newsom
Mrs. Barbara M. Noseworthy
Dr. Hushang M. Payan
Mr. Scott Penzarella
Frank C. Petrulis
Dr. Susan T. Pettiss
Sir John Plowman CBE
Dr. Naeem G. Rathore
Alexander P. Remenchik
Ms. Emmeline Rocha-Sinha
Mr. Michael Rodin
Ms. Doris H. Sasser
Mr. Steven M. Shafran
Mr. Artjan Shani
Mr. William J. Sheehan
Ms. Jennifer B. Shipley
Mr. John Sitilides
Mr. Louis Small
Mr. Norman K. Smith
The Honorable Alan Sullivan
Mr. Nicholas Suszynski
Ms. Jean C. Taylor
Mr. George Thurlow
Mr. Harry Vafiadis
Mr. & Mrs. Sean Wall
Mrs. Judith Weaver
Mrs. Cynthia Weir
Mr. Charles Wilson
Mr. Jason E. Winbourn

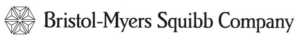